stage lighting

Richard Pilbrow

foreword by Lord Olivier

Revised edition

With contributions by
William Bundy O.B.E. and
John B. Read

Drama Book Publishers
New York

To Viki

also Len Tucker, Herb Anstett representing the best of Master
Electricians in the UK & USA, who have to make it work.

Drama Book Publishers
821 Broadway
New York, New York 10003

© Richard Pilbrow 1970, 1979
Revised edition first published 1979
First edition reprinted 1974 and 1976

ISBN 0-89676-005-7

Library of Congress Cataloging in Publication Data
Pilbrow, Richard
  Stage Lighting
  Bibliography: p.
  1. Stage Lighting I. Title
PN2091.E4P5 1978   792'.025   78-10184
ISBN 0-89676-005-7

0 9 8 7 6 5 4 3 2

Printed in the United States of America

Contents

Acknowledgments

Practical thanks are due to Robert Bryan, who helped to organize this work generally; to Margaret Tabor, for undertaking the amazing task of correcting my English grammar, and Angela Brown with Ann Bryan who typed out—several times—a seemingly mammoth pile of papers.

Visual assistance owes much to Lennart Clemens, responsible for the many sketches throughout the book, Chris Arthur, who provided special photographs, and many other photographers, especially Zoë Dominic, who so often has had the task of providing a management with superb theatrical photography under somewhat gruesome lighting conditions provided by myself.

A special mention is due to Rank Strand who, via *Tabs* and its Editor Frederick Bentham, have kindly lent further photographic material. Any book on stage lighting must pay tribute to Mr Bentham, whose work and writings have been a great source of personal inspiration (despite occasional disagreements!) and have led to many improvements in lighting control in Great Britain.

In the United States, however, I believe the *overall* standard of lighting design leads the world. Much is owed by us all to Mr Edward Kook, founder of Century Lighting, who supported with great dynamism the new profession of the Lighting Designer.

In the United Kingdom two names must be recorded: first, Mr Basil Dean, one of the outstanding directors of this century and a great innovator in lighting, who still casts an acute yet benevolent eye upon our activities. Next Mr Joe Davis, President of the Society of British Theatre Lighting Designers; his lighting for Christopher Fry's *The Lady's not for Burning* did much to open my eyes to the potential in lighting.

Thanks to my colleagues in the Society, particularly John Wyckham, Charles Bristow, Eric Baker, William Bundy, and Michael Northen, and, nearer home, all those at Theatre Projects Lighting led by Robert Ornbo and Bryan Kendall. Lastly, thanks to Studio Vista for patience, foresight, skill and more patience.

Acknowledgments to revised edition

Times change and so do people. To my original thanks must be added Molly Friedel who co-ordinated all the new technical material, John Kennett who added the new sketches and diagrams, Bob Anderson who gave great assistance with the new lantern charts, and Liz Lomas who managed to squeeze in typing all the alterations between her more arduous duties of being my right hand and assistant through these active days.

Especial thanks to Bill Bundy, O.B.E., ex-Technical Director of the Royal Opera House, Covent Garden, then Theatre Projects, and now Technical Director of the National Theatre, whose contribution on the lighting of opera from his vast experience is a most valued addition; and to John B. Read who, after several years with Theatre Projects, has gone on to establish himself as an international figure in the field of lighting for ballet and modern dance and whose wisdom on the subject has allowed the expansion of that section.

Foreword

I can't really grasp how an electric bell works. I once said as much to George Kaufmann who replied, 'The *hammer* is a mystery beyond *my* comprehension.' The word Candlepower is the only one among electronic jargon which has ever reflected in my understanding the faintest glow of appreciation. And now if I can't make out the meaning of the word transistor, I at least know what it aims to mean. To my brothers and sisters who wallow in even deeper ignorance than that which I enjoy, let me say that it means battery, or a kind of battery, or battery as a means of driving power. 'A transistor radio', for instance, is a phrase I bandy about quite carelessly now. Sorry if I'm showing off, but watts, ohms, amps, gnodes, lux, lumens, condensers, thyristors, integrated circuits, digital analogue conversions, ferrite core stores, chips, bits, gates and pots are secrets which are all too safe with me.

But I could once upon a time light a show and do it pretty nicely in the days when this skill was expected of a stage producer, when, if a specialist was brought in, our colleague would be smugly if politely looked down upon by the rest of us.

Only Ingmar Bergman do I know who persists in still practising this lost aspect of our craft. 'Of course I must do my own lightning,' he insists. 'Lightning is *Blixt*,' I explain, '*Belysning* is lighting.' But Ingmar is a Swedish genius and Swedish geniuses are as stubborn as they come, particularly when they have kept up the technicalities, and he has.

As we used to have it before the invasion of the experts, 12 on No. 1 Spot bar or 16 if possible, ditto in FOH, should provide 'a warm' and 'a cool' from each side of the house—together with floats plus No. 1 batten for interior, plus more battens as necessary for exteriors, plus, of course, special effects, hanging pageants or acting areas for streams of sunlight, moonlight, sunset. Special lamps plugged into the dips all round, special 'baby Dietz' in the footlights, for candle-lit scenes, through the fireplace, in the piano, the bookcase, or underneath tables, assisted in the smoothing-out artifice laid on by the practised hand of the leading lady of long standing.

Gentle fades and gentle increases have from time immemorial been employed to accentuate the mood of the scene; also, very commonly indeed, to highlight the entrance of a leading player. I remember an auntie of mine years and years ago saying to me, 'My dear, Henry Irving was such a very great actor that, do you know, whenever he made his entrance you would swear that the entire stage seemed to light up.' (Another example of this very dear lady's memory of the great man came out after a matinée of the Thorndike/Casson production of *Henry VIII* at the old Empire in Leicester Square, in which Wolsey was played by Lyall Swete, '... you see, my dear, Henry Irving wore a gown of real silk and this man had nothing of the kind ... how do I know? Why, my dear, before Irving's every single entrance for several seconds you could hear the swish, swish, swish of the real silk as he walked towards his entrance!')

But I am departing from my subject, which is lighting, and when I say 'my subject' I am attempting to speak of ground which I have already yielded. It is no longer my subject, though it still fascinates me, but it most definitely is Richard Pilbrow's subject. His work which follows this lame introduction is of astonishing completeness and a magnificent exposition of sheer masterliness in the difficult craft that this has grown to be.

It may perhaps be of interest to note the reason behind the beanstalk growth of this aspect of the theatre. It exists in the relation of one sense to another, or the governing of one by another. The effects brought about by Irving and Belasco (incidentally Belasco would shine his spots upwards into a mirror so that a softer glow would fall upon the form and features of Miss Maud Adams) were, according to A. J. Munnings for instance, more soft, more realistic and more plastic than the hurtful glare offered to more modern eyes.

I was caused to reflect upon this when I played in Australia in 1948. In Perth we were, I believe, the first live actors to be heard or seen for some twelve years: none of our audience could understand what we said in the first half of the play, but all expressed gratitude to us for speaking up better in the second half. This, of course, does not represent the facts as they were, but it illustrates the degree to which amplification had been surreptitiously deadening human hearing.

In other words, in Irving's day the lighting could afford to be soft, quiet, more atmospheric, offering denser differences of light and shade, because the audience's ears were sharp and perfectly responsive to the simple impact of the normal human voice and quiet light playing upon the speaker. It is since the development of habitual amplification that more and more complaints have been made concerning the level of the actor's speech and this has only been eased by the ever-increasing voltage of light thrown upon a subject. In other words, you have to see better in order to hear better. The perception of the eye has been deadened along with the sharpness of the ear.

If the same indulgence as that of oral amplification were provided for the eyes, the race would soon be walking about with binoculars strapped to their faces. One may wring one's hands at the pity of these conditions but along with so many other things in civilization, in order not to despair it must be shrugged off in the lame utility cliché of 'progress'. That this situation has been met is thanks to Richard Pilbrow and his like. Your old friends, the actor-managers, would not have had the electronic knowledge necessary to satisfy the senses as it is required these days. The difference is just about the same as that of flying before and during the War 'by the seat of our pants' and the technological expertise required for handling the jumbo jets of today.

19 June 1970   Laurence Olivier

Author's note

This book is divided into two parts. The first, Stage Lighting Design, deals with the role that lighting has to play in a production, the lighting designer's place in the theatrical team, and the processes and procedures that he has to go through in designing the lighting of a show.

The second, Stage Lighting Mechanics, is in the form of a designer's note book and covers briefly some of the technical equipment that the working designer needs to know about. The equipment surveyed is representative of English and American practice with some German. Further information should obviously be obtained from manufacturers' catalogues. This section is an introduction to the necessary knowledge of the craft that must lie at the centre of any practice in the art of Stage Lighting.

For the serious enthusiast anxious to learn more of lighting, I can recommend three courses of action. First, reading (a wealth of accumulated experience will be found in the bibliography). Second, the study of plays. The first interest of the lighting designer should be in the plays that he is called upon to illuminate. The reading of plays and an interest in other productions of every sort can form the best background to one's own practice. Third, practice itself. A lighting designer can only truly learn his trade by doing some lighting. If it is not always possible to find a real stage on which to practise, a model can provide a tremendously rewarding start. From a very small Pollock's model theatre, I gradually built a most elaborate, half-inch-to-the-foot scale model, with a hundred and twenty channel switchboard and with an almost professional quantity of spotlights. These little lanterns (made by Robert Stanbury, tutor in stage lighting at the Wimbledon School of Art) really did give an amazingly accurate representation of the various types of beam to be obtained from focus lanterns, acting areas, pageants, and so on; and one could set up an almost complete professional lighting layout. I remember a production of *Richard II* at the Old Vic, directed by Val May, set designed by Richard Negri, on which we set up every scene and tried out every cue on a model. The production was hauntingly successful from a visual point of view, and every effect had been seen, in miniature, beforehand and discussed. A model, however crude, is an invaluable aid when practising, and every budding lighting designer should obtain one.

Scope of the book

This book is intended for the professional amateur. That is, the man or woman who works either professionally or as an amateur, but who combines the enthusiasm and love of theatre of the dedicated amateur with the professional's compelling drive for the highest standards.

The fascinations of stage lighting are many. The enthusiast needs first and foremost imagination, the ability to conceive visions. Next, the creative and practical ability to turn these visions into reality with light. And finally, dedication. Theatre demands from its servants teamwork, co-operation and commitment. The lighting designer will be required to give peak effort at any hour of the day or night, often in the most unreasonable circumstances. It is at the ever-growing number of such complicated, perhaps crazy, enthusiasts that this book is aimed!

Throughout the book I have used the term 'Designer' when referring to the Lighting Designer. He may be solely concerned with the lighting design or he may also be the director, set designer, technical director or electrician. He is, however, the person responsible for organizing the use of light upon the stage.

Unless specific reference is made to a particular type of dramatic presentation, the word 'play' may be assumed to include any other type of performance, i.e. musical, opera, etc.

Author's note to revised edition

Eight years have passed since the publication of the first edition of this book. In the English theatre things have changed, in many ways beyond recognition. A splendid new National Theatre stands on London's South Bank, and many new repertory theatres dot the country. English theatre 'expertise' is in demand around the world, but the whole world of theatre has become more international, and directors, actors, writers, theatre consultants and even lighting designers are among today's globe-trotters.

It is difficult to take an overview of the state of stage lighting today. In a way that demonstrates both the frustrations of the theatre industry and its opportunities for talent and originality, one sees a situation of 'one step forward, two steps back'. This 'stop-go' has certainly been a continuing source of bedevilment to the modest band of historians of stage lighting, and each generation must have been irritated by the over-acclaimed achievements of the next. Stage lighting is a mix of art and technology, and progress in its practice is influenced by technical developments in spheres quite separate from the demands of theatre directors and designers.

Eight years have seen some remarkable technical advances alongside an infuriating tardiness in other areas. Some new lighting designers have emerged in Britain and in the United States and indeed even the more traditionally oriented European theatre seems at last to be awakening to the lighting designer. However, in some ways the spread of a more general acceptance of lighting has also meant that the designer's work has been taken more casually for granted.

Outstanding stage lighting is still rare: perhaps the average quality has improved only slightly over the last eight years. Certainly lighting has by no means come close to fulfilling its promise in the theatre. Computer technology may have produced spectacular innovations since 1970, yet one suspects that, despite the efforts of the many devoted enthusiasts, there remains much ignorance about lighting's contribution. The potential that lighting has in a theatrical production, as foretold by Adolphe Appia and Gordon Craig (see page 12), has seldom been fully realized.

Introduction

Stage lighting is a remarkable part of modern theatre. Remarkable, because although theatrical productions have been presented for many thousands of years, Stage Lighting, with the ability to actually *control* light, is an entirely new element.

For centuries men have performed plays; they have spoken, sung, acted or mimed stories to an audience surrounding them. Various rituals have accompanied these performances; styles of presentation have changed. Shapes of theatres, scenery, elaborate costume, properties, machinery, all have come into and gone out of fashion. Many so-called innovations are basically only a repeat of something which has gone before; however, electricity, electric light and the control of the illumination by which players are seen, has meant a true revolution in the theatre.

It is only in the last four or five hundred years that theatre has generally been performed indoors and light has had to be used to illuminate the stage and the players. Candles, oil lamps and gas, each in turn, contributed a slightly more sophisticated means of producing this light and allowed some degree of effect. Electricity, when it first arrived, merely imitated its predecessors. Rows of lamps, sometimes of different colours, could be dimmed or made brighter as required. After the First World War the introduction of the spotlight and the development of dimmer control broke through the traditional limitations and led to a new awareness of what controlled lighting had to offer to the theatre and the dramatist.

Without light nothing can be seen: it is one of the primary stimuli to the human brain and we are immensely sensitive to its every nuance. The most hackneyed example is perhaps that of waking in the morning and throwing open the curtains. There are few people who do not react in some way to the prospect of a grey, clouding, drizzly winter morning or a clear sharp brilliant sunlit day. The actual landscape can be identical. The difference is only in the light, which appears to create the *quality* of the air surrounding us.

Our lives revolve around the daily cycle of light and dark. Dark has an immediate subconscious and conscious impact upon us. Variations of light and shade affect nearly every move we make. I find as I write these words that I am sitting by a window: it would be inconceivable to work in the far corner of the room away from the light.

The spotlight and the dimmer have given us control over light. Within any given space we can create artificially any shape and feeling of light that we desire. *Unlike at any time in the past, this light can be created at a distance from its actual source.* We can fill a space with the atmosphere of dull day or sparkling morning; we can use this naturalistically or abstractly. We can fill the stage three-dimensionally as if creating the air that the actor breathes. Yet this new degree of power over light is still in its infancy; despite the everyday advances in technique, despite the theories that have been endlessly discussed, and despite the marvellously imaginative use that has already been made of this new medium.

An aspect of theatre only some sixty years old, the new lighting has already drastically influenced the shape of the theatres themselves. The return to open staging has been strongly influenced by developments in lighting.

For centuries men have written into their plays the light they have experienced in their lives; now this light can be 'manipulated' on the stage. Its visual and emotional effect can be used to accompany and influence the action: its dramatic potential, as new horizons of technique appear, is boundless.

Part 1
Stage Lighting Design

1 Living light for living people

Adolphe Appia and Gordon Craig were the prophets of modern stage lighting and production. Appia defined stage lighting as he found it in the nineteenth century as *Helligkeit*, which meant general illumination. This was produced by rows of border and wing striplights and footlights. Appia found this pitifully inadequate, and he foretold a new kind of light: *Gestaltendes Licht*, a 'form revealing light'. This three-dimensional, directional, moving light would give objects their natural roundness, shape and significance.

Light in nature may, broadly speaking, be divided into two categories: general indirect light (skylight or the light of an overcast sky), and specific direction light (sunlight). By filling the space of the stage within which the actor moves with an appropriate balance of these two kinds of illumination, the lighting designer creates a living space around the actor. This links him with his surroundings and completes the process of making a living environment within which he can perform, thus emphasizing to the audience the full meaning and emotion of the play.

In this chapter I shall draw heavily upon many previous works on lighting—particularly several from America which are listed, among others, in the bibliography on page 175. I do this because I feel that too often the fundamental principles of lighting, which are set forth in these books, are disregarded. In the United States lighting designers, largely inspired by Professor Stanley McCandless of Yale University, have established some 'rules of the game'. These remain a model of clarity to us all and the lighting designer ignores them at his (or the theatre's) peril.

The properties of light

The two types of lighting described above can be said to possess four controllable properties:

Intensity   Colour   Distribution   Movement

Intensity

The brightness of light. This is variable over a vast range from a mere glimmer to the limits of brightness that the eye can stand. This brightness depends in the theatre upon the number of light sources, their size, and whatever switches, dimmers, colour filters or masks are used. There are certain points to remember about brightness.

a *Subjective impression of brightness*
    Illumination can be measured in a number of scientific ways,

which are usually of only academic interest to the stage lighting designer. He is more concerned with the subjective impression of brightness upon the audience: i.e. not how bright the light *is* but how bright it *appears.* A single candle lit upon a dark stage will appear 'bright' while a thousand watt spotlight upon a bright stage may appear dim. Contrast powerfully affects the impression of brightness.

The colour and texture of scenery, costumes, properties and, indeed, the actors' faces, also affect the apparent brightness. The same illumination will give quite different effects on black and white settings.

b *Adaptation*

As the brightness changes, so the eye of the observer adapts itself. A bright scene will appear even brighter, by contrast, if it follows a dim one. But it will gradually appear less bright as the eye adapts itself to the new level. It might, therefore, be desirable gradually to creep up the actual intensity during such a scene to counteract this effect. Conversely, if prior to a dim scene the houselights are slowly dimmed, the audience will adjust more easily, and see more clearly what is happening on the stage.

c *Visual fatigue*

Too much light (glare), too little light or too many rapid changes of intensity may prove tiring to the observer.

d *Visual perception*

The amount of illumination needed to allow an object to be clearly seen depends upon the colour, reflective quality, contrast and size of the object, and its distance from the observer. With a theatre audience, consideration must be given to those in the back of the house as well as those in the front rows. The farther away the spectator, the more light is needed upon the stage.

e *Intensity and mood associated with brightness*

Bright light, allowing greater visual acuity, makes an audience more alert. The old rule of 'bright light for comedy' has much to recommend it.

Colour

Every colour in the visible spectrum is at the command of the lighting designer. Colour on the stage is the product of the colour of light and the colour of every object. Objects can only be seen because they act as reflectors of light to the eye. Delicate tints of coloured light may be used to enhance the actors' faces, or to colour-tone the whole stage. Realistic or stylized colour may be called for by the play, or colour can be used to emphasize, modify or enrich the pigment in costumes or scenery.

a *Visual perception*

The eye sees more clearly in the yellow-green zones of the middle spectrum rather than at the ends of red and blue.

b *Colour and mood*
   Warm colours and tints are often associated with comedy, cool or strong colours with tragedy.

Distribution

All light has form and direction, ranging from a soft shadowless diffusion to a stark sharp shaft of light. The angle of a beam of light and the resultant shadow may be endlessly varied. The eye only provides distinct vision within two or three degrees, beyond that peripheral sight is established by fairly crude stereoscopic vision. *The eye is invariably attracted to the brightest object in the field of vision.*

Movement

Each of the first three properties of intensity, colour and distribution may be altered or changed either quickly or slowly. A room may grow darker, the setting sunlight slowly changing colour and finally disappearing into the soft diffused light of dusk. This can be achieved on the stage realistically, or in any more abstract style that the designer chooses. Nature has conditioned us to an infinite variety of effects, to which we tend to become immune in our day-to-day life. Some of these 'effects', however startlingly beautiful, would appear outrageous on the stage.

The objectives of stage lighting

The aims of stage lighting are fourfold. By keeping them in mind the designer may judge every moment of his lighting. The aims can be used as a check list by which all stage lighting can be evaluated.

Selective visibility

The designer's first and most important task is to achieve visibility. The cardinal rule is: *Each member of the audience must be able to see clearly and correctly those things that he is intended to see.* Those parts of the stage to which his attention should not be drawn can be less brightly lit or left in complete darkness.

Ninety-nine per cent of the time it is the designer's duty to light the actors clearly so that everyone can see them. Only for very particular dramatic effect can the actor be underlit. If the audience have to strain to see the man who is speaking or singing, the lighting, no matter how beautiful it may look, is a total failure. It is said that an actor who cannot be seen, cannot be heard. In fact if an actor cannot be seen, the audience can hear, but they soon become fatigued and gradually begin to pay less attention.

Not only must the actor, and every other object upon the

stage that should be seen, be clearly illuminated, but each must receive proportionally the correct amount of illumination, and the lighting must reveal them correctly.

As we have already noted, the eye will naturally look towards the brightest part of the stage. This brightness is determined by:

a the amount of light,

b the amount of reflection from the object.

Thus a black object upon a bright stage will appear dark, whereas a white object will appear bright even if only dimly lit. For most practical purposes we have an easy reference point, which is the face of the actor. Faces, however, vary in tone: a pale face or make-up will appear lighter than a ruddy or suntanned one in the same lighting.

Almost all the time we will want to make the actor's face appear the brightest object upon the stage, in order to focus the attention of the audience upon him. This requirement determines almost all the basic principles of stage lighting.

During the action of the play different parts of the stage may become more important, different actors may need to appear more dominant. So the balance of visibility may be changed, either subtly or sharply. The balance of lighting may move from one side of the stage to another; an actor in an important speech may be gradually 'highlighted'. In this way the lighting acts as a pointer to the audience, telling them where to look. The well-known follow-spot in a musical is an obvious (if crude) example of this type of 'indication'.

In a naturalistic production of a Chekhov play, there may be several dozen cues shifting the balance of intensity around the stage, none consciously 'seen' by the audience, but all of which subliminally direct their attention towards the key point of the scene. In films or television the camera can track or cut in to a close-up for a dramatic moment. On the stage all the audience see the play all the time in 'long shot'. Adjustment of the 'balance of visibility' help to focus their attention.

We must also remember that colour, which allows greater visual acuity towards the middle of the spectrum, plays a role in determining the visibility balance.

Revelation of form

General illumination alone may produce an even visibility over the whole stage but everything will appear flat and uninteresting. To make an object appear naturally in three dimensions there must be a 'form-revealing' light. Appia said, *'Shade and shadow are equal in importance to light itself.'* The third property of light discussed above was distribution. What the audience should see must not only be lit adequately, but also correctly. Everyone knows the moon is a sphere, but dependent upon the angles of the sun (the light) and the earth (the spectator) it will appear to be a flat disc or a crescent. All

15

objects on the stage may be seen correctly or they may be distorted, their shape flattened or revealed, dependent upon the distribution of light and shade. Most importantly the three-dimensional shape of the actor may be emphasized and he may be set apart from the scenery behind him and thrust into appropriate prominence.

Composition

'Painting the stage with light' is always the most obvious and enjoyable pursuit for both the lighting and scenic designer. Here the overall visual aims of the set designer are realized and perhaps extended. The intensity, colour and distribution of light create compositions of light, shade and colour over the setting and around the actors.

However, it is clearly the lighting designer's duty never to try to achieve an attractive visual picture at the expense of visibility. He has to ensure that the overall pictorial effect is what he intended, and that everybody in the audience can see clearly and correctly what should be seen. It is quite easy to create dramatic visual effects with light: shafts of colour, psychedelic projections, dazzling neo-realistic sunsets. It is comparatively difficult to do this, and at the same time to ensure a clear and correct balance of visibility. This is one of the principal challenges of stage lighting.

The possibilities of creating dramatic compositions in light are, of course, infinite. A brief study of the use of light in the paintings of the great masters can be rewarding. The 'new lighting', made possible by electricity, throws open the challenge of working not in paint, as they did, but in light itself—furthermore this is light and shade in four dimensions.

Light is used as an element of design in space, but this design is not static, as in painting or sculpture. Lighting design is visual design in space *and in time.* The controlled compositions of light may change and follow the play like a musical accompaniment.

Mood

Finally there is the creation of mood. Often one sees the inexperienced designer striving to create mood at the expense of almost everything else. Mood should, in fact, be the result of having successfully achieved the first three objectives. Light has an undeniably powerful effect upon our state of mind and emotions. Clear, warm brightness makes most people feel good, and vice-versa. The playwright uses this instinctively in his writing, making day and night, good and bad weather contribute to the dramatic effect. The designer, by using intensity, colour, distribution and movement, can exploit the emotional and psychological effects inherent in light and increase appropriately the dramatic effect the playwright intended.

A summing-up

The two types of lighting (general indirect and specific directional), possessing four controllable properties (intensity, colour, distribution, movement), used to achieve four objectives (visibility, composition, form, mood), are equally valid no matter what style of production may be embarked upon, no matter what type of theatrical presentation is intended and no matter what shape of stage and auditorium are used. Classical opera, modern naturalistic arena drama, anti-illusionistic staging, dance, circus or open-air musical—all can benefit from the designer having consciously applied these yardsticks to his work.

The content of the play and production style chosen for it by the director will dictate how these criteria are employed.

2 How to do it: an introduction

The black box and an experiment in visibility

Assume that the stage is contained within a large black box. All light is excluded. Darkness. How do we best go about lighting this space dramatically?

First, an experiment. Seat an actor in the middle of the stage. Take a spotlight and shine it on him—from above and from the front. He will be seen quite clearly, even from the back of the theatre, sitting in a pool of light surrounded by darkness. Now turn on all the general 'flooding' lights in the theatre, battens, footlights, even the worklights and the houselights. Obviously there will be much more light upon the actor but, strangely, he will appear no more brightly lit, indeed if there were a light-coloured background he would probably appear less bright, his face and outline tending to disappear against his light surroundings.

From this we may deduce two things. First, the spotlight is of great value for lighting the actor, since it allows us to light him separately from his surroundings. This makes him more visible. Second, we learn that contrast of light and shade is an important factor in determining apparent brightness.

The angle of light and its associations (Pl 2–11)

Continue the experiment, observe more closely how the appearance of the actor is altered as the position of the spotlight is moved: below—to the front—the side—45° above—overhead—behind, and so on. About 45° above appears to reveal the face most naturally. Now try the same angles moving around towards the side of the actor. The most 'natural' angle of all will be seen to be about 45° above and to the side. Farther round to the side the light will appear more harsh and dramatic.

As the theatre is using the human being as a yardstick, and the human situation as the usual basis of its drama, so in theatrical lighting, natural light is the yardstick by which the audience will (subconsciously) react. This must make it the designer's continual guide.

Lighting the actor

We have found that to light the actor's face most naturally the spotlight should be placed roughly 45° above and 45° to the side. Even this, however, may cast rather harsh shadows, particularly when he turns his head away from the front. So next we will want to place another spotlight at an equivalent angle on the other side. Two units 90° apart, 45° above the actor and to the side will illuminate him adequately. He will be free to move around within the limits of the spotlights' beams and still be reasonably lit.

'The Method'

Since a spotlight beam will seldom exceed eight or ten feet in diameter, how do we go about lighting the whole stage? We now embark upon a study of what has been termed a 'Method' of stage lighting. This was first put forward by Professor Stanley McCandless in the United States and in England by Mr Geoffrey Ost in his excellent little book *Stage Lighting*. This 'Method' suggests a basic formula for setting about lighting a scene and, as such, provides an excellent framework. However, in common with most methods, by its very nature it introduces the danger that its 'rules' will be too rigidly adhered to. Perhaps most rules in the theatre—as in life—are really made to be broken; certainly the creators of 'the Method' have always preached that the formula should be loosely and freely interpreted. It is regrettably true that some very dull lighting can result from following it too closely. But, a word of warning: while an individual designer should employ individual methods, varying them for each production, he would be foolish to forget the basic precepts of the Method. Let him vary his approach to lighting (as indeed I will later suggest); but let him beware at all times of ignoring the basic disciplines

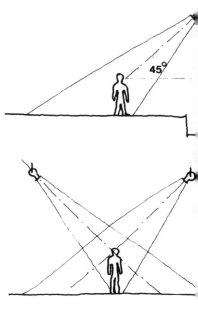

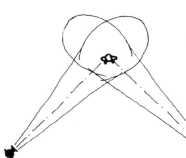

Fig. 1 Lighting the actor

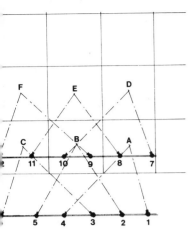

Fig. 2 Lighting the acting area

the Method provides for the fulfilment of the four objectives of lighting. It divides the lighting of a scene into eight categories.

1 Lighting the acting area

Let us now return to the lit actor on the stage. We have next to light the space around him—all the space in which he or his colleagues will want to move during the play.

We must first divide the stage into areas of a size that a spotlight beam at the throw available can fill, and yet not so large as to limit flexibility in their control. We will probably decide on a module of about 2–3·5 m. (6–10 ft.). If we have a proscenium stage 8 m. (24 ft.) wide we might divide it across its front edge into three parts. With an acting area 5 m. (16 ft.) deep it will be two areas deep. For convenience we will letter these A–F (fig 2).

The actor will now be found in Area B centre stage. His two spotlights will be shown at positions 2 and 5. To cover the remaining areas we will add two spots to each area at relatively the same angle.

Spotlights 1–6 will be placed in the auditorium, while 7–12 will very likely be hung on a spotbar behind the proscenium. The distance of these spots in plan from their areas will depend upon their height above the stage. (See mechanics p. 167.)

If the audience is to see the front of an actor, some light at least must come from the front, i.e. from the general direction of the audience. In fig 2 it will be seen that half the illumination is actually coming from the auditorium.

If the two spotlights into each area are both at full intensity the result may be rather flat. We can vary the balance attractively either by altering their intensity slightly or by putting a different tint of colour in one side or the other. Perhaps a very pale blue or cold tint in those lamps on the actor's left and a warm gold tint on the right. There are endless variations of this—but it should always be remembered that these units are lighting the actor's face and should be subtle in colour to avoid distorting his appearance.

Let us apply this acting area lighting to a simple set to be lit naturalistically (figs 3, 4, 5). It is a realistic interior box set with a French window on stage left, fireplace on the right and entrance at the back.

Fig. 3   Typical box set

The acting areas are laid out in the manner described earlier and we see that area F will light the armchair by the fire and areas B and E, the sofa. Note that area D is much reduced by the shape of the setting. Supposing the scene takes place on a sunny morning, we shall assume the main source of light to be sunlight from the window. Accordingly the acting area spots on stage left will be of a light warm tint, gold, pale yellow, or possibly no colour 'open white', while those on the right will be a cool tint taking the colour tone of the walls of the room

19

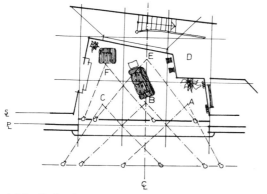

Fig. 4
Plan of typical box set

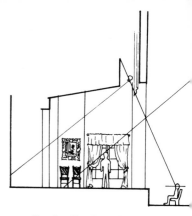

Fig. 5 Section of typical box se[t]

(this light from the right would, in nature, be a reflection of the sunlight from the walls).

A later scene at night may be required, with moonlight coming through the window and two lamps lit around the sofa area. The warm light in the room should now appear to come from the table lamp, centre, the cool of the night from stage left. With a fire in the fireplace, the stage right area C may need warm firelight from the right and lamplight from the left, while area A will want cool moonlight from the left and lamplight from the right. If then the curtains are drawn, the moonlight will have to go, being replaced by another sort of 'reflected' light, this time a reflection of the centre lamps from the walls and closed curtains. To cope with these complications we might double-up the acting area spotlights in various tints for each contingency. With the smaller installation we would choose compromise colours which, at various levels of brightness, could be accepted as apparently warm or cool as necessary.

In principle, then, the acting area lighting builds up a pattern of basic illumination around the actor. This pattern is divided into areas as the designer requires, so that each part of the stage can be separately controlled. Into each of the areas we beam two spotlights, from the most suitable angles for the human face, and by varying their colour and intensity we achieve some variety in the composition and mood of the scene. The size of individual areas need not, of course, be identical, and may have to be adjusted to the position of scenery, furniture—and action.

We must, of course, ensure that each spotlight is spread sufficiently to overlap its neighbour. It is also usually advisable to focus spotlights with a soft diffuse edge to the beam. This will avoid dark spots between the areas and any distracting hard edges of light across the actor's face. The transition from one area to another must be unseen. If, after careful focusing, there are still dark patches, we have obviously made the areas too large, and they must all be readjusted.

Moving into three dimensions

With the foregoing we have probably gone a good way towards satisfying Objective 1—selective visibility.

If the setting of the play is indeed like the interior box set we have discussed, with a ceiling over it, it is likely that the front of house (FOH) and spotbar positions we have chosen are the only places we are able to put lighting equipment. Obviously we cannot backlight the actor if there is a ceiling over his head, but supposing the ceiling were not there, or supposing we were lighting the actor on a bare stage, would we gain anything by using more angles than the two at 45° to his front?

The answer is an unqualified yes. Light is three-dimensional: it fills space, and its angles, the angles of light and shade, of composition can be infinitely varied around the actor to enormous advantage. We have already discussed the 45° angles, which were enough to illuminate the human face pleasantly. Let us now examine in more detail plates 2–11 showing the effect of various lighting angles upon the face.

Light from below (Pl 2)

This casts shadows upwards and appears unnatural, because in nature it is an uncommon angle of light. It is probably the least useful lighting position, which is not to say that it should be scorned entirely.

Footlights are a relic of the old days when the lighting of the stage came from rows of candles. These candles were superseded by oil lamps, then gas jets and, finally, electric lamps. Before the days of spotlighting, the footlights, being on the front edge of the stage (and obviously closer to the actor than the battens hung overhead) were a principal source of light. Then spotlights came to be placed in the auditorium; these lit the actor at the front of the stage far more adequately and from a more natural angle. So the footlights lost their prime function.

But in nature some light does come from below. The childish game of holding a buttercup beneath someone's chin to see the yellow reflection should remind us again that everything reflects light. A man in a green field on a sunlit day will be 'uplit' in green light. The shadows under the eyebrows, nose and chin will be tinged with green. We might want this effect,

Fig. 6 Lighting composition

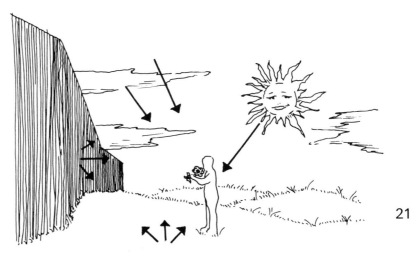

occasionally, on the stage. Footlights can be used at a subdued level to colour-tone the stage and setting. A warm or cool tint can subtly colour shadows, walls and ceiling.

For the simulation of artificial light, or for an arbitrary effect, we often need a low angle of light. Obviously a scene played around a candle or lantern on the floor or on a table should be lit from below. This is often very difficult to achieve without casting unwanted multiple shadows. However, we can be satisfied that the footlights and/or spotlights from below the actor will be needed on occasions—occasions which are demanded by the play or by the type of presentation.

Eye-level from the front (Pl 3)

This flattens out the features almost completely and the actor tends to merge with the background. On its own this is an unimportant angle but, nevertheless, it can be useful. An actor with deep-set features may be too harshly lit from the 45° angle. A lower angle of light from the front of house will 'fill in' over-severe shadows if used with discretion. Again, if footlights are not used (for example on an open stage), this low frontal light can be employed for colour-washing the stage.

Low level from the side (Pl 4)

As the source of light is moved around to the actor's side his face will be more sharply and dramatically lit. Obviously if he looks away from the light only the back of his head will be seen; but if he is facing front or towards the source he will be sharply 'edge' lit. As the angle between the spectator and the light increases, so the effect becomes more dramatic. Contrast and shadows increase until the actor is in complete silhouette. Side- or edge-lighting and 'rim-lighting' (where the light is farther behind the actor) have always been recognized for their dramatic value. Examine some of the paintings of Rembrandt to see the effective use of side-lighting as a dramatic device. A danger inherent in low sidelight is that one actor will tend to cast shadows upon another; it is therefore more common to use a sidelight from above head height. A low sidelight can, however, be immensely useful in lighting ballet or modern dance to reveal fully the plastic values of the moving figure.

The angle around 45° horizontally and vertically (the 'ordinary' or basic acting area angle) (Pl 5)

As the angle through to 90° (i.e. overhead and/or to the side) increases, so the contrasts and shadows grow more pronounced; the light becomes more dramatic but the danger of 'facial' distortion is increased.

The light overhead (Pl 6)

This cannot contribute much to lighting the face but it can create a most dramatic effect. Equally useful dramatically is:

Backlight (Pl 7)

Above and behind the actor. The beams fall upon the actor's head and shoulders, creating a halo-like impression that makes him stand out from his background.

High and to the side (Pl 8)

This has much of the dramatic value of a low sidelight while lessening the risk of actors shadowing each other.

Above, behind and to the side (Pl 9)

A high side backlight. An angle mixing the qualities of back- and sidelight and particularly useful when used as the dominant motivating 'keylight' of a scene.

Low angle side backlight (Pl 10)

For special effect.

Having looked briefly at the values of these angles individually, let us now consider them in combination. The nine possibilities divide simply into three groups, each of which can contribute to three-dimensional lighting.
1 Lights to the front. These light the face of the actor, and roughly 35°–45° horizontally and vertically is to be preferred.
2 Lights from the side. These model the actor. A high angle avoids the shadowing problem.
3 Lights from above (and behind). These complete the modelling and make the actor 'stand out' from the background.

We find that to satisfy both Selective Visibility and Revelation of Form on our basic layout, we need to employ not just two but as many as five spotlights in each area. Pl 11 shows this combination in one area; elaborated over the whole stage it would ensure a highly flexible and exciting lighting set-up.

Once again it must be stressed that this is only a basic method of work. Some plays need backlight, some do not. Some settings allow backlight, others do not. The designer, by thinking in terms of three-dimensional light, will try to encourage the set designer to design his set so as to allow the appropriate light to be used for the play.

2 Supplementary acting area

If we look back to the plan of the interior set (fig 5) we will note that the acting area spotlights have adequately covered most of the stage area. But there are certain places on the stage outside the six areas. For example, the arch upstage is beyond area E and an actor standing outside the French windows would be out of area A. In these cases we should need to supplement the acting area units with 'specials'. Remembering the 45° principle, we would set two spotlights into the arch area upstage. These would probably come from the first spotbar and be placed next to units 8 and 11 (see Demonstration 1, p. 31). Into the French window a single unit would probably suffice, again from the spotbar, adjacent to unit 9. Now we have achieved a complete coverage of the stage and wherever an actor may go we should be able to light him.

3 Blending and toning the acting area

In a small installation with very limited equipment it may not be possible to allow even two spotlights into each of an adequate number of areas. It is likely in this case that some flooding equipment will be needed to wash light softly over the acting area, filling any irregularities there may be. This equipment could be a batten hung beneath the spotbar or perhaps some floodlights—500 watts or smaller—on the bar itself. It will be useful to have hoods on these lamps so we can get the light where we want it—on the actor, and not lighting the top of the scenery.

Flooding equipment in this subsidiary role can also be valuable on the larger stage, without losing the selective quality of spotlighting. A soft wash of light and colour can act as a 'fill-light' affecting the colour tone of the whole stage. The PAR or reflector lamp batten can be very useful here. These units, providing a broad 'sheet' of shadowless illumination, can colour and blend the acting area without unwanted spill on the surroundings.

4 Lighting the scenery

A rather amazing rule to begin with is *don't*—or perhaps, *don't, unless you have to.*

If the lighting of the acting area has been carried out as meticulously as it should have been, much of the set will be well lit by reflection. But some scenery will certainly need its own special light. An area of sky, a cyclorama, an effect of sunlight striking a wall—these and many other effects will call for special treatment.

Returning to the interior set example, we will find almost certainly that the walls of the room itself will need no special lighting. The acting area colour tints should have been chosen with due consideration for the painted colour on the walls and reflection should do the rest. But the backing outside the window will need some units, as will the hallway beyond the

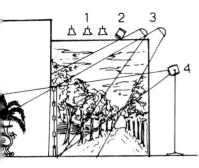

7 Section through window, exterior

upstage arch. Three floods (two for day, one for night) should go outside the window, with perhaps two smaller ones in the hall. These should be fixed as high as possible to avoid casting shadows of the passing actors on the backings. The space in front of the window backing should not be forgotten. This is the area that is supposed to be outdoors. It is within sight of the audience and both downlight and backlight of the actor should be used (fig 7).

We should not always think in terms of using floodlights for lighting scenery, for very often spotlighting will be more effective. The view outside the window may be a painted cloth of countryside, and, if facilities permit, its appearance could be enhanced and the illusion of distance increased if parts of it, e.g. the horizon, are subtly spotlighted.

The designer in his early meetings with the set designer will need to consider:

a Do I have to light the scenery specially?

b If so, how? Is it to be front lit? If so, is there any texture on the set that would be enhanced by lighting from a particular angle? If there is, does the necessary angle contradict any other motivating angle of light called for by the script? If the scenery is translucent or transparent should it be rearlit? From what angle? Should the colour of light subdue or enhance the colour in the set? Are the colours chosen by the set designer suitable to be lit in every way demanded by the play? (For example, it would be unwise to design a green set that is only used in a scene described by the author as lit by a blood-red sunset.)

These and many other questions will have to be posed and answered with regard to sets, props, costumes and everything that makes up the environment of the actor.

5 Motivating light

Now we must consider (at least with any play that is remotely naturalistic) the motivating light. This means any *light sources* used on the stage: candles, gas lamps, oil lamps, electric fittings, fires, chandeliers, braziers and natural sources such as the moon and stars. The sun itself is (luckily) not often called for, since its brightness would obviously be impossible to imitate—but a setting sun or sun seen through mist or cloud would come into this category. Nearly everywhere, the designer will have to re-create the artificial light source electrically. Moreover, if, for example, a candle is required, since most fire authorities will only allow real flame on the stage in exceptional circumstances, the designer will have to use real ingenuity to provide a substitute that is acceptable to the audience. It is slightly ridiculous that one has to go to such lengths to produce an imitation candle flame.

The motivating light, i.e. the source or sources of light on the stage will often be the key to the lighting composition of a

25

scene. It is important that the director and the designers, both of set and lighting, consider carefully the placing of these sources in relation to the placing of the actors. Even more important is that, once decided upon, *these light sources should in turn influence the movement of the actors.* Behaviour is influenced by light. One sits by a light or by a window to read a book. These considerations are too often forgotten in the rehearsal room.

6 Motivated light

Next in importance from the point of view of composition is motivated light. This includes all the special lighting required to give the *illusion of light coming from a chosen source.* This may be one of the motivating light sources (see above), or it may be from off-stage. Very often we will assume that the sun is the off-stage light source, and so the motivating light will suggest the sun's rays. On the interior set example, sunshine is supposed to be coming through the window left. For this we will probably use one or maybe several lamps, either hung overhead or on tall stands, shining through the window. The rays of the sun are virtually parallel, and quite the hardest thing to reproduce on the stage, but we can no doubt assume 'artistic licence' and use a 1000 watt or even 2000 watt Fresnel. If the facilities are available perhaps the best thing would be to use several parallel-beam lanterns, the old 'pageant' lanterns, some 'beamlights' or the American beam projector. Only with these can one get a truly parallel shadow of the window into the room.

The stage lighting equipment available at the moment needs to be supplemented by a range of these parallel beam lanterns, and I suspect their size should not be limited to one or two thousand watts—for why should we not be able to achieve a really blistering shaft of sunlight?

If the time of day in a scene changes—perhaps to sunset— we may need some more 'motivated light'. A similar type of unit but hung lower down would cast the longer shadows of evening across the room. Obviously the motivated light is going to be the most dominant light in the room. The acting area units will be balanced on their dimmers to reinforce the illusion that the sunlight is in fact the source of light. Once again we should see that the director and his team have chosen the position of the window itself with care, and that the director has placed his actors on the stage bearing in mind that his main light source will be coming from the window.

We move on to the next scene. Night has fallen and the lamps are lit. Perhaps we will want to suggest moonlight outside—using similar units to those for sunshine but differently coloured and much much lower in intensity. The lamplight itself, from the fittings on-stage, will be insufficient, so we will hope to colour and set the acting area units in such a way that they will give the illusion of light coming from the light fittings. But it may be necessary to set a 'special' spotlight on to the sofa area to reinforce this impression.

On a more ambitious installation we might use two more spots to supplement each fitting. We must remember that we are trying to give the impression of light *from* the fitting. An actor standing by a lamp should have the warm light, apparently from the fitting, on the near side of his face. We must beware too of casting a shadow of the actual fitting on any nearby surface.

We must then consider other, perhaps less important, sources of light. We may want a glow from the fire: for this we can conceal a small spot or flood in the fireplace. This might be supplemented from a low tormenter-boom side position.

Lastly let us imagine a hanging fitting on the landing at the top of the stairs. If we have a spotlight hung above and beyond it, it will backlight the actors as they go up or down.

7 Special visibility

We have noted most of the types of lighting that might be used for illuminating the actor or his setting. This category is for all 'specials'. In our interior example, the last scene may end with one actor left alone on the sofa at a dramatic moment. The director would like everything to fade except a light on his face. The acting area units will be set too wide for this, so we must focus a special spotlight for the job. A non-realistic production may use dozens of such 'specials', beams of arbitrary light. A follow-spot would come into this category and we must remember that such a spotlight can range from the bright hard-edge follow-spot of a big musical to the most delicately handled softly focused moving light almost unnoticed by the audience.

8 Special effects lighting and projection

The reader may be surprised to find these being considered so low in priority. Special effects include all the wonders and illusions of psychedelic swirling colour, fire and flame, ghosts, clouds, lightning, snow and explosions. These, one might suppose, are the essence of stage lighting. Nothing could be further from the truth. They are fun and games to the designer, effects that have to be handled with great expertise and precision, but which must nevertheless be considered as secondary to the job of lighting the actor dramatically.

An important aspect of special effects, and one that is continually growing in importance, is projection. The projection of scenery is becoming more and more practical and exciting. Cycloramas, backcloths, rear-projection screens, all can be covered with powerful projections of real or stylized images. Great possibilities of projection on to other surfaces, the floor, three-dimensional objects, gauzes, mirrors and so on are creating a new dimension in scene and lighting design (for more details see chapter 6).

The creative concept—a personal approach

The categories we have just explored are the framework of the standard 'Method' of lighting.

However, I must confess that, much as I admire the Method, it is not the way in which I, basically, like to approach lighting design. My own working method runs parallel, but places different emphasis on the various categories. My concept stems from a desire to create a three-dimensional atmosphere of light around the actor. It is founded upon the inspiration of natural light, although the way in which it is developed will allow any type of production style. In practice I take two sections of the Method and consider them in a slightly different way.

When working on a production with a great number of scenes or changes of acting area, the discipline of the Method is almost indispensable. However, where I differ is in the degree of priority given to 'Motivated Light' and the 'Acting Area Light'.

Whether we are in a realistic situation or not, the category of light the Method describes as 'motivated' is the dominant keylight of the scene. Just as sunlight dominates natural lighting, so the dominant keylight of a scene should influence everything else.

Rollo Gillespie Williams in his book *The Technique of Stage Lighting* produced a theory of lighting composition which has influenced me considerably. Considered together with the Method it represents more closely my own approach.

It combines the acting area and motivated lighting and then divides them into:
    1 dominant lighting
    2 secondary lighting
    3 rim-lighting
    4 fill-in lighting

The dominant lighting should set the dramatic key of the scene (in fact I call this light the 'keylight'). If the scene requires it, it should have a clearly pronounced direction, intensity and colour. It might be highlight from the sun through a window, moonlight, the light from a lamp or fire, or a perfectly abstract shaft, with no particular naturalistic significance.

Our earlier investigations into the effect of varying angles of light tell us a lot about how the keylight should be considered. It may come from the front; it may, indeed, be from one of the acting area 45° angles. A frontal angle will give a soft and generally flattening effect. As the angle between the audience's vision and the direction of the keylight increases, the dramatic effect is also increased. The most powerful angles will be found at the side, above and behind the acting area.

This light is all important: it provides the basic construction upon which the remainder of the composition can be built. It can create shadow (which is all too often lost when we start our composition with the acting area light) and everything can be balanced appropriately to the level we choose for the keylight.

Next we consider the secondary lighting. This is in all probability the 'acting area lighting' of the Method. It is supplementary to the keylight and may be quite complex, coming from various angles at various intensities. It will be a counterfoil to the keylight in naturalistic schemes, being the reflections created by it. The amount of shadow that the keylight creates will be determined by the secondary lighting; the brighter this is, the less will be the effect of contrast. It determines, therefore, how dramatic the keylight effect is, and it creates a balanced composition. For an exterior scene, in which the keylight is sunlight, the secondary light will be the light from the sky and reflections from the ground or any adjacent walls (fig 6).

The keylight for a night scene may be the light from a practical lantern, and the secondary light may be moonlight. The latter could be considered a keylight but, due to the composition of the scene, it is making a secondary contribution.

The final two categories are intended to accentuate the actor. First is 'rim-lighting'. This is the highlighting from the back top or sides of the actor, and must be at a higher intensity than the rest of the lighting if its modelling is to be apparent. It will give highlights to the actor's hair and edge-light him to separate him from the background. Sometimes this separation will be neither necessary nor desirable, but whenever it is needed it clearly enhances the actor's appearance.

Lastly, 'fill-lighting'. Fill-light is light, generally from the front, which softens the shadows and blends the key- and secondary lighting. It is also a toning light for the setting. Fill-light from a low frontal position can do this and at the same time perform a more important task, that is, provide lighting into the actor's eyes from a low level to soften any shadows that may result from the overhead lighting.

Summary

These two theories—one demanding an original approach for each production, the other supplying a discipline for all—may be combined to produce a new check list:
1 the dominant keylight
2 lighting the acting area with (a) secondary light (b) rim-light (if required) (c) fill-light (if required)
3 supplementary acting area

4 blending and toning the acting area, if not already dealt with under 2(c)
5 lighting the scenery
6 motivating light source
7 special visibility
8 special effects lighting and projection

Lighting is not a mechanical process; it is neither simply a matter of illumination nor of making effects. The art of creative lighting is to create an IDEA based upon a play, and upon the concept of the director and the set designer. This idea is of light and shade and SPACE which enfold the actor and help him project his story to his audience. Therefore the designer must have a mental image of the overall visual effect of the stage, filled with actors and scenery. This image must be in three dimensions, and in the fourth too—in time—as the lighting ebbs and flows and changes with the drama.

With this idea in mind the designer must start work on the technical realization of his plans, constantly bearing in mind his duty to the actors and the four Objectives of lighting.

He remembers too that it is frighteningly easy to produce startling visual images, and that the real task of the designer is to do this as required, and at the same time to light the actors perfectly, 'in balance' with them.

With a clear dramatic and visual concept painstakingly carried through, the designer's work should fit in to the whole production perfectly. Except in unusual circumstances it will probably go almost unnoticed by the public, but his reward will be a personal satisfaction. His colleagues, the director and set designer, will have had their concepts too—the lighting designer can perhaps satisfy their demands and give them that little bit extra—the 10 per cent extra of which they didn't quite dare dream.

Demonstration 1 Typical Box Set

LANTERN SCHEDULE

Position	Type		Usage
FOH	1	patt 264	Area A
	2	,, ,,	,, B
	3	,, ,,	,, C
	4	,, ,,	,, A
	5	,, ,,	,, B
	6	,, ,,	,, C
Bar 1	1	patt 23	,, E
	2	patt 23	Arch US
	3	patt 137	Softlight
	4	patt 23	Lamp special
	5	patt 23	Area F
	6	patt 137	Softlight
	7	patt 23	Window spec
	8	patt 137	Softlight
	9	patt 23	Arch US
	10	patt 23	Lamp spec
	11	patt 23	Sofa spec
	12	patt 23	Area E
	13	patt 23	,, F
Bar 2	1	Beamlight	Sun to Window
	2	,,	,, ,, ,,
	3	patt 223	Downlight exterior
	4	patt 49	Cloth
	5	patt 49	,,
	6	patt 49	,,

Position	Type		Usage
Boom L	1	patt 23	X Light Warm
	2	,, ,,	,, ,, ,,
	3	,, ,,	X Light cool
	4	,, ,,	,, ,, ,,
	5	,, ,,	Night
Boom R	1	,, ,,	X Light Warm
	2	,, ,,	,, ,, ,,
	3	,, ,,	X Light Cool
	4	,, ,,	Fire X Light
Stage L	1	patt 49	Flood cloth 8' 6" stand
	2	patt 243	Sunset 4' 6" ,,
	3	patt 243	Moon 8' 6" ,,
	4	patt 223	X Hall 4' 6" ,,
	5	patt 123	Downstairs wall brkt
	6		Hanging fitting
Stage R	1	patt 137	Fire glow
	2	patt 123	Firelight
	3		Fire
	4	patt 223	X Hall 8' 6" stand
Onstage	1		Tablelamp
	2		Wall Brkt
	3		,, ,,

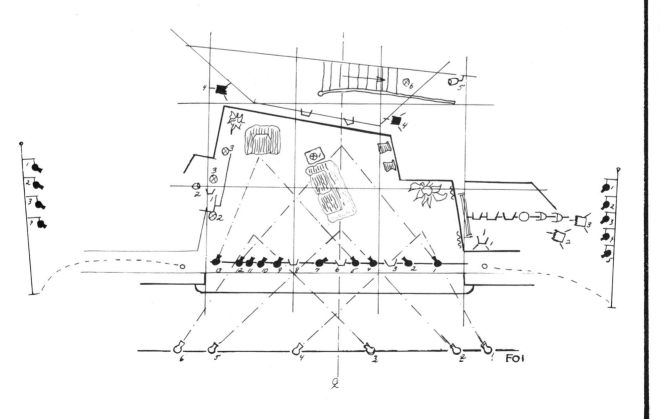

3 Procedure: preparation

The role of the lighting designer

Who should be in charge of the lighting? The English professional theatre has traditionally held the director responsible. In America it has been the set designer's prerogative. But during the last few decades lighting has come to be regarded, in both countries, as a separate element, under the control of a Lighting Designer.

The reason for this is obvious. Lighting has grown increasingly more complex. More equipment has gradually been introduced, with the result that the lighting process has taken more time and cost more money. With more elaborate facilities, more elaborate and sophisticated effects have been made possible. A desire for these effects and an ever-growing recognition of the dramatic potential in lighting, have led in turn to increasing demands being made by the director. New technical possibilities extend artistic horizons—greater creative demands prompt new technological developments. Voices have been raised against this seemingly inevitable increase in complexity; but nothing has stopped it. It is interesting to note that most of this elaboration in lighting has come out of the American and English commercial theatre, which is hardly an area that encourages unnecessary or frivolous expenditure. Yet for many years hard-headed producers have paid out very substantial sums of money for their lighting. They may have been reluctant, but in the end they have found it necessary—and worthwhile.

The specialist lighting designer has emerged, part artist, part technician; he must possess the imagination to grasp the director's and set designer's concept of the production, and the vision to contribute something of his own. He must also have at his command the ability to plan and use light, as well as a knowledge of stagecraft and electricity in order to realize his 'vision'. Finally, he must work efficiently and economically.

Theatre lighting design is now a profession on its own. In England the Society of British Theatre Lighting Designers, formed in 1963, is the professional body devoted to the working conditions of its members, the raising of standards of their work and the improvement in quality of equipment used. Its membership, although still small, is responsible for 80 per cent of the major professional lighting in the United Kingdom. In 1975 this society enlarged its membership to include all designers working in the theatre: scenery, costume, sound and lighting. The new, wider organization has become a special section within Equity, the actors' and directors' union, with autonomy over designers' affairs. In the United States professional lighting designers must be members of the lighting section of the United Scenic Artists Union. To join this union the applicant must pass an entrance examination and these are held annually. The union now ensures that every Broadway production has to employ a lighting designer, and a standard contract of employment, a minimum fee, working conditions, programme credit and so on, are established. Fees range from a minimum of $2000 (£1042), of half the scenery designer's fee plus a minimum of $100 per week and an assistant paid by the producer. In England the working conditions of the profession are less well organized. There are at present few designers able to live exclusively off the proceeds of lighting. Shows are still presented with no one person responsible for the lighting, but these decrease in number every year. About 90 per cent of London productions credit a lighting designer. Incredibly perhaps for a period of galloping inflation, fees, which in 1969 were usually between £150 (then $350) and £500 ($1200), are still in the range of £200 (now $370) to a rare £1250. Royalties are still only grudgingly won. Since this fee may cover three or four weeks' work, a large part of which will be over weekends, often at night, it is obvious that money is not a great temptation to the designer.

In England there is still a serious need for training in lighting design. Whereas in the United States several universities can offer a course in stage lighting, in England there is nothing comparable. In the latter country a knowledge of lighting can only be gained by reading those few books that are available, or by working with a practising designer. Some of the leading English drama schools offer lighting lectures as part of their stage management technical courses, but none can offer a study of advanced practice.

The Arts Council of Great Britain has a scheme whereby one or two young potential designers can receive training for one year by a subsidized 'attachment' to a working designer. This is a modest beginning but much progress has yet to be made to encourage a new generation of lighting artists for the theatre.

The production team

Theatre is teamwork and the director is the leader of the team. It is quite useless for the designer to pursue an idea of his own which is at variance with the director's intention. Wherever there may be disagreement, the lighting designer can, of course, try to persuade his colleagues to his way of thinking, but if he cannot, then he must bow to the director's wishes. It is also clearly no part of his job to do anything but enhance the appearance of the set and costumes. A costume designer has every right to expect the true colours of his costumes to be seen on the stage. The lighting should do this, unless by so doing it is conflicting with the overall intention established by the director.

Planning begins; analysis of the script

Ideally the designer will start work from the very outset of the production. It is far from satisfactory to start work on a production when the set has already been completely designed and the actors are in rehearsal. The lighting designer should be in on the early conferences and discussions between the director and the scenic designer. He will probably be able to make a positive contribution, perhaps pointing out how lighting might influence the staging of a particular scene or suggesting how a solution with light might help overcome a particular scenic problem. The most successful productions are usually those on which the director and designer have collaborated closely.

Since every facet of the lighting will come, in one way or another, from the play itself, the first step, obviously, is to read the script. The designer should first read a script through quite rapidly to get the feel and atmosphere of the play and then go through it again, painstakingly making a synopsis of the action. In this scene-by-scene breakdown every reference, either in the text or in the stage directions, to any lighting effect should be noted, as well as those scenes in which the lighting may make a special contribution.

The time of day of each scene, any reference to the weather or season of the year and any indication as to whether the lighting should change during the act with the passing of time or to underline any change of atmosphere should also be recorded (fig 8).

Lighting. Scene Synopsis

MISTER by Stanley Eveling
Theatre Projects Trust

Basement room in Whitechapel. Window below street level.
Time: February March.
Prologue. 5 am. "grey light of early morning illuminates face & figure of Lord Nelson, making it difficult to see whether it is real or not."
Very cold dark – passing car lights

Tom staggers very ill, downstairs through door (light from landing) into room. falls over furniture.
Daddy wakes in cubicle. Bed side light on.
rush around room – Daddy turn on overhead light.

Tom to kitchen. Lights stove to boil kettle (iii)
scene at kitchen table. "halflight" (isolated in space)
"Morning-watch ..... sea just beginning to light up round the coast, silver & grey."

Daddy to bed Tom to sofa "it's cold" (ix)

f.b.o. [or change-light on pipes above to sc.1]

Fig. 8 Scene synopsis

When every detail has been extracted from the script itself, discussions can proceed. First, it is vital to establish why and how the play is going to be directed. What is the intention of the director and what style has he chosen for his staging? Is it to be realistic or naturalistic? Stylistic or expressionistic? It is unlikely that the style can be labelled in any of these convenient ways, but it is important that each person knows quite clearly what is in the others' minds.

Each scene will be discussed and the lighting designer may suggest how the light called for by the author in a particular scene could influence how or where it will be played and how the set may best be used. Probably the director and set designer and the set and lighting designers will need to meet separately on details that only concern themselves, but there should be a continuous interplay of ideas until the time when the final decisions are made.

The set will probably be discussed with the model and the lighting designer must ensure that whatever is being designed is practical from his point of view. He must see that sufficient space is left for lighting equipment, and that the set is correctly fitted on to the proposed stage. It would be foolish to allow the set designer to cover the whole stage with a huge ceiling right down to the proscenium wall if it is absolutely essential that overhead lighting is used. It is no use, except in extremely unusual circumstances, allowing the designer to design a part of the set that is impossible to light. If the intention of the production is that the actors should be very harshly cross lit, to make them stand out sharply from their surroundings, then the designer must allow space for the sidelighting.

Every now and again a production crops up where there appears to be almost no way of fitting in the lighting equipment at all. One such was the musical *Jorrocks* at the New Theatre, London (director Val May, set designer Disley Jones), which had such an enormous quantity of complicated flown scenery that there was no room for overhead lighting bars at all. Most of the flown scenery consisted of solid built pieces, and eventually I reached a solution whereby the lighting bars were built in to the underside of these (Pl 12). When the scenery was in use at stage level, the lighting bars were touching the floor, but when the piece was flown out the bars became a convenient overhead lighting position. In *She Stoops to Conquer* at the Garrick Theatre, London (lighting by David Hersey), the set was a very low-ceilinged room, and so small lighting units had to be built into the ceiling itself in place of the usual lighting bars.

Rehearsals

As soon as possible the designer must watch the actors' rehearsals. The director will have discussed how he intends using the stage, but he has to have absolute freedom to do

35

what he likes once he begins work with the actors themselves. The designer should log in his script all the principal moves around the stage. By the time he comes to the lighting rehearsals, he should know the actors' positions as well as the director does. During rehearsals he may find that the director has staged a scene in a way that is not only contrary to the original intention, but so different from it as to make it almost impossible to light as intended. The designer should point this out, for it may be that the director has simply overlooked the change, or he may have deliberately wanted to do something quite different. The designer, having made his comment, will adapt his plans accordingly.

The theatre and its equipment

Many shows in the commercial theatre are planned and rehearsed before the actual theatre is arranged. Of all the departments on a production, the lighting is probably most affected by the theatre in which the show is staged. The theatre will affect not only space on and around the stage and the position of most of the lighting in the front of house, but also the type and size of control system that will probably have to be used. In the United States this is rather less of a problem, as each show will travel its own switchboards, but in England, where a switchboard is normally permanently installed, the lighting designer is very much dependent on what he finds at the theatre.

The designer should find out, as soon as possible, which theatres may be visited. He should then try to obtain an accurate plan and section through the building, on which he can double check the position of the set and the places where he can rig his equipment. He will need to know the details of the permanent lighting, the type of switchboard, the number of circuits and how they are distributed, and what, if any, extra power is available.

Paper work, plots and plans

Now the formal process of design can begin. The designer will have a clear idea of what the play is about and the contribution that his lighting can make to the production ideas of his colleagues. He will have seen some early rehearsals and he will know what facilities and space he can expect in the theatres that the show is going to visit. As well as all this, he will have to have some idea of the scale upon which the lighting is conceived. Obviously every production has its limits. A school production of *Julius Caesar* with a twelve-way dimmer board might, if it is a gala occasion, use as many as twenty or thirty spotlights; a major musical at the Theatre Royal, Drury Lane in London, might use three or four hundred. Everything has to be considered in proportion, but the same rules of good lighting apply to all productions.

The designer has now to convert his ideas into plans and plots that will allow his equipment to be prepared.

The process of lighting is a strange contradiction. In performance we are dealing with a totally insubstantial medium: light is so difficult to contain, describe or confine. Yet when we employ it in the theatre, it is essential that every detail be precisely planned in advance. Every single part of the lighting can be calculated and considered on paper. Only by preparing all the physical aspects of the lighting, i.e. the equipment, in great detail, can we get sufficient creative freedom on the stage itself. Sloppy and inefficient planning will only lead to confusion on stage: time and money will be wasted and both will always be at a premium. The first priority in any theatre is for the actors to have sufficient time to rehearse: they should not have to wait for a designer who has not done his homework. Furthermore, good planning will ensure that the designer is able to spend the maximum available time on the creative part of his lighting.

The lighting design, set down on paper, can be described in three or four documents.

1 *The lighting layout plan* (fig 9) —a plan of the stage and the set, on which the layout of equipment will be marked accurately and to scale.

Fig. 9

Lighting layout plan

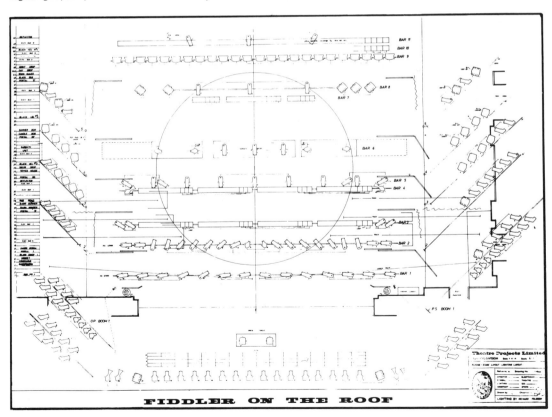

FIDDLER ON THE ROOF

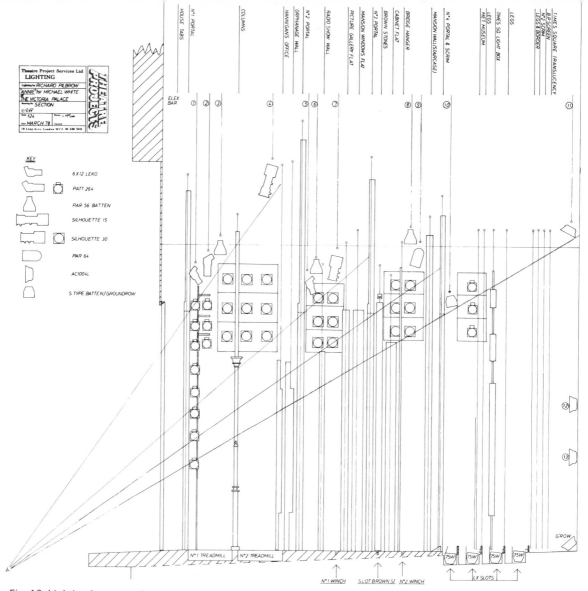

Fig. 10 Lighting layout section

2 *The lighting layout section* (fig 10) — a cross section of the stage showing vertical sightlines and the position and height of all the lighting equipment.

3 *The lighting layout schedule* (fig 11) — a list of every piece of equipment, lantern by lantern, giving details of its type, wattage, the use to which it will be put, the colour media it will require, the way in which it will be rigged and plugged, details of any special accessories that might be required and the number of the control board channel to which it is connected.

4 In the United States another plot is necessary, the *'Hook-up' schedule* (fig 12). This is a list of all the dimmer circuits, showing which lanterns are connected to which dimmer and their type, wattage, function and colour. This is particularly necessary, since American practice is to use a fairly modest

THEATRE PROJECTS (LIGHTING) LTD.

PRODUCTION: Back to Methuselah

THEATRE: Old Vic

POSITION	NO:	TYPE	SETTING		FOCUS	COLOUR	CIRCUIT
Bar 1	1	p223	ULC/LC	I/L	1/2	(50-50)	101
	2	p223	All L upstage edge revolve half stage off eclipse		3/4	(43)	102
	3	2p23	Straight down	pattern DL/LC	gobo H	(16)	103
	4	p223	All C/UC	J/M	3/4	(50-50)	104
	5	2p23	Straight down DL to C		gobo H	(40)	105
	6	p223	URC/RC		3/4	(50-50)	106
	7	2p23	Straight down	pattern all C	gobo H	(6)	107
	8	p223	ULC/LC	I/L	3/4	(40)	108
	9	2p23	Straight down DR to C		gobo H	(40)	109
	10	p223	All C/UC	J/M	3/4	(40)	110
	11	2p23	Straight down	pattern DR/RC	gobo H	(5A)	120
	12	p223	All R upstage edge revolve half stage off eclipse		3/4	(43)	127
	13	p223	URC/RC	K/N	1/2	(40)	128
Bar 2	1	p243 BK	X to LC/C		3/4	(50-50)	111
	2	p58	UR revolve			(42)	118
	3	p243	Backlight DL		3/4	(8)	112
	4	2p23	Straight down	edge revolve - outer to C - inner	gobo H	(5A)	114
	5	p243 BK	Backlight DLC to C		3/4	(8)	140
	6	p243	X to C/RC		3/4	(50-50)	119

Fig. 11 Lighting layout schedules: **a** English, **b** American

---

	INSTRUMENT SCHEDULE						ZORBA

R2

POSITION	No.	TYPE	FOCUS	COLOR	DIMMER	GANG. WITH	NOTES
BOX LEFT	1	6×12" 750W LEKO	WARM CENTRE	805	2	L2 R1.2	(3)
	2	"	"	805	2	L1 R12	
	3	"	SUN LEFT R	804	6	L4 5	(16)
	4	"	" RC	804	6	L3 5	
	5	"	" LC	804	6	L34	
	6	6×9" 750W LEKO	WARM LEFT	805	3	R7 8	"
	7	6×12" 750W LEKO	WARM RIGHT	805	1	L8 R6	(2)
	8	"	"	805	1	L7 R6	
	9	"	COOL APRON	517	4	L10 R9 10	(5)
	10	"	"	517	4	L9 R9 10	
*	11	"	COLOR APRON	815	5	L12 R11 12	10b (22)
*	12	"	"	815	5	L11 R11 12	
BOX RIGHT	1	6"×12" 750W LEKO	WARM CENTRE	CLEAR	2	R2 L12	
	2	"	"	"	2	R1 L12	
	3	"	SUN RIGHT L	"	7	R4 5	(17)
	4	"	" LC	"	7	R3 5	
	5	"	" RC	"	7	R3 4	
	6	6"×9" 750W LEKO	WARM RIGHT	"	1	L7 8	
	7	6"×12" 750W LEKO	WARM LEFT	"	3	R8 L6	
	8	"	"	"	3	R7 L6	
	9	"	COOL APRON	844	4	L10 L9 10	

ZORBA

No 1 Board Hook up 14 Plate 15/3000W

SWITCH	POSITION AND UNIT No	TYPE	FOCUS	COLOR
1	AUX MASTER 011 012 013 014 (1 BOX LEFT 3.4. RIGHT 3 2 PIPE 13)	3.8"x11" 750w LEKOS / 1.6"x9" 750w LEKO	SPECIALS	CLEAR 809
2	1 BOX LEFT 5.6 / 2 BOX RIGHT 5	2.6"x12" 750w LEKO / 1.6"x9" 750w LEKO	WARM RIGHT	805 CLEAR
3	1 BOX LEFT 1.2 / RIGHT 1.2	4.6"x12" 750w LEKO	WARM CENTRE	805 CLEAR
4	1 BOX RIGHT 1.2 / 2 BOX LEFT 5	2.6"x12" 750w LEKO / 1.6"x9" 750w LEKO	WARM LEFT	805 CLEAR
5	AUX MASTER 501 502 503 504 (1 BOX LEFT 7 8 RIGHT 6 7)	4.6"x12" 750w LEKO	COOL	517 849
6* 011 36	3 PIPE 1.3.5.7	4.8"x11" 750w LEKOS	NIGHT HI-LITE	805-850
7	AUX MASTER 701 702 703 704 (RAIL 1.3.7.9)	4.6"x12" 750w LEKO	LEFT WARM	825
8	RAIL 12.14.18.20	4.6"x12" 750w LEKO	RIGHT WARM	552
9	RAIL 6 10 11 15	4.6"x12" 750w LEKO	BLUE WASH	856
10	↑ RAIL 5.8.13.16 / ↓ 2 BOX LEFT 10.11 RIGHT 10.11	4.8"x11" 750w LEKO / 4.6"x12" 750w LEKO	HIGH BLUE / APRON COLOR	856 / 815 508
11	NON DIM 111 112 113 114 (RAIL 2.4.17.19)	4.6"x12 750w LEKO	COLOR WASH	841 815
12	↑ AUX 121 122 123 124 125 126 MAST (TORM L&R 1 2 ORCH PIT 1 2) / ↓ 8 PIPE 1 10 PIPE 2 4 7	4.6"x12" 750w LEKO / 2.3½"x400w Q-LEKO / 4.6"x9" 750w LEKO	SPECIALS / TOWN NIGHT	805-850 856
13	↑ 6 PIPE 9.12.15.18 / ↓ 7 PIPE 1.3.5.6	4.8"x11" 750w LEKO / 4.6"x9" 750w LEKO	BOUZOUKI / BACK ROSTRA	818 828 / CLEAR
14	↑ AUX MASTER 141 142 143 144 (8 PIPE 3 10 PIPE 1.3.5) / ↓ 3 PIPE 2.4 6.8	4.8"x11" 750w LEKO	TOWN DAY / KHANIA B/L	CLEAR / 819 821

Fig. 12 Hook-up schedule

number of large capacity dimmers with several lanterns ganged up to each dimmer. Its equivalent in England would be a 'plugging schedule'. On a large installation it is often helpful to have a list of circuits with the lanterns connected to them. This can be helpful at a lighting rehearsal when one cannot in an instant, perhaps, find a particular number on the layout plan. It becomes essential if there are any re-pluggings during the performance: then a separate plugging schedule should be prepared for the use of the electricians concerned and the designer himself.

I usually work from a 1:25 scale plan and section of the stage, or with a very large installation 1:50. (In the US 1:24 is used.) Once I have decided from where I will be lighting each area, I draw on the plan the bars (pipes) from which the equipment will be hung. There are several different ways of indicating lanterns on a ground plan, and there is now an internationally recognized set of symbols that can be used (see Mechanics p. 166). I prefer the system which I introduced in England (suggested by American practice). This is a set of stencils, which are accurate scale representations of each lantern. I find this accuracy of the greatest importance when a large quantity of units have to be stacked together along a bar. By drawing each to scale, one can tell exactly how they will be fitted in to the space available.

With stencils, ground plan and section, the designer can begin to build up a pattern of lighting equipment. Each scene has to be carefully considered with regard to the keylight and acting area lighting for each part of the stage that is used in the action, the motivated, motivating lights and so on. When all this has been considered and roughly noted scene by scene on the drawings, the designer will probably find that he has an enormous quantity of equipment; perhaps far more than his producer is willing to provide, and possibly more than he can fit on to the switchboard in the theatre concerned! Now he can go back over each scene, rationalizing and simplifying and compromising as he goes. It is very likely that several lanterns provided for one purpose in one scene can quite satisfactorily perform another function later on. Some cool acting area spotlighting in a night scene could double as a shadow fill-light in a bright midday scene. Through this type of planning the designer can reduce his layout to the absolute minimum with which he is confident he can achieve his objectives.

When the layout has been completely rationalized and the designer is sure that every lantern is doing as many jobs as possible, he can begin to draw them out carefully on a working plan and section. Now he knows how many lanterns will need to be hung in each position, he will lay them out as neatly as possible. It is helpful to the electrician to space them regularly, but if for any particular reason the spacing is irregular, this should be made clear and the appropriate dimensions indicated.

While the plan is taking shape the designer must also work out how each lantern will be connected to the control board. If the number of circuits available is limited, he will have to loop several lanterns together on to single circuits. If some lanterns are only used in one or two scenes, he may need to have these patched, re-plugged or cross-switched. This should be kept to the minimum, however, for the more circuits that have to be changed during the performance, the more likely it is that a mistake will occur and the wrong lantern be connected.

When working out which lanterns should be fed from which circuit, it is advisable to consult the electrician in charge and his board operator. It may be that by careful arrangement of the plugging, certain operations on the board might be simplified. Their opinions, and the designer's knowledge of the play and of the way the board has to be operated, must be combined to produce the most rational and practical layout of circuits.

When the plan and section are complete, the lantern schedule can be drawn up. This is a detailed analysis of the layout and a work instruction to the electricians preparing the equipment.

Particular care must be paid to any non-standard items. If the designer wants to use some special lantern made for the production, he must note this on his schedule and, probably, supply working drawings for its construction. Any practical light fittings used in the show, such as chandeliers or oil lamps, must also be listed. The set designer will probably want to select these, but the lighting designer must liaise closely with him to make sure that whatever is chosen is suitable from a lighting point of view; and he must then make sure that appropriate electrical arrangements are made.

Obtaining the equipment

Each production will, of course, have different needs as regards equipment. A production in a major repertoire theatre will probably be equipped entirely from the organization's own resources. A commercial show in the West End of London and many amateur or school productions will possibly need to acquire extra equipment. This can be purchased or hired from various companies. (Some of these are listed on page 174.) Wherever the equipment is coming from, the designer and his electrician must make every effort to ensure that it is delivered to the theatre absolutely ready for speedy erection. Providing that the designer has done his planning homework, almost every part of the equipment can be pre-set by the supplier before it is delivered to the theatre. Bars and booms can be made up with all the clamps and feed cables in the right position, lanterns, colour, accessories can be packed or crated bar by bar so that everything that is required is immediately to hand. If a show is to tour for a long period it may be worthwhile making up all the equipment so that the lanterns are not even taken off the bars. When moving theatres they are simply broken up into manageable lengths, dropped into crates and packed off to the next date.

Planning the tour

If the production is going on tour, one has to face some complications. Obviously it is unlikely that any two theatres will be the same. The designer must find out what facilities he is going to meet at each date and shape his plans accordingly. He may have to talk to his director about compromising on some of his effects at some of the less well-equipped theatres. If a compromise has to be made the designer must remember that, no matter how fond he may be of any particular visual effect, the one thing that cannot be compromised is the lighting of the actors.

Final rehearsals

During the last few days before the production weekend, the designer must get to see as many rehearsals as he can. He knows that right up to the last minute the director may be making changes in his handling of the actors and he must be up to date with every development. The problem is that he will have had to finalize his equipment requirements long before the actors have finalized their performances. He will thus have to make sufficient allowance for any reasonable changes that may occur.

At the final rehearsals the designer will be able to make a note of the probable timing of his lighting cues and approximately how much time there will be between each cue. This will allow him to up-date his script breakdown into a *lighting cue synopsis* (fig 13). This is a list of all cues in the production, scene by scene, with each cue number, stating the time to be taken with the cue, the effect to be achieved, and noting how long after one cue the electrician will have before the next. This cue synopsis will be used as a guide by the designer during the lighting rehearsal and a copy should also be given to the stage manager and the board operator. The stage manager will have it for information and the board operator will need it so that throughout the lighting rehearsal he will know where he has got to in the show; he will know which cues are very close to each other and how long he has to prepare for the next sequence of changes.

When all is finally ready the designer can pack his bags for the first production weekend. Plots, plans, whisky, glucose and patience! If he takes his pyjamas, he must remember he may not need them!

Fig. 13 Cue synopsis

```
THE HERO                                              CUE SYNOPSIS

DIRECTED BY:  PETER COE
DESIGNED BY:  MICHAEL KNIGHT
LIGHTING BY:  ROBERT ORNBO

CUE        SPEED

                        ½ hour  preset on poster
                        verbal - houselights
1          5S           build to R.A. announcer
2          2S           x fade to backlight
f/o        5S           build to total DC for Matthew
f/o        7S           lose headlights
3          15S          x fade to Christine apartment
4          40S          close to DC when they are established on floor (!)
5          3S           x fade to back and x light
f/o        30S          build full
6          3S           lose FoH
f/o        10S          build all
7          7S           x fade to House of Commons
8          5S           build FoH for Prime Minister
f/o        7S           build all D.S.
9          5S           x fade to backlight - strobes
f/o        10S          build to full day
9A         3S           strobes out
10         5S           x fade to cabinet room (+ proj.)
11         15S          build all   (end of lecture)
12         5S           fade to C only
12A        3S           f.b.o.

verbal                  Houselights  - preset

13         3S           House to ½ build press conference
14         7S           x fade to Christine's apartment
15         7S           x fade to Cragg's house
16         3S           all FoH out
f/o        7S           build all
```

Demonstration 2

Juno and the Paycock
by Sean O'Casey
National Theatre—Old Vic
Dir. Sir Laurence Olivier
Des. Carmen Dillon
Light Richard Pilbrow and John B. Read.

CUE SYNOPSIS (ABRIDGED)

ACT I	Living room of the Boyle family in a Dublin tenement. Morning. Sunlight from back OP bright clear. Fire burning/votive light.	
p 1.16	Joxer/Boyle scene. Close to table DC. Lose sunlight exterior cooler foreboding. (Keep in door area L.)	
p 1.25	Will reading. Recover sunlight.	
ACT II	Few days later. 6 p.m. Sunset from low back PS. Light from window left cross table to fire. Warm afternoon.	
p 2.3	Through scene. Slow fade to twilight.	
p 2.5	Table lamp lit and dresser lamp. Gas brackets lit. *follow on* slow fade exterior to night. Close to table/fire acting area.	
p 2.8	Cheat in cool bed area DL for Johnny.	
p 2.10	Streetlamp below back on (uplight on ceiling to create strange 'false' dimension). *follow on* cheat up interior acting area for 'party'.	

p 2.15 Start fade to cool/funeral—emphasize door L.
p 2.20 X fade to cold 'reality'—Johnny and the Mobilizer. Very gaunt skeletal—emphasize to fire RC.

ACT III 2 p.m. November. Cold sun grim gaunt. Table/sofa to door.
p 3.10 Mrs Boyle entry fade—close to C.
p 3.18 Furniture men. Fade 2. Very shadowy. X-light window.
p 3.21 Johnny taken. Lose sunlight to cold silhouette. Clock strikes. X fade to very low key sunset from PS.
p 3.23 Mrs B. exit. X fade to night. Joxer and Boyle just seen at table.
p 3.24 Fade to very low bed L to table. Room dark, stark, empty.

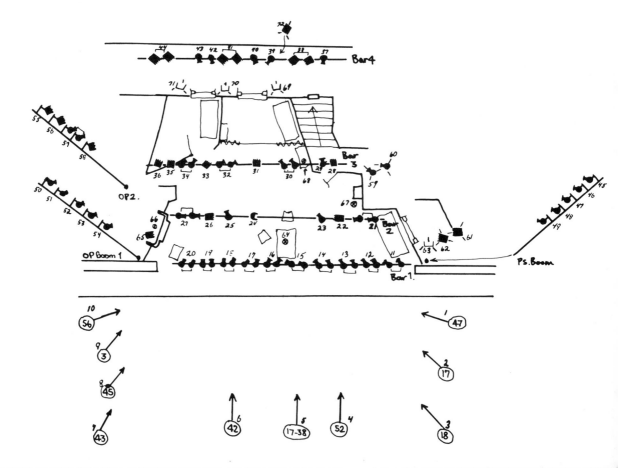

JUNO AND THE PAYCOCK
LANTERN SCHEDULE

	Position	Type	Function	Colour
1	FOH sides	2 patt 264	X light DS	47
2	FOH high side	6 patt 264*	Acting areas DS	17
3	,, ,, ,,	2 patt 264	Night wash DS left	18
4	front	3 patt 264*	Warm frontlight	52
5	,,	3 patt 264*	Cool ,,	17–38
6	,,	2 patt 264	Twilight wash DS	42
7	high side	2 patt 264	Night wash DS right	43
8	,, ,,	3 patt 264*	Acting area	45
9	,,	5 patt 264*	,, ,,	3
10	FOH sides	2 patt 264	X light DS	56
11	Bar 1	2 patt 23	Acting area	67
12		,,	,, ,,	3
13		,,	,, ,,	52
14		,,	,, ,,	67
15		,,	,, ,,	3
16		,,	,, ,,	17
17		,,	,, ,,	50
18		,,	,, ,,	17
19		,,	,, ,,	50
20		,,	,, ,,	3
21	Bar 2	2 patt 264	Night backlight DS	18
22		patt 223	Lamplight C	4
23		patt 264	Cool US	17
24		Beamlight	Sun X to bed DL	50
25		patt 264	Warm fire to chair	9
26		patt 223	Lamplight C	4
27		2 patt 264	Night backlight DS	18
28	Bar 3	patt 223	Hall and stairs shadow	27–47
29		patt 23	Stairs	60
30		2 patt 23	Acting area US	17
31		patt 223	,, ,, ,,	56
32		2 patt 23	Lamp on dresser	2
33		patt 223	Night US	18
34		2 patt 23	Acting area US	67
35		patt 223	,, ,, ,,	55
36		patt 223	Bed alcove UR (shadow fill)	38

	Position	Type	Function	Colour
37	Bar 4	patt 264	Backlight stairs	17
38		2 patt 243	Sunset to windows L & R	47
39		patt 264	Moon to ,, L	40
40		patt 264	Cool sun to ,, L	17
41		2 patt 243/2kw	Sun to ,, L	50
42		patt 264	Moon to ,, R	40
43		patt 264	Cool sun to ,, R	17
44		2 patt 243/2kw	Sun to ,, R	50
45	Boom L	patt 264	X light DS cool	67
46		,, ,,	,, ,, ,, lamplight	3
47		,, ,,	,, ,, ,, night	18
48		,, ,,	,, ,, ,, fill/shadow	55
49		,, ,,	,, ,, ,, sunset	47
50	Boom R 1	patt 264	X light DS cool	17
51		,, ,,	,, ,, ,, lamplight	2
52		,, ,,	,, ,, ,, night	43
53		,, ,,	,, ,, ,, fill/shadow	56
54		,, ,,	,, ,, ,, firelight	4–B 11
55	Boom R 2	patt 243	X light US night	18
56		patt 243	,, ,, US sun	50
57		2 patt 23	,, ,, US lamplight	3
58		patt 223	Bed alcove UR	9–56
59	Stage L	patt 264/stand	X stairs	17
60		,, ,,	X stairs	47–60
61		patt 243/stand	Through DL window sunset	53–56
62		,, ,,	Through DL window cool	60
63		patt 49/stand	DL window backing	60
64	Onstage	patt 123	Tablelamp	
65			Firelight	4–B 11
66			Fire	
67			Votive lamp	
68			Dresser lamp	
69	Backstage	patt 49	Backcloth	18
70		,, ,,	,,	60
71		,, ,,	,,	18
72		patt 223	Streetlamp shadow on ceiling	17–50

B = Broken colour
* = On separate circuits.

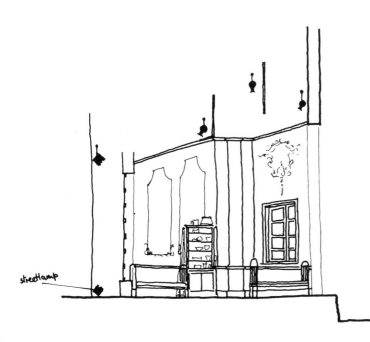

streetlamp

4 Procedure: production

The get-in and fit-up

The day of the get-in arrives. All the weeks of theoretical work are over and theory has to be turned into reality.

In the professional theatre the time taken between the closing of one show and the opening of another has to be kept to the minimum. Every night the theatre is 'dark' an audience is lost. This often means that the fitting up of scenery and lighting will go on around the clock, day and night, until complete. A well-planned production will try to work to a more rational timetable, allowing the crew reasonable breaks for rest and meals, but in any event speed and efficiency are essential.

Since the lighting always has to be done after everything else, the lighting designer has to become used to working at any hour. All too often he will find himself focusing his lamps at perhaps 4 o'clock in the morning; then, after eight hours on his feet, he will have to start lighting the production, beginning the really creative work in a dirty, hungry and exhausted state. The wise designer will try to ensure some refreshment for himself and his crew, but ideally he will try to see that a programme is arranged that avoids the need for this manic effort.

There is, however, one advantage in having to light late at night or in the small hours. At this time most other people have gone home. If one of the problems the designer has to face is fatigue, the other is interruption. Only on one show in twenty will he be able to get on with his job quietly and without interference.

All too often the scenery takes longer to put up than anticipated, or something else will have gone wrong. The designer, first focusing, and then doing the actual lighting, will be constantly hindered. The electrician's ladder will be used by someone else; a painter will be working in the spot the designer needs to reach; he starts focusing as an electric saw starts merrily shattering the eardrums. A special piece of scenery may need to be flown in to have a lamp focused on it— but all the flymen have broken for a visit to the nearest bar. Eventually with the laborious job of focusing finished, he starts lighting. He calls for darkness; a horde of people will produce imperative reasons why they must have some working light. At last, he begins—with a sickening crash some zealous stage hand, 'tidying up', crashes a flat into a lovingly focused boom— and so on.

I repeat, there are many advantages in doing the lighting when everybody else has gone home!

There is, of course, a better solution. A well-planned accurate timetable, ably supervised by a team who work well together and who help each other—stage manager, carpenters, electricians, scene and lighting designers.

For the purpose of this chapter we shall assume that we are working on a production in a theatre like those in the West End of London where little or no permanent equipment is installed. In other words, we must take all the equipment into the theatre and rig it according to our plan before we start lighting.

During the get-in and fit-up, the designer, if he is working with a good electrician, will have little to worry about. But he should know what is going on and, since on a small production he may be acting as his own electrician, he should know how to do the work himself.

As we discussed in the last chapter, the major part of the preparation of equipment should have been done before it arrives at the theatre. The only thing now left to be done is to take the equipment in and to rig it speedily.

It is important to bring the scenery and lighting into the theatre in a logical manner and to place it where it will be most conveniently to hand when wanted.

A large part of the lighting equipment will be hung over the stage. It is therefore usually possible to hang it out of the way before the carpenters start on the scenery.

If the production uses a false floor with a revolve or sliding wagons, it is convenient to lay the floor first. Next, the flown lighting should be hung while the engineers are rigging any mechanism under the stage; then the sets should be built and the side lighting rigged. Finally, the set should be dressed with props and portable lighting equipment placed on stage. Any lighting equipment in the auditorium can be rigged either when the floor is being laid or the scenery erected—in other words, the whole fit-up is planned as a 'leap-frog' process.

The first step is to measure out the set accurately on the stage. Obviously in a well-run theatre there will be plans and sections of the stage showing the exact position of all the hanging lines. From this the designer will have worked out which set of lines or which counterweight bar is to be used for each lighting bar (or pipe). It is always worth checking the accuracy of these before actually starting. It is tedious to have to move a lighting bar after it is flown. The master carpenter will be asked for the first bar wanted and the flyman will fly it in. The designer should have told him the number of lanterns that he is going to hang on it. If he has not, he should give him an indication of the weight he can expect, so he can begin to load the counterweights.

In collaboration with the carpenter he will decide in what order the hanging should be done. Perhaps the electrical work could start downstage with the carpenter's work at the back, or vice-versa. In order to work as quickly as possible, the bars can be first laid out on trestles, the lanterns hung from the bars, cables connected and neatly strapped along the bar's length.

BEFORE the bar is flown out each lantern should be carefully checked for the following:

1 The lantern has a lamp and is working correctly.
2 Any shutters, colours, accessories are fitted and working easily and correctly.
3 The clamp holding the lantern to the bar is fitted solid and tight.
4 The safety chain (if any) and feed cable are fitted with sufficient slackness to allow movement of the lantern in any direction.
5 The offstage ends of all feed cables have been tested through and clearly marked with the circuit number.
6 Nuts or locking handles are firm and *correctly* tightened. Much time is wasted on focusing if some enthusiast has so tightened the locking nuts that the lantern is immovable.

I find that it saves time later to 'rough set' each lantern— pointing it in the direction you expect it to go. This is particularly important on a very tightly packed bar, since it allows you to check that each lantern is sufficiently clear of its neighbour. If the equipment has been correctly prepared in the workshop it will only take a matter of minutes to assemble and prepare each bar; each lantern can then be quickly checked and rough set and each feed checked before the bar is flown out. There is nothing more frustrating than being held up in the middle of focusing by an electrician perched twenty-four feet up a ladder trying to find a fault in a circuit, or clear a jammed shutter, or loosen a lantern which has been tightened as solid as the Rock of Gibraltar. Three minutes' work and foresight on the ground can save half an hour on the top of a ladder.

Once all the overhead equipment is flown out of the way— well out of the way to clear any scenery being hung—the stage crew can take priority on the stage. The electrics staff can probably split into groups (if there are more than two, that is) and work elsewhere.

One pair of men can probably begin to rig any extra equipment in the auditorium; one pair begin to make ready any sidelighting equipment such as booms (tormenters) or ladders, and one pair can start to plug up the overhead flown equipment, connecting it to the dimmer control.

In the commercial theatre in the United States it is very likely that all the dimmerboards will also be installed afresh for each show. Setting these up is a major task and all cables have to be fed from the boards to each lantern. In Europe it is more common for the theatre to have a permanent control system installed. This will be wired out to sockets around the theatre, thus reducing the lengths of temporary wiring needed.

When the erection of the scenery is almost complete, the electrics can rig the sidelighting equipment and any lights or electrical effects actually on the scenery—such as practical lamps, etc. Then every circuit should be tested individually. When all is working the designer is ready to start.

1 Theatre Projects model theatre 1958

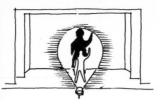

2 Below—front

3 Front—direct horizontal

4 Sidelight—source same height

5 Front 'acting area' light—both sides

6 Top light—straight down

7 Backlight—high source

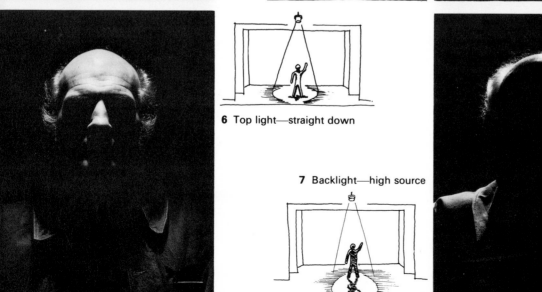

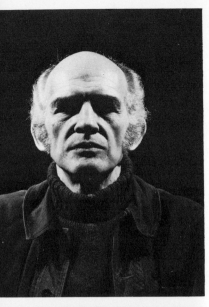

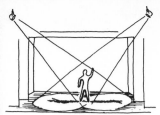

8 Sidelight—high source both sides

9 Side backlight—high source

10 Side backlight—source same height

11 Front keylight
Front—direct horizontal fill
Side backlight—high source
Side backlight—source same height

2-11 Lighting the actor's face

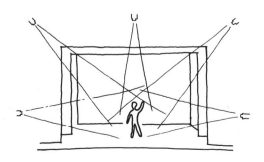

Elevation

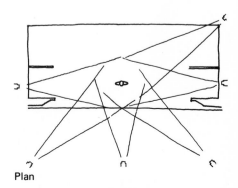

Plan

12 *Jorrocks* New Theatre, London 1966
Dir, Val May Set, Disley Jones Light, Richard
Pilbrow Overhead bars hung within flown scenery

opposite top
14 *Blitz* Adelphi Theatre, London 1962
Set, Sean Kenny Light, Richard Pilbrow

opposite bottom
15 *Blitz* Victoria Station. Use of 24v beamlights

13 *Blitz* FOH lighting positions

16 *Three Sisters* Beamlights provide sunlight through windows

17, 18 *Three Sisters* National Theatre Old Vic, London 1967
Dir, Sir Laurence Olivier Set, Josef Svoboda Light, Richard Pilbrow Acts I, IV

19 *Danton's Death* 59 Theatre Company Lyric Theatre, Hammersmith
Dir, Caspar Wrede Set, Malcolm Pride Light, Richard Pilbrow

20 *Brand* 59 Theatre Company Lyric Theatre, Hammersmith
Dir, Michael Elliott Set, Richard Negri Light, Richard Pilbrow

21, 22 *Oliver* New Theatre, London 1960
Dir, Peter Coe Set, Sean Kenny Light, John Wyckham

23 *Juno and the Paycock* National Theatre   Old Vic, London 1966
Dir, Sir Laurence Olivier Set, Carmen Dillon Light, Richard Pilbrow
See Demonstration 2

24 *Rosencrantz and Guildenstern are dead* National Theatre Old Vic, London 1967
Dir, Derek Goldby Set, Desmond Heeley Light, Richard Pilbrow
See Demonstration 3

25, 26 *One Over the Eight* Duke of York's Theatre, London 1961
Dir, Paddy Stone Set, Tony Walton Light, Richard Pilbrow.
First major use of scene projection in U.K.

27, 28 *On the Level* Saville Theatre, London 1966
Dir, Wendy Toye Set, Malcolm Pride Light, John Wyckham Projection, Robert Ornbo

29, 30 *Macbeth* Washington Arena Theatre
Dir, Edwin Sherin   Set, Robin Wagner
Light, Jules Fisher
Arena stage using 52 30w 6v PAR pinspots

29

30

31

31, 32, 33, 34 *The Storm* National Theatre Old Vic, London 1966
Dir, John Dexter Set, Josef Svoboda Light, Richard Pilbrow
See Demonstration 4

32

33

34

35, 36 Thorndike Theatre, Leatherhead
Architect, Roderick Ham Lighting consultant, Richard Pilbrow

Focusing

Accurate focusing is the key to successful lighting. Each lantern has to be directed with great care to do its chosen job, and this has to be done quickly. Every minute saved now becomes valuable rehearsal time later.

Obviously the easiest show to focus is the one on which the lanterns are all in easy ladder reach, the stage floor is flat and uncluttered and there is a permanent set on to which to focus. If the lanterns are out of reach, another way of getting to them must already have been devised. In the United Kingdom an extremely useful device called a Tallescope is almost universally used (fig 14). The largest version of this allows a (tall) electrician to reach some thirty-six feet. For a still higher reach—seventy feet, if the stage floor is clear—the same company manufacture Zip-Up Staging, which is a squared-planned modular scaffolding kit.

Another way of getting a man up to a high bar is to pull him up in a bosun's chair. At its simplest this is a seat like a child's swing hung from the grid by two or more lines. Under the supervision of a senior flyman, the electrician is lifted alongside the bar and, by taking up or letting out the appropriate lines, he can be moved across the stage. This is obviously an extremely dangerous operation and it must be well supervised. While a man is aloft, the stage should be in silence and one man alone must give the orders. At all times, at least two ropes *must* take the weight and these ropes must be in first class condition. I shall never forget trying to catch my friend and colleague, Robert Ornbo, when he fell thirty feet in a bosun's chair from a broken line. The flyman had allowed the second line to go completely slack. By a miracle his fall was broken and he survived uninjured—but, as in all theatre work, it was a never-to-be-forgotten reminder of the need for care and discipline.

There are several variations on the bosun's chair. Ian Albery developed (for the production *The Man of La Mancha* in London) a form of cradle suspended on a flown track. If a very high bar has a lot of lanterns on it, it may be well worth hanging alongside it a temporary scaffolding bridge along which the electrician can work.

If the floor is not level it can present a further hazard to the conventional ladder, although the Tallescope's adjustable legs will cope with up to 2 ft. 6 in. (6·4 cm.) differential and any reasonable angle.

A complication arises with a multiscene show. Each lantern may be used for a different purpose in each scene. Some may be used only in one scene, some only in another. Obviously one doesn't want to have to change the set every time there is a move from one lantern to another. The designer will have to work out which lanterns can be focused in one set and which by calculation will do for another; and which lanterns must be focused specially on to a certain set—or piece of it—when it is in position.

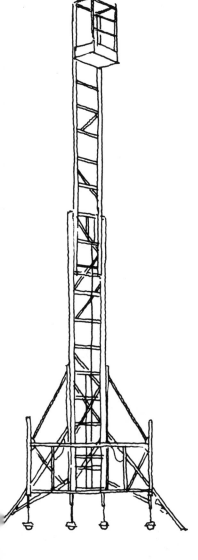

14 Tallescope

It is important to realize how long the focusing is going to take. An average show might take two minutes for each unit. If access is good and the focusing straightforward, this should be reduced to one and a half minutes. Most shows will have a complication somewhere. For every spotbar that you can rattle along at great speed, there will be an awkward lamp that is just out of reach.

Much credit for the speed at which the job can be done will, of course, go to the electrician doing the work. Here should be true teamwork: the designer on stage, quite clear about the function of each lantern; the electrician at the top of the ladder, his equipment prepared, the appropriate tools to hand, his 'ladder crew' holding him firmly and ready to move him at his orders, his board operator prepared to bring in the next circuit immediately it is required.

The lighting designer or his assistant must have direct (if possible, talk-back) communication with the control board when calling for circuits. The less shouting, the better. With a competent electrician, I prefer to use signals to indicate my detailed requirements while focusing a lantern. When the first circuit is called for, and the working lights are extinguished, I stand on the spot where I wish the beam to fall. So that I will not be blinded by the beam, I stand with my back to the lantern and by signs show the electrician where to set it, until the centre of the beam is on the back of my head. When set, a 'thumbs-up' will tell him to tighten the locking nuts so the unit is fixed solid. Further signals can indicate a widening or narrowing of focus or movement of shutters until the beam is exactly adjusted. The whole process is carried out in silence.

As the designer focuses he is rapidly reconciling the actual effect of the light, which he is seeing for the first time, with the image of it he has carried in his head through the planning stages. Now he can begin to tell if it will contribute to the overall effect he imagined. Has he chosen the right lantern; is it the right colour and at the right angle? He must calculate how it will fit with other settings and combine with other lights. Quite possibly he will have to modify or alter slightly his original intention as he goes along, to meet some unforeseen eventuality.

He must remember all the various uses to which the lantern will be put. While each will normally be set head high, there are also sitting or even lying positions to be remembered. Usually each spot has to be set so that it blends unobtrusively with its neighbour. For this the edges have to be softly focused and the beam has to be large enough to provide an overlap. The designer has to remember that some lanterns, e.g. the Fresnel or focus lantern, become less bright the wider the beam is spread. In some places the beam of the spot will fall upon part of the set. Unless he deliberately intends to preserve it, it will be best to soften the resultant hard edge of light.

Lamps depicting sunlight pouring through a window not

only have to look right, they have to light an actor standing in a certain position in a certain scene. The designer must also ensure that any mirrors, panes of glass or pictures with glass in them are not casting unpleasant reflections into the audience; also that any lanterns off-stage are not in sight by reflection. Lights on backings or lamps off-stage must not cast un-welcome shadows of actors who might be waiting to make entrances, or cause hot-spots on them as they walk on to the stage.

Next comes the setting of the front of house (FOH) lanterns. The designer must be quite sure how high or how far upstage he wants them to be set—particularly those coming straight into the stage from the front of the circle. In order to avoid shadows on the back wall, he will probably want to set these lamps fairly low but he must be careful that they light an actor sufficiently far up stage. If the front of house lanterns are set so low that they only light the very front edge of the stage, the area upstage will only be lit from the spot bar overhead and without fill-light may appear to be too top lit; the actors' eyes will disappear in shadow and faces will look distorted.

Sidelighting from the front of house must be carefully judged. In a multiscene production some lamps may need to be cut off at different depths of the stage for different scenes.

As each lamp is set, the designer should double check that no spill or ghost light is coming from it. Unwanted glows on the proscenium or a border or box-front must be avoided. An incorrectly focused profile spot may send a ring of spill light on to an adjacent backcloth, or a faulty lantern may send an irritating leak of light almost anywhere. If this is not corrected while focusing, it may cause embarrassment at the lighting rehearsal, while the designer tracks down the cause of that unwelcome spot of light.

I am continually surprised, even in a show using many hundreds of spotlights, at how accurate one has to be with focusing. Even a few inches' error can show up later in rehearsal. Indeed, however carefully the focusing session is carried out, I find that after the first rehearsal one has to go back and readjust to secure the exact desired effect.

If the lighting is going to be used more than once, it is very important to remember the exact position of each spotlight. In a long run play, units may get knocked; in repertoire they will probably have to be reset continually. The only way to log the setting of a lantern is by the painstaking plotting of its position. Let us now consider a useful method of doing this.

This stage is measured off in 2 feet squares and calibrated accordingly, upstage from the setting line and left and right of the centre line (fig 15). This grid is shown on the layout plan and marked on the stage in chalk on centre line and proscenium line.

On the *focus schedule* we will now be able to log the exact

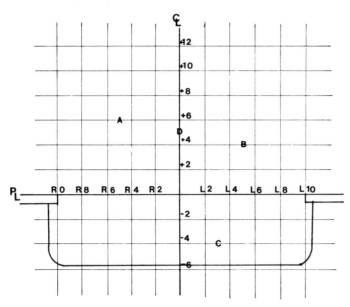

Fig. 15 Plotting grid

position of each lantern. If the first spot is aimed at position A,
we will describe this as being set to '+6R5'

Position B +4L5
          C −4L3
          D +5CL

This will describe the centre of the beam at head height. If there
are no alterations to the beam shape this indication of position
may be sufficient, with a note as to how wide or narrow or soft
or hard the focus should be. If the beam has to be shaped we
need more detail (see fig 16).

Let us take our first example. We are standing at A, described as
+6R5. Next we describe the top of the beam, the bottom, the
left, then right:

Unit No.	Position	Focus
5	+6R5	R8/R1/+4/+8 soft

If the beam is of a complex shape and cut at a diagonal, a
sketch on a small plan may help to clarify it.

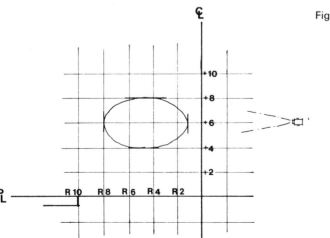

Fig. 16 Detail of plotting grid

If the focus is related to any object such as a wall, door or piece of furniture, this can obviously be more easily described. The description 'Stand behind centre of sofa/cut at left end' is probably quite sufficient. Any combination of grid numbers and description can be satisfactory.

While the designer is focusing, he or an assistant can note the settings. I usually prefer to do the detailed plotting after the show has opened, when time is not at such a premium, and when the lighting has been finalized.

Although speed is essential, the electrician should always be allowed enough time to make sure each lamp is securely locked before moving on to the next. It can be somewhat irritating to find during later rehearsals that all the beams of light are slowly sinking toward the floor.

When all focusing is complete two things remain to be checked. First, the practical fittings: the designer should see that each is working and that the lamp being used in it is sufficiently bright. If it's not connected to a dimmer that is suitable for its small wattage, he should ensure that it is not in fact too bright. Second, all the lights that are placed off stage should be turned on to see that the set is 'light-tight', in other words, that no light is leaking through holes or gaps in the scenery, or glowing through the scenery itself. If there are any problems, the scene designer or master carpenter should be able to help solve them.

The lighting rehearsal*

Everything is now ready to begin lighting. The wise designer will have equipped himself with a desk from which to work, which he will place either in the stalls or dress circle, where he has an ideal view of the stage. I prefer doing the initial lighting from a stalls position, but wherever the designer chooses, he should remember that in later rehearsals he must wander round the theatre and check that his lighting is correct from every part of the house. The desk should be large enough to take his layout plan, plots, script and other amenities such as ash-trays, cups of coffee, bottles of whisky (not recommended in American practice) etc. It is also useful to have a little extra space for the stage manager or producer to use when necessary. Most important, however, are the facilities for communication with the team of electricians who are actually going to carry out the lighting.

It is essential to avoid having to shout up to the electrician. The lighting process requires thought and concentration and these qualities are not ideally mixed with the need to bellow instructions. As already mentioned, the ideal communication is some form of talk-back. There are many new pieces of

*For discussion of lighting with advanced memory systems see chapters 8 and 10.

equipment becoming available, but the one that has to be handled least is usually the most convenient. Certainly the board operator should be able to reply to his designer without touching the equipment. If the production is a complex one, the designer may want to be in touch with other parts of the theatre, lighting bridges, follow-spot operators etc. It may be useful for the designer to be in talk-back contact with the stage manager (although this link should only be used sparingly during rehearsals, when the stage manager may be involved in giving some other vital instructions). Earphones must be substituted for the talk-back loudspeaker during dress rehearsals to reduce any noise which may disturb the cast on stage.

Finally, of course, the designer has to be able to see at his desk, so a shaded light must be provided. If possible, this light should be on a dimmer so that its brightness can be adjusted to match that of the stage. Otherwise, the designer and those sitting around him may be dazzled by the glare.

Now the designer is at his desk, the electrician will be ready at the switchboard, equipped with pencil and paper to take notes and to write out his plots; the stage manager or his assistants will be on stage, armed with the prompt copy in case any information is needed.

A word about time. Lighting rehearsals are, by tradition, rather prolonged affairs. They can be very absorbing to the designer and director and, if correctly conducted, a fairly busy time for the board operator. It is very important that everyone in the theatre knows what is going on and what is going to happen next. If sets have to be changed, the stage management should be warned well in advance when the designer is going to be ready. The designer must also remember that everyone working in the theatre is human; everyone needs to eat, sleep and take occasional breaks; bars close and last trains often run on time. It is usually surprising how much more can be achieved if problems of this nature are taken into account, and a break at the right time can often mean that much better work is done afterwards.

It is usually best to start from a blackout, with all the working lights turned out, any doors to the outside closed, all lights in the auditorium off. In other words, start with a blank slate. A note of warning here. It is wise to turn on any emergency lights or exit lights that have to be kept on during a performance. Similarly, if the show has an orchestra, these lights should be turned on before lighting starts, otherwise some quite unexpected and probably unpleasant light may intrude later.

Once darkness has been achieved, it is a good idea to check quickly through one circuit at a time. This is the final check that everything is working, and it allows the designer to see for the first time, from the auditorium, the effect that each spotlight is going to give. He must make a note of anything that looks like a possible problem: any too obtrusive colour, any spill light that escaped his attention, any hard edge of light where it is not wanted. Then he should tell the board operator that he is going to start and call for the first state of lighting, according to the cue synopsis. Presumably, he is starting from the beginning of the show, and he must explain to the board operator exactly how it will start. He may want to take the curtain up on a dark stage and then fade in the lights; or the curtain may rise on a scene with pre-set lighting. Whichever is the case he will start by plotting the first state of light.

There are, of course, as many different ways of lighting a show as there are different results, so the following can only be an expression of my own personal preferences.

We would begin by calling for those lights that represent the keylight of the scene. Thus, taking the simple example in chapter 2 (the interior realistic set), we would first call for the exterior lighting, the sunlight coming through the window and the light representing skylight illuminating the backing. These circuits have to be brought up to the intensity at which they are likely to be used. If we are starting the play with all the lights coming up to a bright level in which the actors can perform, we should probably set the keylight to a level that appears very bright when seen on its own, remembering that when all the other lighting in the room is added it will probably look correctly in balance. If the play starts with a more atmospheric opening, to enhance the pictorial effect we may keep the lighting within the set to a lower level. This will probably allow us to create a more dramatic visual picture; then, as soon as the curtain has risen, we can slowly creep up the acting area lighting until the level is sufficient for the action of the play. With our example, supposing the play is a bright cheerful comedy, it is likely that the sunshine will be used at full; but at this initial stage it is perhaps best to set it to point 8* on the dimmer so there is some 'extra' in reserve.

When the exterior is nicely balanced for the best visual effect, we can begin to build the secondary lighting. We will bring up each circuit on the acting area, all the while attempting to keep the correct balance, using the keylight through the window and trying to make the effect of the acting area spots follow through the feeling of daylight coming from that side of the room. As soon as we feel we have roughed in a balance of lighting over the stage, one of the stage management can walk through each actor's moves in the scene. We may discover that the whole thing is a little too dim for the play at this point and we will have to make all the acting area slightly brighter. In this case it can be done without undue alarm, because the backing and sunlight can also be brightened to avoid losing the pictorial balance. Once this is done, the stage management can again cover all those parts of the stage that

*References to dimmer levels assume a dimmer calibrated 0–10, with 10 providing full light.

the actors use. We should then find that, wherever they are, they are correctly, attractively and appropriately lit, and that even from the farthest part of the auditorium they can be seen clearly. As they walk towards the window they become more obviously in the direct light of the sun; and the side of the face away from the sunlight will look as if it is lit from the natural reflection in the room. As they move around the stage there should be no feeling that they are going from spotlight to spotlight; indeed, all the beams should merge together, creating the three-dimensional feeling of real space and real air that we have been attempting to achieve.

If there are parts of the stage that are not used we need not be afraid to leave them underlit, provided that this does not detract from the atmosphere of the scene. Remember that shadow is as much a part of interest in lighting as is light itself (provided we do not have actors walking through quite unnatural black spots). In the less important parts of the stage a shadow can give depth to the set, and these 'natural' areas of shadow may be made even more interesting by the subtle addition of a complementary or contrasted colour tone.

We must ensure that all the colours used blend together suitably and that there are no sudden or unnatural changes. If there are, it may be a question of adjusting the intensity of the offending lamp, or even of changing the colour we are using.

Any soft light or fill-light from front of house lanterns or footlights must then be added. Too much will tend to flatten out the stage picture, indeed too much light from the footlights may cause distracting shadows over the upper part of the set; too little will mean the desired colour-toning effect is not achieved.

If any part of the stage is very bright, a light fitting or a bright sky-backing, for instance, it may be that an actor standing in front of it will appear underlit by contrast. It may be possible to cure an underlit point on the stage by reducing the brightness elsewhere.

I find it useful, as I call for each circuit, to make a note, either myself or with an assistant, so that as the picture on the stage builds up I have a record of the circuits used and their intensity. The most convenient way of doing this is to have a pad of cue sheets (fig 17), each of which has a list of all the numbers of the lighting channels. As each is called, I note against it in pencil the level to which it is brought. I find it tremendously helpful, while looking at the stage and considering the picture that I have created, to be able to see it at the same time on paper (it is almost like seeing an X-ray of a body). This can show up a discrepancy—some lantern that has been left on un-necessarily, or one that is too bright or too dim—when a look at the stage will merely indicate that *something* is not quite right.

When everything is to the designer's satisfaction the opening light is complete. The electrician should then be told

THEATRE PROJECTS LIMITED. Production: FIDDLER ON THE ROOF

CUE NO: 4 TIME: 10 sec. NOTES: Autos "D"

1	31	61	91	121
2	32	62 7	92	122
3	33 6	63 7	93	123
4 7	34 F	64	94	124
5 5	35	65	95	125
6 5	36	66	96	126
7	37 6	67 F	97	127
8 7	38 5	68	98	128
9	39 5	69 7	99	129
10	40 6	70 F	100	130
11	41	71	101	131
12	42 7	72 F	102	132
13	43 7	73 F	103	133
14 7	44 7	74 F	104	134
15 7	45	75	105 7	135
16	46	76	106 7	136
17 7	47	77 6	107	137
18 7	48	78 6	108	138
19	49	79 6	109	139
20 7	50	80 6	110	140
21	51	81 7	111	141
22	52	82 8	112	142
23	53	83 7	113	143
24	54	84 8	114	144
25	55	85 6	115	145 6
26	56	86 6	116	146
27	57	87 7	117	147 6
28	58	88 8	118	148 7
29	59	89 6	119	149
30	60	90 6	120	150 7

Q5 5 sec. small build

38 39 49 50 81 / F

86 106 118 152 / F

12 119 / F

Fig. 17 Cue sheet

to 'plot' it and be given the time to do so. Different control boards can be plotted in different ways but sufficient time must be allowed to get the whole thing written down clearly.

The most exciting developments created by the introduction of memory control systems, of course, make this tedious business of writing down the whole plot unnecessary. With these systems the electrician plots a cue by simply pressing a button to memorize it. This speeds up the whole process of lighting, but it also demands that the lighting designer works faster than he has had to in the past. While the electrician is plotting he can be double checking what he has done so far, and be getting himself ready for the next cue. Similarly, the stage manager can be noting down the principal effect of the cue so that he can ensure that it is accurately repeated at every performance.

The electrician should be able to see from his synopsis how the cue is to be operated, its duration and the time between one cue and the next. The designer anyway must make this quite clear, and if rehearsal time is not too limited he may want to go back and have the cue rehearsed several times to get the timing exactly established.

When the board operator is quite clear about everything, the designer can continue with the next cue. First, he must tell the operator what he wants to achieve—i.e., whether it is a fade or a build or a cross-fade and how long it should take—and then rebalance the lighting on the stage accordingly. It is at this point that some knowledge of the control system and its operation becomes desirable. A good electrician can probably perform almost any cue on a switchboard that he is used to, but there are many boards on which it is difficult to achieve certain effects. The designer must have enough knowledge to be able to judge what is possible. It is obviously useless spending hours plotting a complicated series of cross-fades if they are beyond the ability of the operator or the capability of the machine. However, many cues which at first sight seem appallingly complicated can after a few days' practice become quite simple, and memory systems open new vistas of potential.

In this way the entire show is worked through, cue by cue, state of light by state of light. During this rehearsal it is much better if the director and the scenic designer sit alongside the lighting designer. They should comment freely and positively about what the lighting designer is doing. They should all have confidence in one another as a team, and the lighting designer should simply be putting into practice what they have all visualized. The director will naturally be interested in how well the actors can be seen, and the set designer will be biased toward thinking that the only priority is the attractiveness of his set on the stage. The lighting designer has to satisfy both their demands. Inevitably there will be conflict and on many occasions he must attempt to reach a compromise. The creative designer is the one who can overcome a problem with a new solution which is more satisfying to everyone.

The designer should always remember that a lighting rehearsal is only a rehearsal; it is a waste of time to spend hours and hours fiddling in tremendous detail, trying to achieve 'absolute perfection'. This first session is much better thought of as a 'roughing-in' process. The old days of the lighting rehearsal which went on hour after hour and day after day are best forgotten. The aim of the first session is to achieve broadly all the desired results; inevitably when the actors are seen on the stage, certain things will have to be altered.

The advent of thyristor dimmers and the consequent ease of remote control has seen the introduction of the portable lighting control for rehearsals. Early examples of this were seen in England at the Glyndebourne Opera House and the National Theatre at the Old Vic. With this, one pre-set of the switchboard (a 'Rehearsal Wing') can be set up at the lighting designer's control desk in the stalls. Thus, instead of talking to the operator over an intercom, the two men can sit side by side and be in immediate communication. The lighting can be set up, modified and altered very rapidly without the need to pass instructions. Under ideal circumstances the lighting designer can even do the job himself. The instantaneous memory system inevitably carries this process even further, allowing stalls controls at the service of the designer to be commonplace.

With this facility available, the lighting can be done during the first costume-technical rehearsal, with the actors on the stage. A lighting rehearsal with the stage management in their ordinary day clothes never really indicates the final effect. The first rehearsal with costumes is very often very slow, for the director will be taking the actors back over entrances and exits and pieces of business. While this is going on, the designer, particularly if he has a 'rehearsal wing', can lay in his lighting and so see from the beginning exactly what he is doing. It is never worth taking up too much of the actors' time for lighting at this type of rehearsal; and if the director is working fast, any finer details should be deferred. A brief lighting rehearsal later can tidy up the plot and put in the finishing touches.

This way of working will only succeed if the lighting design has been carefully considered in advance. If this has been done, and if the show has been carefully and well focused, the designer can go into the first rehearsal with actors and light with a good deal of confidence. The latest control systems allow the designer to improvise his lighting more freely still, and yet from a carefully planned and prepared design.

Technical rehearsals

Each production period will be planned in a different way, but if the play has more than one scene, a technical rehearsal must be held before the formal dress rehearsal. This is a stopping rehearsal, held either with or without the actors, to practise the scene changes and to try out the lighting and sound cues. It is valuable for the lighting designer, for it is the first time that he will have had a chance to run through the lighting cues in succession. After a long extended first rehearsal he may have mistakenly lit a scene with too great a contrast to the one preceding or following it. While the stage crew and technicians are rehearsing their part, he will now have a chance to see the thing as a whole, going from scene to scene without pause. Now he can also see how the board operator copes with the various changes (although he must allow time for the missing dialogue), and, perhaps most importantly, he can supervise any physical movement of lanterns that has to be done on stage. Lanterns may have to be repositioned or moved from scene to scene and now is the moment to see that the assistant electricians know their job and can reposition them with the necessary degree of accuracy.

The dress rehearsal

If there has not been a rehearsal such as the one I have just discussed, this will be the first time that the designer will have seen the whole thing come together, actors, setting, costume, lighting and sound. First, he must remember one vital point: this will also be the first time that the electrical staff have worked the show with the actors performing on the stage and with their cues coming at them in rapid succession as they will during performance. While the actors may have been rehearsing for several weeks, the electrical staff will have only rehearsed once or twice before. The designer must be patient with their mistakes and defend them from the possible impatience of others. It may be hard for the director and producer or even the actors to appreciate that somebody with such a vital role as the board operator is coming to the show afresh. He will have to be given time to rehearse, just as they have had time; the designer must ensure, on behalf of his operator, that the rehearsal is not so rushed that it sends him into a panic.

This may also be the first time that the designer sees the lit actors in costume. During lighting and technical rehearsals, before the costumes are used, I usually find myself very depressed. But, if all the homework has not been in vain, when the costumes come on to the stage everything suddenly fits into place: the whole thing begins to take on the expected degree of sparkle and brightness. Some things, however, may still not be working. A lighting colour may conflict with the delicate tones in a costume. Some scenes may look too bright with the actors in position and some not bright enough. Adjustments will have to be made. The timing of cues will be seen for the first time, maybe a five minute fade is a little too fast, or maybe a build at the beginning of the scene is a little too slow: all must be corrected. The designer must be on the watch for the stage manager's mistakes. Perhaps the moment a cue is given may have to be altered slightly to accommodate a piece of business or a different timing on stage. The director will probably want to go back and try various parts of the play again. On some older switchboards it is extremely difficult to go back two or three cues. The designer must cope with the director's impatience and attempt to help the board operator find himself in his plot. As switchboard design improves, this problem should be reduced.

During the dress rehearsal the lighting designer must go all over the theatre. He must see his lighting from the stalls, the gallery and every other part of the house, ensuring that everything he means to be clearly visible is clearly visible from the farthest seat. Whenever he is in doubt let him err on the side of visibility; rather overlight for the first few rows than underlight for all the rest.

During dress rehearsals lots of people will comment upon the lighting, some informed and some, perhaps, ill-informed. Lighting is a subject about which almost everybody can have an opinion. A designer should pay scrupulous attention to the comments of his colleagues in the team, the director, the set designer and so on. If he finds himself in disagreement with them he may attempt to persuade them to his own point of view. If he fails with the director he must accommodate him, for the director is finally in charge and his wishes have to be realized. Comments from other people may well be much less important. The designer must always remember his initial concept of the lighting. He must remember that this was produced as a result of collaboration with and understanding of his director's and set designer's intentions, and he must question continually his fidelity to these intentions. He must be understanding, flexible and accommodating about any changes introduced by his colleagues and must apply his own standards of good lighting, seen always in the context of what the production needs and what the production is all about. A piece of theatre is never a static and final piece of work; it is alive and open to change. The designer must be continually aware of this and receptive to it, even if it means altering his own carefully considered plans.

The designer should not forget, during the dress rehearsals, such details as the handling of the house lights, the lighting of the curtain before the show and in the interval, and the curtain calls. He should remember that the speed at which the house lights are dimmed will affect the impression the audience get when the curtain rises. He should also remember the effects of a sudden change of light and the rules of contrast. The house curtain warmly lit before the performance will build (in the audience) a feeling of theatrical warmth and anticipation; and the colour chosen can affect the colouring of the scene immediately following.

All these details contribute to a smooth and efficiently run show, and thus add to the audience's enjoyment.

The first night

When the curtain rises on the first night the lighting designer's job is virtually over. Perhaps the most important thing he can do now is to keep calm. The performers will all be on edge, and so too will the stage management and the electrical crew. If minor mistakes are made, it is always best to leave them; simply note the error and discuss it the following day.

In the case of a major error, for example if the working light or the house lights are left on when the curtain is taken up, then obviously something must be done. If the error is one that is really going to spoil the whole scene, the designer should act rapidly but calmly, telling the stage management or the operator exactly what is wrong in a clear and concise manner. Before doing so he should make quite sure that they are not engaged in any other cue at the time, never interrupting if there is a danger that by so doing he will upset the show even more. Some control boards are extremely difficult to work, and even more so when it comes to correcting a mistake. A knowledge of how the board is being operated will help the designer make a constructive and useful suggestion in the case of dire emergency.

The show is on

After the first night, if the show embarks on a run or goes into repertoire, the designer must check that all his plots and plans are completely up to date and that all the last-minute alterations have been included. He must make sure that copies of these are given to those people responsible for the standard of lighting throughout the run of the play. These will normally be the electrician and the stage manager. Both should be given copies of the lighting layout plan and schedule, a focus schedule and a cue plot. It is useful when a production has been lit to transpose all the cue sheets on to a cue graph plot (fig 18). With the aid of this one can see clearly how much use is made of each circuit and whether any rational economies can be made. One can also see 'at a glance' which lanterns are contributing to each effect. This is informative to the designer and essential if the lighting is ever to be reproduced elsewhere. With these it should be possible for the staff on the job to double check the lighting and correct any mistakes that are made. If any further changes are made to the lighting during the run, these changes too must be noted in the master plots. Thereafter the designer must ensure that he visits the theatre regularly. Lighting can so easily change: lanterns can be knocked or moved slightly out of position, the timing of cues can, over a period of weeks, gradually alter. The designer must be quite clear that only he can be responsible for maintaining the standards that were set on the first night.

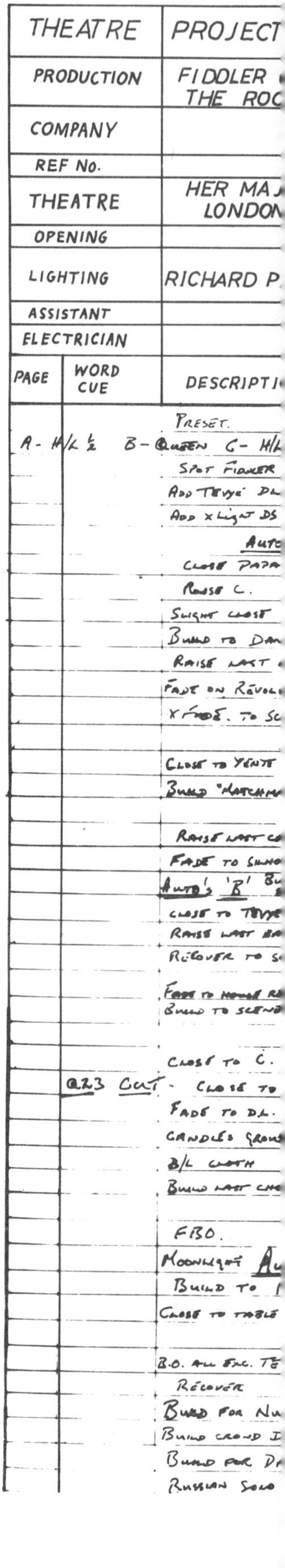

Fig. 18 Cue graph plot

THEATRE	PROJECT
PRODUCTION	FIDDLER THE ROO
COMPANY	
REF No.	
THEATRE	HER MA LONDON
OPENING	
LIGHTING	RICHARD P.
ASSISTANT	
ELECTRICIAN	

PAGE	WORD CUE	DESCRIPTI
		PRESET.
A - H/k ½		B - QUEEN C - H/L
		SPOT FIDDLER
		ADD TEYE DL
		ADD X LIGHT DS
		AUTO
		CLOSE PAPA
		RAISE C.
		SLIGHT CLOSE
		BUILD TO DA
		RAISE LAST
		FADE ON REVOL
		X FADE. TO SC
		CLOSE TO YENTE
		BUILD "MATCHMA
		RAISE LAST CO
		FADE TO SILHO
		AUTO'S 'B' BU
		CLOSE TO TEYE
		RAISE LAST BA
		RECOVER TO S
		FADE TO HOUSE RE
		BUILD TO SCENE
		CLOSE TO C.
	Q23 CUT -	CLOSE TO
		FADE TO DL.
		CANDLES GROU
		B/L CLOTH
		BUILD LAST CHO
		FBO.
		MOONLIGHT AU
		BUILD TO
		CLOSE TO TABLE
		B.O. ALL EXC. TE
		RECOVER
		BUILD FOR NU
		BUILD CROWD I
		BUILD FOR DA
		RUSSIAN SOLO

	F.O.H. UPPER CIRCLE	F.O.H. BOOM PS	F.O.H. BOOM OP	DRESS CIRCLE	BAR 1

N (channels):

F.O.H. UPPER CIRCLE: 1+2 21-22 | 3+20 | 4+5 | 6 | 7 | 8 | 9 | 10 | 11 | 12 | 13 | 14 | 15 | 16 | 17 | 18+19

F.O.H. BOOM PS: 1+3 LR | 4 | 5 | 6 | 7 | 8+9 | 10

F.O.H. BOOM OP: 1+2 3 | 4 | 5 | 6 | 7 | 8+9 | 10

DRESS CIRCLE / BAR 1 – LEKO's: 1+2 3 | 4+5 | 6+7 | 8+9 | 10 | 11+13 | 12+14

(264 series noted across Boom sections: 264 264 264 264 264 264 264)

R (circled): 51, 45 | 67, 36, 57, 67, 51, 57, 40, 67 | 17, 3, 52, 17, 52, 62, 78, 17 | 43, 3, 76, 2, 9, 3, 00, 49, 3, 17

Notes row:
- STEV'S HOUSE S.R. / S.L.
- WASH STGH GAUZE PS + OP — OFF PORTALS
- WASH D.R.
- DL CUT TOP AT DAY / DROP BOTTOM / DLC
- DL
- TEV'S HOUSE
- LOW GAUZE L
- DR CUT TOP AT DAY / DROP BOTTOM
- DL
- LOW GAUZE C
- TEV'S HOUSE
- DR CUT TOP AT DAY / DR DROP BOTTOM
- DRC
- DR
- WASH DL + DLC
- DC / DL / DC / DC / DR / DC / DR
- DL / DLC / DL / DR / DL / DC / DC
- WASH FRONT GAUZE PS-OP — OP PORTAL
- L/LC SHUTTER OFF TEV'S HOUSE ROOF
- APRON & DS TRUCK TO EDGE OF STAGE
- DLC TO EDGE OF STAGE
- DC/R OFF TEV'S / DC / DC/L
- TEV'S HOUSE OP / DC / DR (STREET)
- LC & TEV'S HOUSE

T (totals): 106, 105, 77, 78, 79, 80, 81, 82, 83, 84, 85, 86, 87, 88, 89, 90 | 146, 148, 150, 152, 145, 147, 151, 149 | 118, 120, 122, 124, 117, 119, 123, 121 | 107, 5, 7, 11, 6, 9, 12, 10, 8, 37

Q (cue sheet):

Cue rows (left column labels): (top), L, 2, 3, 4, 5, 6, 7, 8, 9, 10, 11, f/o, 12, 13, f/o, 14, 15, 16, 17, 18, 19, 20, 21, f/o, 22, 24, 25, 26, f/o, 27, 27A, 28, 29, 30, 31, f/o, 32, 33, 34, 35, 36, 37

Demonstration 3

Rosencrantz and Guildenstern are Dead
by Tom Stoppard
National Theatre—Old Vic
Dir. Derek Goldby
Des. Desmond Healey
Light Richard Pilbrow

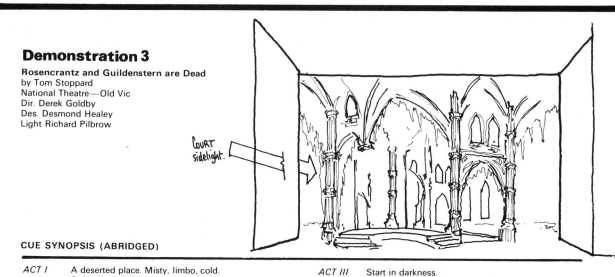

Court sidelight.

CUE SYNOPSIS (ABRIDGED)

ACT I   A deserted place. Misty, limbo, cold.
Build bleak empty day—moorland.
Players' entry. Warm toward sunset. Continue fade
to exaggerated twilight.
End scene 1 fade to night.
Build castle Very flickery lamplight, ghostly,
golden, chiaroscuro.
Increase forestage to bright 'battle of wits'.
Return to court.

ACT II   Snap on full court.
X fade to 'rehearsal'. Weird hot red.
Close to death mime—close to Guildenstern on steps R.
DBO.
Court—dark night—all revealing sunrise (FOH).
X fade to exterior with distant castle. Cold bleak
close to Hamlet 'tableaux'.

ACT III   Start in darkness.
Build to ship—sail—golden morning.
Sunset through to night—exchange of letters.
A new day—players discovered.
Battle with pirates—hot—smoke—confusion
DBO.
Restore ship—late afternoon.
'The sun's going down.'
Fade sunset—continue to surrealistic red dream—
nightmare of players' dominance.
Mime of deaths—intensify to low backlit red effect
on player king.
Rosencrantz and Guildenstern in pin 'face' spots only,
DL and DR.
Restore to court. Night all blue, cold, 'purged' for
Hamlet end.
Very slow fade to blackout.

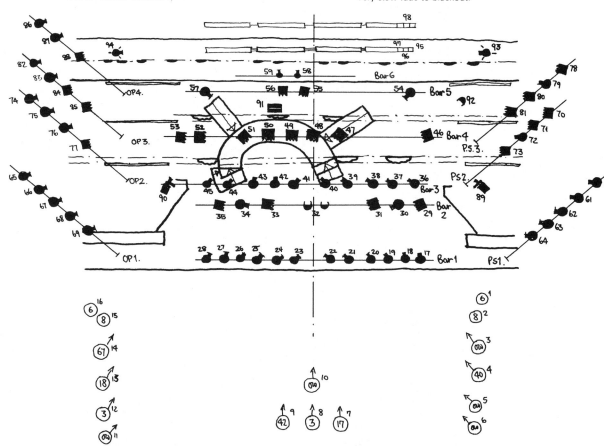

RIDGED FOCUS SCHEDULE

Position	Type	Function	Colour
FOH left	Beamlight	'Nightmare' red forestage RC	6
	3 patt 264*	Sunset left	8
	6 patt 264*	Acting areas DS	OW
	2 patt 264	Night wash forestage	40
	1 patt 93	Rosencrantz pinspot DR	OW
FOH Centre	,, ,,	Guildenstern pinspot steps R	OW
	3 patt 264*	Front wash cool	17
	,, ,,	,, ,, warm	3
	2 patt 264	,, ,, twilight 'violet'	42
	2 beamlights	Front dawn	OW
FOH Right	1 patt 93	Guildenstern pinspot DL	OW
	3 patt 264*	Acting areas DS warm	3
	2 patt 264	Night wash forestage	18
	5 patt 264	Acting areas DS cool	67
	3 patt 264	Sunset right	8
	Beamlight	Red forestage LC	6
Bar 1	patt 264W	Acting area left	3
	,, ,,		17
	,, ,,	,, ,, centre	3
	,, ,,		17
	,, ,,	,, ,, right	3
	,, ,,		17
	,, ,,	,, ,, left	17
	,, ,,		3
	,, ,,	,, ,, centre	17
	,, ,,		3
	,, ,,	,, ,, right	17
	,, ,,	,, ,,	3
Bar 2	patt 243	Night backlight forestage	18
	2 patt 264	Backlight forestage white 'verbal battles'	OW
	patt 243	Backlight court rich gold	4
	2 beamlights	Downlight red forestage	6
	patt 243	as 31	4
	2 patt 264	as 30	OW
	patt 243	as 29	18
Bar 3	patt 264W	Rostra L cool	17
	,, ,,	Rostra C white	OW
	,, ,,	Players' rehearsal 'spook-light'	1
	,, ,,	Rostra warm court	3
	,, ,,	,, ,, ,,	2
	,, ,,	Rostra R cool	17
	,, ,,	Rostra court	38
	,, ,,	as 38	1
	,, ,,	as 37	OW
	,, ,,	Rostra C cool	17
Bar 4	patt 243	Court backlight X RC	4
	,, ,,	Red backlight	6
	,, ,,	Night downlight LC	40
	,, ,,	Court downlight	38–60
	,, ,,	Night downlight RC	40
	,, ,,	Red backlight	6
	,, ,,	Court backlight XLC and sail	4
	,, ,,	Rostra X light	OW

Position	Type	Function	Colour
54 Bar 5	patt 264	Opening rostra high side backlight	17
55	patt 243	Backlight rostra	17
56	,, ,,	Backlight sail	OW
57	patt 264	as 54	17
58 Bar 6	2 patt 23	Light arches above gauze cool	17
59	,, ,, ,,	,, ,, ,, ,, warm	52
60 PS Boom 1	2 patt 264	X light forestage warm	OW
61	,, ,, ,,	,, ,, ,, cool	17
62	2 patt 23	,, ,, ,, night	40
63	,, ,, ,,	,, ,, ,, court	38
64	,, ,, ,,	,, ,, ,, sunset	34
65 OP Boom 1	2 patt 264	X light forestage warm	OW
66	,, ,, ,,	,, ,, ,, cool	17
67	2 patt 23	,, ,, ,, night	40
68	,, ,, ,,	,, ,, ,, court	38
69	,, ,, ,,	,, ,, ,, sunset	34
70 PS Boom 2	patt 223	X light below rostra warm	OW
71	,, ,, ,,	,, ,, ,, ,, night	40
72	2 patt 23	,, ,, ,, ,, cool	17
73	patt 223	,, ,, ,, ,, sunset	34
74 OP Boom 2	2 patt 264	X light front court arches	2
75	,, ,, ,,	,, ,, ,, ,,	18
76	2 patt 23	X light below arches cool	17
77	patt 223	,, ,, ,, sunset	34
78 PS Boom 3	patt 243	X light rostra court	2
79	patt 264	,, ,, ,, cool	17
80	patt 243	,, ,, ,, night	18
81	,, ,,	,, ,, ,, sunset	34
82 OP Boom 3	2 patt 264	X light middle court arches	2
83	,, ,, ,,	,, ,, ,, ,,	18
84	patt 243	X light rostra cool	17
85	,, ,,	,, ,, ,, sunset	34
86 OP Boom 4	2 patt 264	X backlight court arches	2
87	,, ,, ,,	,, ,, ,, ,,	18
88	patt 243	,, ,, ,, ,, sunset	34
89 Stage left	patt 252	Cloud effect on gauze (opening)	17
90 ,, right			17
91 ,, centre	Tubular ripple	Ripple effect on gauze (ship)	15
92 ,, left	3 beamlights	Low side backlight to player King's death (end ship)	6
93 ,, left	patt 264	X light above gauze off cloth	17
94 ,, right	patt 264	,, ,, ,, ,, ,, ,,	17
95 Backstage	Ground row	Frontlight cloth	32
96			34
97			17
98 Backstage	Ground row	Rearlight cloth	OW

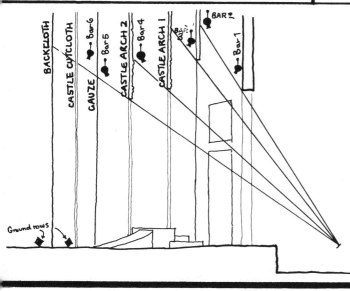

5 Design problems: colour

The next chapters discuss various design problems that will arise with various types of production being staged in various types of theatre. Before getting down to the specific, we must discuss one important subject that applies to every sort of show in every sort of theatre. It is colour.

The use of colour and coloured light is an important part of lighting for the stage. With it the designer can suggest the time of day or the season of the year. He can underline the mood of a scene and he can enhance or destroy the effect of the scenery and costumes. Indeed to a great many people stage lighting means colour, and the fact that the most popular selling colour in Cinemoid is No 6 Red (by a very substantial margin) indicates how brashly colour is all too often used. On the other hand, in the professional theatre, recent years have seen something of a reaction against the excessive use of colour. There has been a call, largely stimulated by the 'Brechtian' theory of stagecraft, for a return to the use of white light. Colour has been considered by some directors as anathema and a symbol of everything that is old fashioned. Sir Tyrone Guthrie, in his *A Life in the Theatre*, has protested against stages bathed in a 'weak solution of apricot jam'. This reaction has been in many ways a healthy one and, as with so many things in life, I suspect the real truth lies somewhere in the middle. No doubt far too many plays were performed bathed in a soup of pale gold. On the other hand, how does one actually define 'white' light? The light produced by the conventional theatre spotlight is a very different white from that of an English sunlit morning, and the colours of a natural sunset often far outdo the most lurid theatrical effect. In fact, I happen to be writing this chapter while on holiday in the Hebrides. As I write, the sun is setting and there's a large bank of storm cloud building in the east. The last rays of the sun fill the air with a colour something closely akin to the well-known No 8 (Cinemoid colour). The shadows are warm blue, the sea two quite separate colours, ranging from a greeny-blue to a deep purple-brown under the almost indigo coloured storm clouds. I would hesitate before offering any director such a technicolour vision on the stage!

When thinking about how much or how little colour to use, the choice may seem to be between stark Brechtian whiteness, a psychedelic morass of multi-coloured sensation, or an attempted distillation of the colours of nature. The guide line seems to lie in the simple rules that we have tried to follow throughout this book: first, what does the playwright call for, and second, how does the director intend to re-create his work on the stage? Taking the natural world as our inspiration we can certainly assume that there need be little call for the apricot jam solution.

For *Love For Love* for the National Theatre Company at the Old Vic in London, director Peter Wood and set designer Lila de Nobili wanted very deliberately to create a varnished, crusted, 'old-master' feeling over the stage. Here the apparently clear sunshine was 50 or 50-50 (Cinemoid colours); the shadows, 52, 53 through to 7 and even 42; the sunset, various combinations including 8, 7, 47 and lamplight 3, 2 and even 4 and various complications thereof. This was an example where one strove deliberately for the marmalade effect! By contrast, I remember a production of *Richard III* at Stratford-on-Avon for William Gaskill, with a set by Jocelyn Herbert. For this the effect of white light was wanted. The result, with which I think we were all pleased, was part white but part variations of 17, 67, 55, 50, 60, and so on. The colours were used to model and modify the real white light, which in fact appeared quite yellow. This complex battery of off-whites combined to give the stark effect required, and yet provided a very subtle degree of visual variety.

Some years later I had the privilege of working with the Berliner Ensemble when they did a season at the Old Vic Theatre in London. Their famous version of 'white light' was very different from that imagined by the English Brechtian disciples. First, although they found that the Old Vic permanent equipment provided them with the brightest stage area that they had met outside their own theatre, they nevertheless boosted this with some thirty or forty kilowatts of twenty-four volt beamlights. Then every lantern on the stage was coloured with 67 Cinemoid. This was the authentic version of Brechtian whiteness. Rather sadly it also blotted out almost entirely the marvellous textures of the scenery, but this, we found later, was the unfortunate result of the rushed conditions under which they were working on their tour.

I approach colour from an entirely subjective point of view. I have no preconceived ideas about how it should be used. If the lighting is designed to satisfy the four functions we have discussed and if, as a result, it has achieved the link between the actor and his environment, if it has created the air in which he moves, if it has revealed all parts of the stage in perfect proportion, then the choice of colour follows quite naturally.

Some notes on the basic laws and rules about colour and its use are found in Mechanics pages 147 and 148. The various Demonstrations throughout the book will illustrate some actual uses.

Apart from rules about how coloured light and pigment behave, what are the other things that influence the designer in his thoughts about colour?

Of the four properties of light discussed in chapter 1, colour is probably the most potent when it comes to evoking an emotional or psychological response in the audience. Changes of intensity, the distribution of light or its movement have, of course, an emotive effect, but colour, which can be applied so subtly and with such complexity, provides an unparalleled opportunity for the designer.

An interesting production from this point of view was *Rosencrantz and Guildenstern are Dead* by Tom Stoppard, directed by Derek Goldby, set designed by Desmond Heeley. The setting was a textured low rostrum, standing in front of a backcloth. Into this area there was flown, for the Elsinore scenes, a series of three-dimensional arches, and for the ship scene, an enormous sail. The production had a bizarre, theatrical quality; the two protagonists seemed to pass through a sort of wonderland. We evolved a scheme whereby the lighting would take this idea and, largely through the use of colour, amplify it. For example, the play opens in a 'no-man's land' on a barren heath. The light slowly built from darkness with a suggestion of grey mist and the stage was gradually lit in a cold, mysterious, mournful tone. This slowly lightened, until the entry of the group of players who were to become a pivotal element in the development of the play. They brought on with them their own new light, but a light that was still keyed to the reality of the deserted moorland. It increasingly suggested a setting sun through the mist and then twilight. As the play became more bizarre and the spell of the players seemed to enfold Rosencrantz and Guildenstern, so the lighting became hotter and more aggressive. When the players went on their way the scene ended; there was almost a feeling of relief as the stage disappeared into a strange blue backlight of night. Out of this came the Court: dusty, mysterious, encrusted arches dimly seen as if by a flickering torchlight. At times Rosencrantz and Guildenstern moved almost in a world of their own, with brilliant games of verbal tennis, in a style that was little short of music hall. For this the lighting in which they worked grew clearer, whiter and brighter, as if cocooning them in a sharp clear light of their own. When the players again intruded the lighting took their hot bizarre tone, eventually, at the play's climax and the players' deaths, resorting to stark shafts of pure red, cutting across the stage from bizarre angles (see Demonstration 3 and colour Pls 51, 52). This play used colour aggressively, perhaps outrageously, and yet it proved to be in tune with the director's intention. Its success in London and New York perhaps proved its justification. At the other end of the scale, the most subtle variations of white—cool white, warm white, brown white, grey white, green white—can all build toward a thrilling result.

A very obvious note of warning here: the designer should use strong colour only with the greatest care, remembering that the first function of lighting is Selective Visibility. An actor under normal circumstances cannot be considered truly visible if he has a bright green face. Only in exceptional circumstances can there be any justification for using anything but the subtlest colour on the acting area, except as an underlying deep colour wash to affect the overall tone of the stage. When he comes to lighting the setting or background, the designer can obviously take more licence, provided that he is enhancing the work of the set designer and not simply trying to 'improve' it without reference to the original intention. The scene designer has every right to expect to see his scenery and costumes the way he intended them to appear.

Colour mixing on backcloth or cyclorama

The designer frequently has to decide whether to light a cyclorama with a single colour medium to give exactly the colour required, or whether to blend several colours, for example the primaries, until the desired tint is achieved. The answer to this depends upon the degree of variety of effect that one has to achieve. If a cyc has to go through every colour in the spectrum, obviously a three colour mix of the primaries is essential. If, on the other hand, all that is needed is a blue sky that fades to a sunset, it would be far more economical to have two circuits of blue, perhaps one light and one dark, and one circuit of a sunset colour. An additive mix of deep colours is very wasteful of light since, while the result may be white or a light tint, it is only achieved by a small part of the light from each circuit coming through the saturated colour medium. Wherever possible, it is best to use the palest colours that are consistent with providing the required range of effect.

Subtractive mixing

Subtractive mixing means that if one combines several colours in a single frame for a single spotlight, a new colour is created that will have been subtractively mixed in the same way as one mixes pigment. The sixty or so colours in each colour range provide for most of the colour variations that a designer may require; however, it can be rewarding to experiment and develop one's own colour from combinations of these. Subtractive colour mixing is an experiment that can obviously be done at home and there are many fascinating combinations of colour to be found. The 1959 production of *Brand* at the Lyric Theatre, Hammersmith, London, directed by Michael Elliott and designed by Richard Negri, used a great deal of subtracted colour. The play, which was set almost entirely in the Norwegian mountains, seemed to call for an enormous range of pale greys, pale browns, pale greens, pale blues, pale yellows, most of which were combinations of colour.

Broken colour

This means that instead of using two completely different sheets of colour in front of a lantern, one cuts either or both of them in a certain pattern so that each colour can be seen both separately and in combination. Different types of spotlight will react to this in different ways, dependent upon their lens system, but great variety can be obtained. I found it particularly effective in the Royal Shakespeare Company's *As You Like It* (again with Michael Elliott and Richard Negri). I used a considerable number of units with broken colour in combinations of various greens and yellows. These, together with a quantity of gobos, produced a quite enchanting forest-like impression.

Fluorescence

Fluorescence provides a way of changing the light of one wavelength into that of another longer wavelength. We usually see this used with ultra-violet (UV). These rays, which are almost invisible, will cause certain substances to fluoresce in various vivid colours. The fluorescent colours are available in paints, dyes and stage make up. Some of them are visible under white light, but change in quality under UV. Some are almost invisible and only appear in UV light. Particularly exciting use was made of UV in the National Theatre's production of *Love's Labours Lost* for the National Theatre at the Old Vic, London (directed by Sir Laurence Olivier and designed by Carl Toms). The set was a formalized pattern of trees that were moved into various formations from scene to scene. The trees were green and leafy as if in full summer, but invisibly painted with ultra-violet paint. At the very end of the play, as the stage faded to night and the last haunting words were heard, the normal stage lighting faded out, leaving only the fluorescent UV lamps. The entire scene was magically transformed: the trees were stripped of their leaves and looked as though they were covered in snow.

6 Design problems: staging

Backdrops, front-cloths and cycloramas

These usually need special lighting treatment. Sometimes, when used as a neutral background to the stage, they can be left unlit, but usually they will represent sky, a distant scene or some purely visual piece of design.

Cloths hung toward the back of the stage are usually lit from battens (X-rays) or floodbars. Which of these methods is used

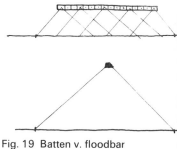

Fig. 19 Batten v. floodbar

Fig. 20 PAR batten to light bottom of

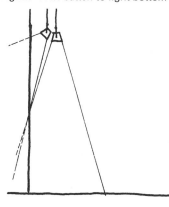

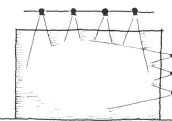

Fig. 21 Spotlighting a cloth

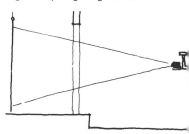

Fig. 22 Spotlighting cloth from FOH

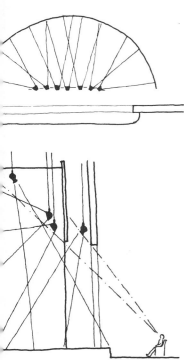

Fig. 23 Cyclorama lighting

depends upon the brightness required and the amount of space available between the lighting position and the cloth. If considerable brightness is needed and if the space is five or six feet or more, then a floodbar can be used. Closer than this, it will probably be found that the cut-off from each flood will show in a series of ugly lines that can only be removed (with difficulty) by using a heavy frost diffuser. The batten will give a good colour mix at a much closer range but with less brightness (fig 19).

When space is limited or when the cloth is a very high one, it is always difficult to get the light down to the middle of the cloth. This can be overcome in various ways: a second batten with a more directional light pattern, e.g. using PAR lamps (fig 20), can be hung alongside the first, or on its own, or the centre of the cloth can be spotlighted from the top, sides, or the front (fig 21). We have noted already that the dress circle front-lighting position can be very useful for flooding a front cloth (fig 22).

We may find that we do not want to flood a backcloth overall with light and the use of spotlighting with Fresnels is becoming more popular. Fresnels can be obtained with an oval-shaped beam and are extremely useful for lighting down to the centre of a cloth from a bar placed close to its top.

The cyclorama, wrapping itself around the sides of the stage, presents a different and more complex problem. It is extremely difficult to light it from nearby. For a large cyc it is essential to get well away and to use powerful 'floods' and/or Fresnels. If the cyc is combined with borders it is almost impossible to get a satisfactory match of intensities between each border and this combination is best avoided by set designers. The best position from which to light a wrap-around cyclorama is well down-stage (fig 23).

Fig. 24 Lighting gauze

Gauzes

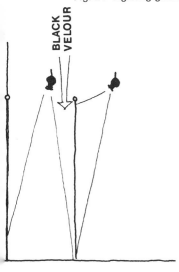

Theatrical gauze has been aptly described as 'holes tied together with string'. It has the quality of appearing solid when lit from the front but transparent when a scene behind it is lit. The description quoted is a good reminder of how to use it. The holes are always there and it is the careful control of light that gives different results. If the front of the gauze is flooded, a lot of light will go through the holes and illuminate the area behind it. If the gauze is to be completely opaque it should be lit carefully from an oblique angle that will not send spill through into the scene behind. Similarly, when the gauze is to be transparent, the light behind has to be very tightly controlled. To make quite certain of the opacity of a gauze (for example, if a scene change has to take place behind it) it is best to back it with another cloth. A black velvet curtain is best, and this can be flown out or opened just before we wish to dissolve through the gauze (fig 24).

Gauze has other uses apart from that of creating spectacular effect. Used in front of a cyc or backcloth it will give a misty quality of distance. Used as part of a standing set it can create rooms or acting areas that can be made to appear and disappear at will. In all cases the techniques for lighting are the same.

Gauze used with projection can be fascinating. A front projection shone through a gauze will give the effect of a double-image, the projection being seen both on the gauze and on the surface behind it. I once saw a remarkable production of *Under Milk Wood* in Berlin. In this a suggestion of the wooded hillside around the little Welsh village was projected on to a vast cyclorama and very slowly a series of gauze borders were dropped in. As each came into sight it repeated the projected image until the whole stage was wrapped in this abstract pattern of foliage, creating the most extraordinary visual effect.

A dark gauze in front of a rear projection screen will slightly darken the whole picture, but it will also make the blacks in the picture stand out with greater contrast and reduce the amount the picture is dissipated by reflection from the acting area.

There are two types of gauze in common use. One, very thin and delicate, is known as 'English gauze' and should be used when its chief function is its transparency. The other, which originated in America, is known as 'Hanson' or 'Sharks Tooth' gauze. This has much thicker 'string' and should be used if the primary purpose of the gauze is to be 'solid'.

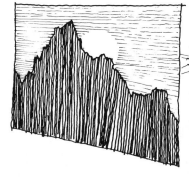

Fig. 25 *Brand* rearlighting

Translucency

Another important scenic device is the translucent cloth which is intended to be lit from the rear. This demands a translucent material which can be made in very wide widths to avoid unwanted seams appearing in the design. The uses to which translucency can be put are endless. The section on musical lighting in chapter 7 mentions two uses of the technique which are typical of a great deal of American musical scenic design. Equally fascinating are the variations one can achieve with an almost blank translucent screen and varied lighting. The ideal surface is a plastic rear-projection screen but various other materials make a satisfactory substitute. Revues and ballet often give the opportunity for exciting and startling variations of back light; the use of gobos, perhaps with colour-changes creating moving shapes and colours of light on the screen, can be fascinating.

On a more sober note was Ibsen's *Brand*, for the 59 Theatre Company (fig 25). For this the predominant scenic effect was a plain white translucent cloth hung behind a dark gauze. Behind these a series of shapes were suspended which, used singly or in combination and back lit, gave a staggering impression of misty views of the mountains and fiords of

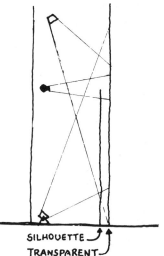

SILHOUETTE
TRANSPARENT

88

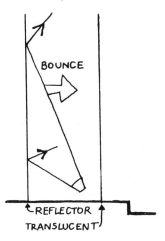

Fig. 26 Reflector drop

Norway. Pairs of 500 watt profile spots were used to suggest the sun or moon as seen through mist: one was focused to give a hard circle and its partner focused softly to create a watery halo. They were set to coincide with the clefts in the silhouette shapes. Out of nothing but light, the shadow of unpainted cut-outs and the translucent screen all the required mysteries of Norway were evoked.

A translucent cloth can be partly painted on the front, and by a combination of back and front lighting great variations and illusions of depth can be obtained. A translucent cloth is always helped by hanging a white reflector drop upstage of any back lighting. This can be a plain white cloth or even the back wall of the theatre if it is painted white: by its reflection of any spill light it will substantially increase the brightness of the cloth itself (fig 26).

Scenic projection

The success of projection depends on an exceptional degree of collaboration among the design team and an understanding of its problems and limitations.

There was a time, many years ago, when projection was considered a rather dangerous venture. The result was rather fuzzy and diffuse and the pictures never quite came out the size predicted.

Having read books written in the late 'twenties and early 'thirties about projection, I became determined to see it satisfactorily used in England once again. My visits to Germany had shown me that a large and comparatively bright picture could be obtained, and I refused to believe that the smaller theatres and different lighting conditions in England meant that projection could never work there satisfactorily. My theory was, on the contrary, that a small theatre could be a positive advantage for, assuming that sufficiently wide angle projection could be achieved, the projector would be placed so close to the screen that the image would be very bright indeed.

I decided, therefore, to import a German projector, the largest then available, of 5000 watts, from Reiche and Vogel of Berlin. The production was a revue for Michael Codron, called *One Over the Eight*, and it was to be staged at the Duke of York's theatre in London. The stage was only about twenty-five feet deep; front projection was mandatory and eventually, together with Tony Walton the designer, I evolved a scheme whereby two projectors, sited on high towers built into a false proscenium on either side of the stage, would shine on to the opposite sides of a curved cyclorama (fig 27). The resulting image was twenty-five feet high by about fifty feet wide.

The next step was the preparation of the slides. We wished to project about forty or fifty different scenes. These were all to be in colour, some were cartoon-like and some were abstract paintings by Tony Walton. The traditional method of making slides, which the German experts also used, was to set up the projector in the position it would be in in the theatre, shine a blank slide on to the cyclorama and then mark the slide until the correct shape required on the stage was established. Unfortunately in our case the production was starting on tour and we were only able to start assembling our projectors in the theatre on the Sunday morning before the Monday night on which the show was due to open. In the thirty-six hours at our disposal there was no time to establish the required distortion by trial and error; but I was convinced it could all be done photographically and checked mathematically. Our German advisers were sceptical (one might almost say hysterical)!

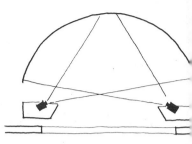

Fig. 27 *One over the Eight* projection p

To cut a long story short, it worked. Robert Ornbo, an artist and mathematician, who has since become the outstanding expert on projection work in England, helped me make all the slides. Then, with our hearts in our mouths, we tried them out. Each picture, projected from its acute angle, came out fair and square. The short throws of the projectors produced a bright and clear-cut picture and the considerable gamble that Michael Codron had taken (there was no other scenery had the projection not worked) came off. The critics, almost without exception, praised 'the multitude of brightly-coloured back-cloths'. Many people were not even aware that projection was used at all: the show indeed appeared to be backed by an amazing quantity of highly-coloured cloths. Since then an enormous amount of projection has been used, some highly successfully and some with disappointing results. Strangely enough, the failures can usually be attributed to the same series of problems, all of which we managed to overcome on that first attempt.

First, intensity of image. If a picture is to be crisp and decisive, it must be *bright*. There is a universal complaint about the lack of brightness in existing projection equipment, and this is undoubtedly justified. A far higher intensity is badly needed, and the use of new light sources such as the PANI H.M.I. projector offers great possibilities. Without advanced equipment one has to extract the maximum power out of what is available. This can be done in two ways. First, by control of the artwork, i.e. of the picture to be projected (the lighter the picture, the more light travels through the slide on to the screen: the more contrasted the picture, the more effective the result will be). Second, and most important, the inverse square law must be remembered: the closer the projector can be placed to the screen *the brighter the picture will be.* For this a very wide-angle projector is necessary, as well as, of course, a large slide, the German 18 cm. (approx. 7 inches) being most satisfactory.

Besides a powerful projector placed as close as possible to the screen and the right artwork, certain other factors contribute to success. One must also, for example, ensure that the rest of the light on the stage has the minimum effect on the projection. It is absolutely essential that as much as possible of the spill light from the acting area is cut out before it hits the screen. In *One Over the Eight* the stage had no other scenery and the action took place right up to within five feet of the screen. To cut any bounce-light down to an absolute minimum, the floor was covered with inverted hardboard which was then painted a matt brown-black.

We experimented in a production in New York of *Golden Boy*, once again designed by Tony Walton, with a matt black floor paint which was claimed by its manufacturers to be 98 per cent light absorbent. They unfortunately omitted to mention, however, that people couldn't walk on it without picking it up on their shoes and leaving black footprints wherever they went.* An equally effective method of reducing spill is to place some scenic element between the stage and the projection. In *A Funny Thing Happened on the Way to the Forum*, the American musical seen on Broadway and in London, again designed by Tony Walton, there were several buildings and high ground rows around the acting area that effectively caught most of the bounce light. As this was an American musical, lit in New York by Jean Rosenthal, the acting area was extremely bright; but even so the projections stood out vividly whenever they were required to.

The angle of light into the acting area is obviously important. Whenever possible light should be directed so that it will not bounce toward the screen. With a screen across the back of the stage sidelighting becomes particularly important. Finally, of course, the sheer quantity of light has to be carefully controlled and balanced in proportion to the screen. As we have seen throughout this book, the impression of brightness is not necessarily achieved with actual brightness. It is usually helpful if the person responsible for projection is also the lighting designer. Unfortunate results can arise when the two jobs are separated.

It goes without saying that the darker the acting area, the more effective the projection can be. Josef Svoboda, the Czech scenic designer, has often demonstrated the enormous potential of projected scenery, yet, while I was lighting for him in London, I was reminded of the need to achieve a balance which avoids the projection becoming too bright for the stage and too dominant. Svoboda's hauntingly beautiful sets for Ostrovski's *The Storm* (Pls 31—34 and Demonstration 4), directed by John Dexter at the National Theatre, used a series of screens, some of gauze, some opaque, set at various angles, and a large number of photographic projections of trees, water and sky. These fused into a fascinating mosaic, creating a luminous and haunting atmosphere around the love story; but on occasions the projections had to be subdued to keep them

*This according to the manufacturers, has now been corrected.

in correct balance with the action. Projection, like every other aspect of lighting, is a matter of balance, proportion and taste.

The ultimate success of projected scenery depends upon the use to which it is put and the skill with which it is employed. Projection cannot be considered a cheap way of producing scenery (indeed it is only cheap if an enormous number of scenes are required); it is simply another way of creating pictorial images. The images produced have a certain luminosity and character and the ability to dissolve from image to image provides a very fluid scenic environment.

The surface upon which the projection is thrown needs careful thought. It is useless having a powerful projector if too much light is wasted by an inefficient screen. Here there are no rules. A few hours' experiment are the only answer. I have found that a very white and highly efficient screen brings its own problems because it reflects, with equal efficiency, the spill light from the acting area.

Rear projection (fig 28)

This requires a greater stage depth than does front projection but when the production only requires a small acting area rear projection comes into its own. This means that a rear projection screen can be placed far enough down stage to allow the projector to stand behind it. If space is limited, the projection can be diverted via a mirror, although some light is lost in the process (fig 28b). An advantage of rear projection is that it gives a brighter picture than front projection because light is transmitted through the screen rather than reflected off it. The production of *In White America*, directed by Peter Coe, lighting by Robert Bryan, at the Arts Theatre in London, used a large rear projection screen on a very tiny stage. The picture was so bright that an actor could perform almost against the screen and still be front lit.

The Travails of Sancho Panza, designer Tony Walton, for the National Theatre at the Old Vic in 1969, used rear projection on a large scale: six 5000 watt Reiche and Vogel projectors behind a thirty-foot wide screen, the face of which was covered by a Hanson gauze on a track. The gauze moved across the projected image and, with a changing balance of front light on the gauze and the rear projection, a whole series of different effects were produced (Pl 40).

A drawback to the use of rear projection in the theatre arises from the width of the viewing angle from the auditorium. Most BP screens transmit the light in a straight line through the screen; thus from a position directly facing the projector one gets a clear bright image, while from the sides of the auditorium the image tends to fade. A careful choice of screen can reduce this problem but, generally speaking, a rear projection screen at the side of the stage or at an angle to the stage front has to be used very carefully to succeed.

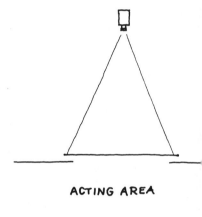

ACTING AREA

Fig. 28a Back projection

Fig. 28b

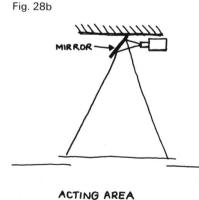

MIRROR

ACTING AREA

Multi-screen projection

If the space available for rear projection is limited, if a multi-image projection is required, if small projection screens (perhaps combined with other scenic elements) are to be employed, or finally if only a low-brightness image is needed, a smaller projector, or a number of them, can be used. The most commonly employed is the Kodak Carousel, and variations of this excellent unit are available with higher powered light sources ranging from 1200 watt incandescent to Xenon. Two advantages become immediately apparent: first, the projector is small and compact; second, and most importantly, it can be operated by remote control with eighty slides in a magazine, and there is thus no need for an electrician to be in attendance on each machine. This clearly makes economic sense, allows projectors to be used in hitherto inaccessible positions, and allows far more complex multi-screen effects to be achieved, thanks to centralized control. Control can range from a manual pre-set board with thyristor remote dimmers for lamp intensity and push buttons for slide change, to fully automated memory consoles incorporating slide change, fades, dissolves and so on.

Two complex multi-screen productions will suffice as examples. Firstly, *I and Albert*, a musical by Charles Strouse and Lee Adams, at the Piccadilly Theatre, London, directed by John Schlesinger, designed by Luciana Arrighi, with lighting and projection by Robert Ornbo (fig 29, Pls 59–61). This musical was a pageant of the life of Queen Victoria with dozens of scenes that had to flow with a film-like quality from one to another. The design concept was for a semi-permanent set giving levels and staircases, backed by a three-dimensional 'wall' of variously shaped rear projection screens. All the forward screens were shaped like picture-frames—square, rectangular, oval—while behind them hung a large screen containing holes shaped to coincide exactly with the 'pictures' in front. Thus, some or all of the pictures could be rear-projected to produce, for example, a gallery of royal portraits hanging in space. Most ingeniously, another battery of projectors could rear-project on the 'wall' surrounding them, thus providing, among other effects, a richly patterned wallpaper upon which the pictures appeared to be hung; at the end of the scene this could dissolve to another wall or vanish. Each picture could dissolve individually, collectively, or in a rippling or random manner, to another image, or disappear. Furthermore if a single image were projected across all screens, the 'pictures' vanished and the whole back of the stage became a single vista—used to much effect for the Crystal Palace scene. Finally all the screens could fly out—as they did at the end of act one. The thunder of the Crimean war burst across the theatre as the stage filled with smoke, the screens miraculously disappeared, and 38 projectors projected a massive Union

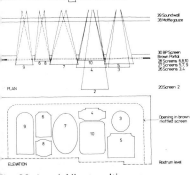

Fig. 29 *I and Albert* multi-screen projection

93

Jack flag through the flickering, swirling smoke, that seemed to envelop the audience. These projectors comprised 19 pairs of 1200 watt Carousels employed on a scaffold against the theatre's rear wall. Because of the noise from their 38 fans, a sound-absorbing wall with glass projection ports had to be built down-stage of them.

Our second example is the sadly shortlived musical *Shelter* in New York, designed by Tony Walton with lighting and projection by myself (Pls 62, 63). A different series of problems required new solutions. The musical told of a young TV advertising executive who was so obsessed by his work that he lived on the job. He lived in a small house with a garden, all artificial and built (for filming commercials) in a TV studio. The studio was run by a computer—a friendly computer. Here he sheltered from the world, his wife, and other complications: for with the aid of the computer's studio technology he could transport the house and change its environment to anywhere in the world—or universe. The set was a mock TV studio, grid extending through the proscenium, galleries and spiral stairs, video and sound equipment and all around a cyclorama upon which could be projected literally any image or environment. The house, taking up two thirds of the stage, was a realistic TV setting with window and porch; the garden had grass and a willow tree. At a word from our hero the whole scene could appear to be set on a sunlit day in New England, a moonlit night in the Bahamas (good tactics, this, for the new girl friend) or in a blizzard right at the top of Mount Everest. Scale could be enlarged or reduced and every sort of image, realistic or phantasmagoric, summoned up.

So far so good—and great fun. Then technical problems emerged. The stage was very shallow: most of the cyclorama had to be front projected, but parts of it could not be reached. The water tank of the house and the willow tree were in part an obstruction. The house window had to be almost against the cyc, but luckily there was a minute amount of space behind. So a combination of front and rear projection was involved (fig. 30). The stage right part of the cyc (#2) and the top above the house (#1) were covered each with two 5 kilowatt projectors mounted high on a stage right down-stage tower, using 18 cm. slides, predistorted for horizontal and vertical angle, curved screen and to avoid shadows of tree and house. The left end of the curved angle cyc (#3) was rear projected from pairs of high-power carousels placed upstage left, and the window (#4) from up-stage centre. (Note the window screen is cheated downstage of the main cyc to obtain sufficient throw.) All those different projectors from different angles and different throws, some front, some rear, merged together to create what was apparently a single vista. Two additional small screens hung over the stage at angles, showing images merging with or counterpointing the main action. These were rear projected by pairs of carousels concealed in a dummy air-

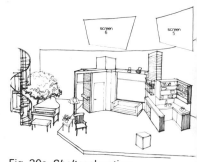

Fig. 30a *Shelter* elevation

Fig. 30b *Shelter* plan

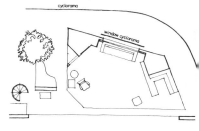

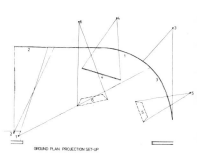

Fig. 30c *Shelter* plan of projection set-u

Fig. 30d *Shelter* screen elevation

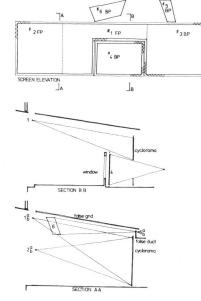

conditioning duct running beneath the TV grid. An amusing show with charm and lots of visual humour, but it closed within a week. Such is theatre.

The rapidly developing world of industrial or commercial conferences uses audiovisual, slide/sound multi-screen techniques with ever greater complexity. Multi-media 'experiences' seem to proliferate in many aspects of entertainment. In the music industry, pop and rock shows and theatrical manifestations of the same continue to appear; for example, *Beatlemania* in New York, directed, lit and co-ordinated by Jules Fisher, and *Elvis* in London, lighting and projection by David Hersey. Projection, which is light literally creating the whole visual image, is a healthy infant, with every likelihood of rapid growth.

Film

There are many problems, both technical and artistic, surrounding the use of film in live theatre, and the occasions on which it is successfully used are all too rare. Svoboda, with his Latterna Magica, used very low light levels on the stage. *The Apple Tree* in New York, directed by Mike Nichols, set designed by Tony Walton, had an entire sequence backed by an enormous BP screen with what appeared to be a full-scale Cinerama film upon it. As with slide projection, the key to success is a powerful projector, correctly placed, with sympathetic lighting.

Optical effects

A whole series of optical effects—fleecy clouds, storm clouds, waves, flame and smoke—have become so much a part of the theatre and television scene that they are now no more than clichés. I have found that the only way to make an optical effect work is to muddle it up. One flame effect looks quite ridiculous, four look better and twenty look superb; add a little smoke, a few flickering lamps and perhaps some fluttering silk and the result is dazzling! Lionel Bart's *Blitz*, which became noted for its fire-raid sequence, used quite simple effects. The secret was that there were lots of them from all directions. The same applies to clouds and snow: jumbling up quantities of projections will achieve the most effective results. I should like to make here another point arising from the *Blitz* example. In all the roaring of air-raid sound effects, whirring of effects motors, trundling of vast scenic units, pumping of smoke, away at the back of the stage there was a rear projection of the silhouette of St Pauls, a famous news photograph from the Blitz itself. That simple and familiar image stirred the memory and imagination of many of the audience, filling in and making allowances for the comparative crudity of the remainder. Effects are illusion and illusion is trickery. Something very simple can often be the key that captures the imagination of the audience.

Demonstration 4

The Storm
by Ostrovsky
National Theatre—Old Vic
Dir.   John Dexter
Des.   Svoboda
Light Richard Pilbrow

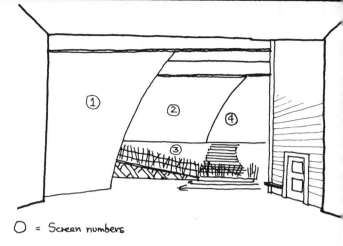

◯ = Screen numbers

ACT I   A public garden high above the Volga. Evening.
              Fade to evening. Close Katerina bench DSOP.
              Cheat in ramp US fade toward storm. Lose bench.
              Close Katerina foot of steps.
              Fade to projections.

ACT II Sc. 1   Room in the Kabanov house. Interior bright sun
                  through small windows (not shown).

ACT II Sc. 2   Street in front of Kabanov's house. Evening.
                  Fade to twilight. Close to ramp US.

ACT II Sc. 3   A small overgrown ravine above the Kabanov garden
                  and a wicker gate. Later the same evening—night.
                  Very poetic—romantic—lovers' meeting.

                  Close to love scene centre.
                  X fade to parting picture.

ACT III Sc. 1   An arcade round an old decaying building. In the
                  background the banks of the Volga.
                  A storm coming up.
                  Rain passes and scene lightens.
                  Storm develops again—lightning.
                  Lightning—fade to severe storm.

ACT III Sc. 2   A public garden, bleak cold evening.
                  Close to Katerina.
                  Suicide attempt.
                  Crowd on with torches centre.
                  Close to Katerina's body·centre.

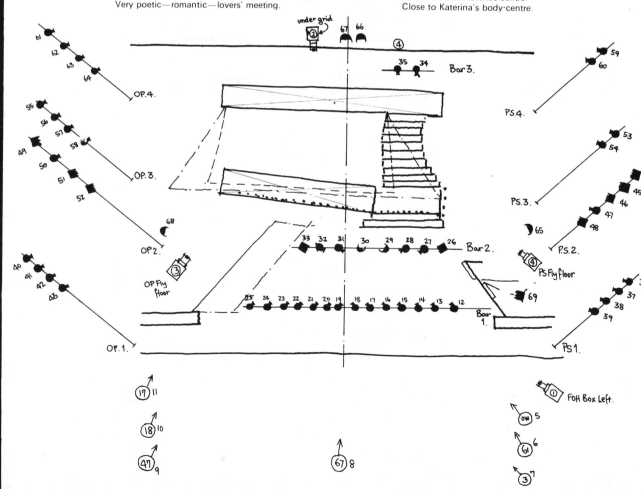

FOCUS SCHEDULE

	Position	Type	Function	Colour
1	FOH Circle L	5 kw Projector	Screen 1	
2	Undergrid back gallery	,, ,, ,,	Screen 2	
3	OP fly floor	,, ,, ,,	Screen 3	
4	PS fly floor	,, ,, ,,	Screen 4	
5	FOH left	6 patt 264*	Acting areas DS	OW
6		2 patt 264	Night gobo wash DS	61
7		1 patt 264*	Katerina body lamplit C	3
8	FOH centre	4 patt 293*	Cool front fill	67
9	FOH right	2 patt 264	Sunset/warm DS fill	47
10			Night gobo wash DS	18
11		6 patt 264*	Acting areas DS	17
12	Spotbar 1	patt 264W	Centre (Katerina body)	3
13		,, ,,	Gobo around bench RC	40
14		,, ,,	Acting area LC/L	OW
15		,, ,,	,, ,, LC cool	40
16		,, ,,	,, ,, C	OW
17		,, ,,	,, ,, RC/R (bench)	OW
18		,, ,,	,, ,, RC cool	40
19		,, ,,	,, ,, L cool	17
20		,, ,,	,, ,, L warm	51
21		,, ,,	,, ,, C cool	17
22		,, ,,	,, ,, C warm	51
23		,, ,,	,, ,, R cool	17
24		,, ,,	,, ,, R warm	51
25		,, ,,	Gobo all LC	40
26	Bar 2	patt 243	Night forestage	18
27		patt 264	Cool storm backlight	17
28		,, ,,	Leaf downlight gobo	61
29		Beamlight	Lightning shaft	17
30		,,		17
31		patt 264	Leaf downlight gobo	61
32		,, ,,	Cool storm backlight	17
33		patt 243	Night forestage	18
34	Bar 3	patt 264	Backlight stairs day	OW
35		,, ,,	,, ,, night	40
36	PS Boom 1	2 patt 264	X light forestage cool	67
37		,, ,, ,,	,, ,, ,, warm	52
38		2 patt 23	,, ,, ,, sunset	47
39		,, ,, ,,	,, ,, ,, night	40
40	OP Boom 1	2 patt 264	X light forestage cool	17
41		,, ,, ,,	,, ,, ,, warm	3
42		2 patt 23	,, ,, ,, sunset	47
43		,, ,, ,,	,, ,, ,, night	40
44	PS Boom 2	patt 223	X light foot stairs night	40
45		,, ,,	,, ,, ,, ,, cool	17
46		,, ,,	,, ,, ,, ,, warm	3
47		2 patt 23	X light centre warm	52
48		patt 223	,, ,, ,, night	40
49	OP Boom 2	patt 223	X light centre to steps	OW
50		2 patt 23	,, ,, ,, warm	51
51		patt 223	,, ,, ,, cool	17
52		,, ,,	,, ,, ,, sunset	47
53	PS Boom 3	patt 264	X light bridge warm	52
54		,, ,,	,, ,, ,, cool	17
55	OP Boom 3	patt 264	X light bridge to L day	OW
56		,, ,,	,, ,, ,, ,, L night	61
57		,, ,,	,, ,, ,, ,, RC day	50
58		,, ,,	,, ,, ,, ,, RC sunset	47
59	PS Boom 4	patt 264	X back rostra day	OW
60		,, ,,	,, ,, ,, night	40
61	OP Boom 4	patt 264	X back rostra night	61
62		,, ,,	,, ,, ,, day	50
63		,, ,,	,, ,, ,, sunset	47
64		,, ,,	,, ,, ,, night UR	8
65	Flys left	Beamlight	Lightning 'shaft' forestage	67
66	,, back	,,	Backlight 'cloud'	67
67	,, back	,,		67
68	,, right	,,	Lightning 'shaft' C	67
69	Stage L			3

* On separate circuits.

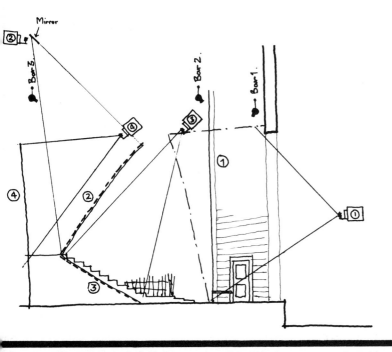

7 Design problems: the behaviour of light

In this chapter we shall be concerned with an extension of the ideas on lighting naturalistic settings discussed in chapter 2.

The interior—natural light

I should like to explore further the question of motivating light and its effect on our design ideas for this type of setting.

Once inside the room we should observe carefully how light behaves: observation of the real world will be helpful.

All the light in the room should appear to come from the window. The wall on the side opposite the window will be brighter than the others. This may need a special lift from a supplementary lantern on the spotbar or from the perch position. The surface of the ground outside the window will also affect the pattern of light in the room. Supposing the ground is covered in snow, the ceiling inside will be brighter than normal by reflection from it. If we are by a lake or river, the reflection might even be a moving impression of reflected ripples.

Since we are attempting to be realistic, we should be fastidious in choosing the angles of light. Sunlight should not really come streaming in through windows on opposite sides of the same room at the same time; and a dawn on stage left should not really come from the same direction as a sunset. I suspect that reactions to natural light are so deeply ingrained that more people notice such discrepancies than is sometimes realized.

As evening falls in our room, the exterior and dominant light can cross-fade to the lower angles and warmer tones of sunset. Within the room the shadows should lengthen, the colour perhaps change softly as the level of reflected light naturally drops. The acting area and fill-lighting should be reduced, leaving a greater emphasis on the keylighting perhaps supplemented by cross-lighting from the side which would be at an angle more in keeping with the sunset.

What if the day is dull, or if the scene is in cold early morning? The overall colour tone should be colder, and the overall level softer. We want to create the impression of an overall diffusion of light. The keylight, which should now be in a cold tone from the window, will be hardly any brighter than the light in the room. It certainly should not show as a clear shaft.

Interior artificial light

If the action calls for one or more artificial light sources to be turned on (table lamps, wall brackets or chandelier), we shall have to supplement their light from our stage lighting and yet somehow maintain the impression that all the light is radiating from these fittings.

In the case of a chandelier, or anything above head height, this can be done comparatively easily. The production of *The Three Sisters* for the National Theatre at the Old Vic had a large chandelier hung upstage in the dinner party scene. This was supplemented by eight lanterns, some upstage, some down-stage of it, which cast a pattern of light that appeared to radiate from the chandelier itself. We should not ignore the light that comes from the fitting itself. This can be as bright as we can afford to have it without dazzling the audience. Sometimes a real light fitting will cast light where we do not want it: for instance, a table lamp will send a lot of its light straight up to the ceiling. As we want to keep the attention of the audience at stage level, we can cheat and mask out the top of the fitting without this being visible from the audience.

Fittings on tables or below eye level are the most difficult to reinforce, because most of the spotlighting comes from overhead. It may be possible, if we need it, to conceal some small unit, such as a 100 watt Fresnel, in the furniture adjacent to the fitting.

All light fittings that have to be switched on during the action should actually be switched from the control board. The actor simply mimes the operation, while the switchboard does the work. This is the only way in which one can achieve a really satisfactory coordination between the fitting and its covering spots. A battery-operated oil lamp should be fitted with a rheostat for the actor to use rather than a switch. Lamps which have to be carried about the stage probably present the greatest problem. They are a test of the manual dexterity of the board operator, since they necessitate a series of rapid cues. And here, incidentally, we have another argument for position-ing the board operator where he can see the stage and see what the actors are doing.

It is always extremely difficult to produce a battery lamp that is bright enough, particularly if it has got to stay on through a long scene. I recall a production of *The Father* with Trevor Howard, directed by Casper Wrede, set designed by Malcolm Pride, where an oil lamp had to be carried on, placed on a table and burn for almost forty minutes. It was impossible to get a battery lamp strong enough to remain bright for that length of time and eventually we constructed one that was both battery and mains. It was carried on under battery power and placed on two mains contacts fixed in the table. The mains supply was then faded in to take over from the battery.

Particularly in a 'dramatic' production like *The Father* one can afford to be bold about the amount of covering light needed in an artificially lit scene. Light from the front can be reduced to an absolute minimum and a truly claustrophobic effect achieved within the room by restricting the illumination to the pool of light around the fitting. This is a moment where the 45° angle becomes positively undesirable. Perhaps my favourite lighting moment was in a production of *Measure For Measure* for Michael Elliott at the Old Vic. In this, one entire scene (five minutes of dialogue) was played around a lantern on a table: the only illumination came from this lantern. Inside was a 25 watt bulb, the light of which was only allowed to escape from two little ports on either side and only just illuminated the two hovering conspiratorial faces.

Moonlight

As with sunlight, one should try to suggest the parallel rays of natural light, but in this case it should be very dim and of a cool tint, avoiding some of the more flagrantly romantic colours that sometimes pass as moonlight on the stage.

Firelight

Firelight can add sparkle and interest to a scene. The fire itself is usually of little importance, and may be masked from the audience by its grate or stove. The light from the fire can be imitated by well-concealed miniature spots. Several 100 watt lamps will be more effective than one larger one, for it must be remembered that firelight spreads out across the room. The colour of fire is not red but rather yellow and amber. I like to use broken colour, and a mixture of 4 or 5 with broken 10 or 11 can be useful. It is usually best to avoid any movement in the firelight itself for this can be distracting, but a few neon flicker lamps built into the fire and partially obscured can be amazingly effective. For something special, this, together with some smoke and some strips of silk blown by a fan, can be more realistic than the real thing.

Exteriors

The realistic lighting of exterior scenes is extremely difficult, for here the light really has to be used in three dimensions. That the effect so often falls short of the designer's intention seems to me to indicate that lighting design is still at a stage of infancy. With 1000 or 2000 watt lanterns, how can we hope to suggest the sun itself? In nature on a sunlit day, everything is lit up, but the human eye does not see everything, it only looks at what it wants to see: thus we have to direct the audience's attention on the stage. We are attempting to create the *essence* of sunlight. Ideally the set is so designed that it allows us to strike a part of it with a very powerful shaft of sunlight and to create shadow. If the side of a house or a piece of wall can be strongly sunlit, this will be the key for the remainder of the scene.

A dull day can present even greater problems. Without a

dominant light to present the idea to the audience it is all the more difficult to prevent the scene looking artificial and 'stagey'. With spotlighting (or perhaps the addition of some soft fill-light) we have to create the effect of reflection and diffusion. A cool colour will be needed, with a very delicate balance of light from all directions. Real reflection and truly diffused light might seem the ideal solution, though I've personally never found this so. For even under these circumstances the illumination still has to be *selective*, and truly diffused light would illuminate everything indiscriminately.

When creating the illusion of dawn or sunset, it is important to decide where the sun is coming from. Is it from the sides, the back or front of the stage?

Dawn and sunset are all too often associated with rather technicolour shafts of light. My favourite dawn was in the production of the musical *Jorrocks.* In a scene set on a deserted heath (a bare stage in front of a large wrap-around backlit cyclorama) darkness gave way to a low-lying, very cool greeny-grey diffused light that was gradually, in its turn, cut across by a faintly growing glassy yellow-white sidelight.

Exterior night

Realistic exterior night scenes are the most difficult to light because they should, in nine cases out of ten, actually be dark! The lighting designer obviously has to effect some compromise between reality and what is needed theatrically. The larger the stage area, and the darker the surrounding scenery, the easier is his task. Whenever possible, the designer should try to introduce some clearly defined source of light, be it a lamp, street light, fire or whatever. If the eye has one light source on which to focus, the remainder of the stage will appear darker by contrast. Similarly, a few stars in the night sky, with just a faint touch of deep blue, can make the whole scene recede amazingly in the imagination. If moonlight is called for, the parallel beam of natural light requirement will apply again. Several small lanterns with parallel beams will be far more effective than one large one dimmed right down, unless the setting is a very open one with a cyclorama, when it may be possible to suspend a lantern sufficiently far away to give the impression of hard edge shadow and almost parallel rays.

Demonstration 5

Miss Julie
by August Strindberg
National Theatre—Chichester
Festival Theatre
Dir.   Michael Elliott
Des.   Richard Negri
Light Richard Pilbrow

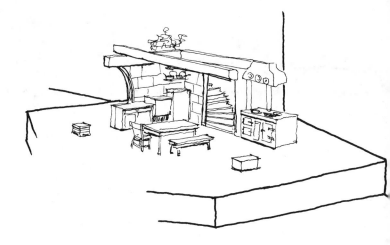

A large kitchen—window stage right to garden—lilac tree.
A stove with hood—kitchen table—sink.
Evening. Very soft warm sunset (from right) Golden-lilac shadows.
Fade very slowly to strong sunset—Miss Julie and Jean the valet.
Christine room candle lit.
Christine room candle out.
Fade through to cool twilight (Jean story of childhood).
Fade all to cold evening—continue to night (NB Scandinavia never dark).

Peasants' entry. Open stove—room filled with firelight.
Jean lights lamp over table—keep area tight around table.
Very slow build cold before dawn.
Dawn (left).
Lamp out.
Sunrise cuts across room, hard crystal clear.
Build to maximum bright sunrise for Julie exit.

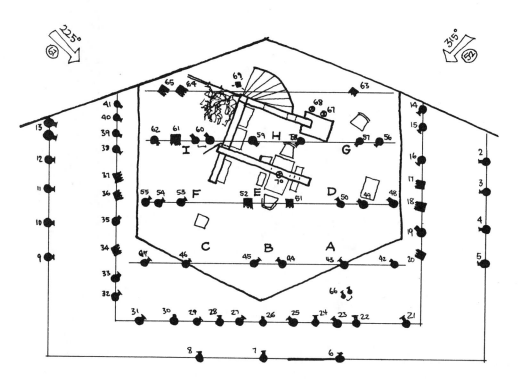

	Position	Type	Function	Colour
1	Side auditorium left	3 Beamlights	Sunrise left	OW
2	Outer left	patt 264	Side wash cool	45
3		,, ,,	,, ,, firelight	4–B11
4		,, ,,	,, ,, cool	45
5		,, ,,	,, ,, firelight	4–B11
6	Centre	,, ,,	Front wash cool Area A	67
7		,, ,,	,, ,, ,, ,, B	67
8		,, ,,	,, ,, ,, ,, C	67
9	Right	,, ,,	Side wash warm twilight	42
10		,, ,,	,, ,, cool	45
11		,, ,,	,, ,, warm twilight	42
12		,, ,,	,, ,, cool	45
13		2 patt 293	Sunset through window	47
14	Inner left	patt 264	Acting area G 315°	52
15		,, ,,	,, ,, D 315°	52
16		,, ,,	,, ,, A 315°	52
17		patt 223	Night side wash US	43
18		,, ,,	Cool to table area	45
19		patt 264	Acting area G 45°	OW
20		patt 223	Night side wash DS	43
21	Inner centre	patt 264	Acting area A 45°	OW
22		,, ,,	Lamp table to UR	3
23		,, ,,	Acting area B 45°	OW
24		,, ,,	Front wash cool DE	67
25		,, ,,	Acting area C 45°	OW
26		,, ,,	Lamp table C	2
27		,, ,,	Acting area A 135°	3
28		,, ,,	Front wash cool EF	67
29		,, ,,	Acting area B 135°	3
30		,, ,,	Front special garden	38–17
31		,, ,,	Acting area C 135°	3
32	Inner right	patt 264	Cool special table L	17
33		,, ,,	,, ,, ,, R	17
34		patt 223	Night side wash DS	18
35		patt 264	Acting area I 135°	3
36		patt 223	Night side wash US	18

	Position	Type	Function	Colour
37		patt 223	Garden cool	17–38
38		patt 264	Acting area C 225°	67
39		,, ,,	,, ,, E 225°	67
40		,, ,,	,, ,, F 225°	67
41		,, ,,	,, ,, I 225°	67
42	Overstage 1	patt 264	Acting area D 45°	OW
43		,, ,,	,, ,, E 45°	OW
44		,, ,,	,, ,, F 45°	OW
45		,, ,,	,, ,, D 135°	3
46		,, ,,	,, ,, E 135°	3
47		,, ,,	,, ,, F 135°	3
48	Overstage 2	patt 264	Lamp right of table	3
49		,, ,,	Acting area H 45°	OW
50		,, ,,	Fire special	2–B11
51		patt 223	Downlight	42
52		,, ,,		32
53		patt 264	Lamp left of table	3
54		,, ,,	Window night special	18
55		,, ,,	,, day ,,	52
56	Overstage 3	patt 264	Acting area B 315°	52
57		,, ,,	,, ,, E 315°	52
58		,, ,,	,, ,, C 315°	52
59		,, ,,	,, ,, A 225°	67
60		2 patt 264	Garden downlight	17–38
61		patt 243	,, ,, night	41
62		patt 264	Acting area B 225°	67
63	Overstage 4	patt 243	Downlight upstage	56
64		,, ,,	,, garden	42
65		,, ,,	Moonlight to tree	40–50
66	Vomitorium L	2 patt 23	Fire uplight	5a–B11
67	Backstage		Stove—cooker	
68			Stove—interior light	2–B11
69		patt 123	Christine window	3–B55
70			Centre hanging oil lamp	

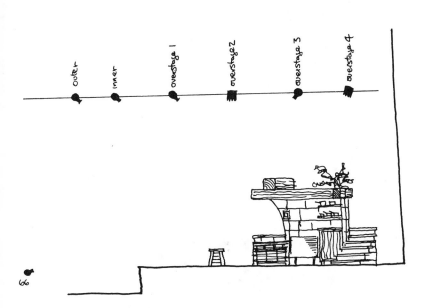

8 Design problems: lighting musicals, ballet and opera; the repertoire

The musical can encompass many different styles of production. The designer may be called upon for pure dance light, for the naturalism of straight drama or for all the effects of grand opera. However, there is generally a demand for brightness and sparkle, a need to make the actors stand out vividly from their background. Jean Rosenthal, the brilliant American designer, described the lighting of the musical as an attempt to make the actors appear 'jewel-like'. Certainly no other country can compete at the moment with America when it comes to producing musicals; and the lighting of the best American musicals would seem to have reached a pinnacle within the genre.

The supply voltage in the United States is 110 volts, which allows greater lamp efficiency, and the American lamp manufacturers themselves possess a far more pioneering spirit than their European counterparts. Thanks to their research, a considerable range of more flexible and powerful lanterns has become available in that country. This, together with a much larger budget for his lighting, has meant that the American designer has greater quantities of more powerful equipment at his disposal.

The shape of the Broadway theatres themselves only allows front of house lighting from a very low frontal position on the balcony rail and from booms in the boxes to the side of the stage. Without an 'acting area lighting position' in the front of the house, the tendency has developed toward using rail lighting straight into the stage as a frontal fill-light, while all the modelling is achieved by units behind or adjacent to the proscenium. The first and second pipes, immediately behind the proscenium or show portal, usually provide acting area lighting, both directly downwards to the fore stage as well as towards areas farther back. The lanterns are almost always 'double hung'. Thus, instead of having one lantern at either side of each area, there are two, making four lamps to each, one pair in one colour tone and one pair in another (probably warm and cool). This is supplemented by sidelighting (ellipsoidal spots or the more powerful beam projectors) which adds plasticity, gives extra colour effects and links the acting areas together. As well as this, down lighting and/or back lighting is added, probably with 8 inch 750 watt ellipsoidal spots, beam projectors or PAR battens. The PAR batten can be obtained in

37, 38 Setting for Prospects Productions' *Edward II* Dir, Toby Robertson Light, John B. Read
Above Assembly Hall, Edinburgh *Below* Mermaid Theatre, London

39 *Blitz* Adelphi
Theatre, London 1962

40 *The Travails of
Sancho Panza* National
Theatre Old Vic,
London 1969
Dir, Joan Plowright
Set, Tony Walton
Light, Richard Pilbrow
Rear projection

41 *Back to Methuselah* National Theatre Old Vic, London 1969
Dir, Clifford Williams Set, Ralph Koltai Light, Robert Ornbo

42 *Camelot* Theatre Royal, Drury Lane, London 1964
Dir, Robert Helpmann Des, John Truscott Lighting, Richard Pilbrow (photo by Barnet Saidman)

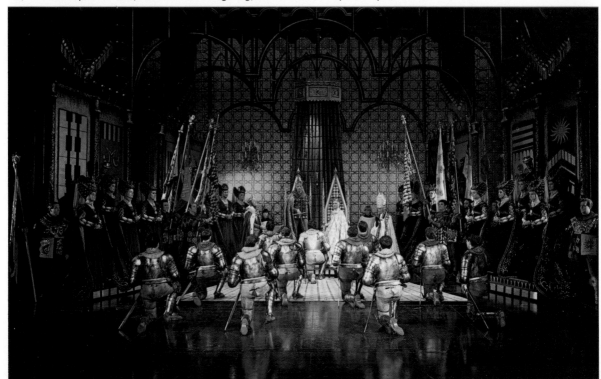

43, 44, 45 *Miss Julie* National Theatre at Chichester Festival Theatre 1965
Dir, Michael Elliott Set, Richard Negri Light, Richard Pilbrow

46 *Fiddler on the Roof* Lex Goudsmit at Her Majesty's Theatre, London 1969
Dir, Jerome Robbins Set, Boris Aronson Light, Richard Pilbrow.

47 *Peer Gynt* Old Vic Company 1962
Dir, Michael Elliott Set, Richard Negri Light, Richard Pilbrow.

48, 49, 50 *Zorba* Imperial Theatre, New York 1968.
Dir, Harold Prince Set, Boris Aronson
Light, Richard Pilbrow

49

50

51, 52 *Rosencrantz and Guildenstern are dead* Alvin Theatre, New York 1967 *Above* Attack on ship *Below* Death of player King

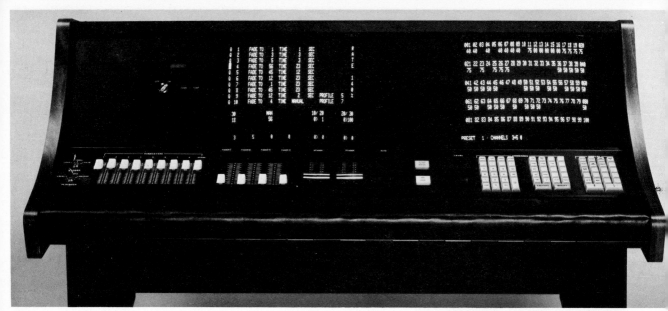

53

55

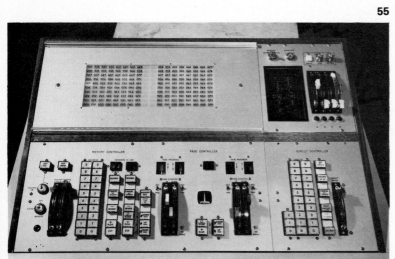

56

54

53 Strand Century Light Palette

54 Strand Electric System CD console

55 Rank Strand System DDM memory control

56 Thorn Theatre Q-File memory system

57 'Fish-eye' lens shot of the
Olivier Theatre, National Theatre,
London (1976),
from the back of the acting area
(photo by Chris Arthur, Trans
World Eye)

58 Lighting for *Gone With the
Wind* Theatre Royal, Drury Lane,
London 1973
Dir, Joe Layton Set, David Hays
and Tim Goodchild Light,
Richard Pilbrow (photo by
courtesy of TABS, published by
Rank Strand Electric)

59, 60, 61 *I and Albert* Piccadilly
Theatre, London 1974
Dir, John Schlesinger Set, Luciana
Arrighi Lighting and projection, Robert
Ornbo

60

61

62, 63 *Shelter* Golden Theatre, New York, 1973
Dir, Austin Pendleton Set, Tony Walton Lighting, Richard Pilbrow Projection, Pilbrow, Ornbo, Bryan

63

64 *Annie* Victoria Palace, London, 1978
Dir, Martin Charnin Set, David Mitchell Lighting, Richard Pilbrow (photo by John Timbers)

65 *A Chorus Line* Theatre Royal, Drury Lane, London 1977   Dir, Michael Bennett
Set, Robin Wagner Lighting, Tharon Musser (photo by Zoë Dominic)

66 *The Cunning Little Vixen* Wedding scene Glyndebourne 1977
Dir, Jonathan Miller   Set, Patrick Robertson Lighting, Robert Bryan

67 *Così fan tutte* Glyndebourne, 1978
Dir, Peter Hall   Set, John Bury   Lighting, Robert Bryan (photo by Guy Gravett)

68 *Nabucco* Covent Garden 1972
Prod, Václav Kǎslík   Set, Josef Svoboda   Lighting, William Bundy

69 *Nymphéas* First performed at Theatre
Royal, York
London Contemporary Dance Company
Chor, Robert Cohan Set, Norberto
Chiesa Lighting, John B. Read (photo by
Anthony Crickmay)

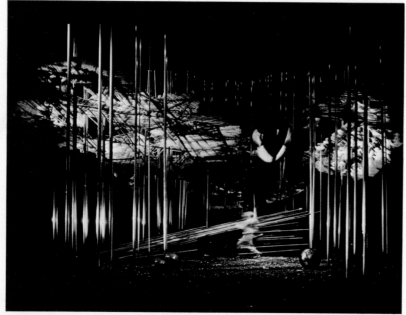

70 *The Ring* Coliseum, London 1971
Dir, Glen Byam-Shaw and John
Blatchley Des, Ralph Koltai Lighting,
Robert Ornbo

71 *Rock Nativity* British Tour, 1976
Dir, Gareth Morgan Set, Martin
Johns Lighting, Andrew Bridge

72 *Jesus Christ Superstar* Palace Theatre,
London, 1972
Dir, Jim Sharman Set, Brian
Thompson Lighting, Jules Fisher

73 Rank Strand Lightboard Mark II,
Deutches Oper, Berlin

74 *Evita* Prince Edward Theatre, London, 1978
Dir, Harold Prince Set, Timothy O'Brien and Tazeena Firth Lighting and projections,
David Hersey (photo by Zoë Dominic)

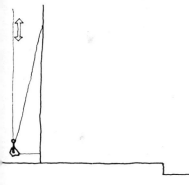

Fig. 31 Flown ground row

sizes up to a thousand watts, and the new tungsten-halogen lamps give even greater power. A large musical can use as many as twelve or fifteen spotbars, and six or eight tormenter booms on either side. This adds up to a very considerable amount of equipment, more than is customary in Europe, but in the skilled hands of such designers as Abe Feder, Jules Fisher, Martin Aronstein and Tharon Musser the results can be truly superb.

A great deal of use has been made in musicals of the translucent backcloth. It was used to particularly good effect in *Fiddler on the Roof*, directed by Jerome Robbins, set designed by Boris Aronson. A skycloth in front of which was hung a gauze with applied cut-outs represented the village of Anatevka. This was lit in London from the rear by PAR battens at the top and bottom. Since the bottom lamps had to be struck, to allow scenery to be set from the back of the stage, the battens were hung from a counterweight bar, with the lamps shining upwards instead of downwards, and the bar was lowered right to the stage floor. This ground row could then be struck in a matter of seconds by flying it away (fig 31).

A far more elaborate rear lighting problem was posed in *Zorba*, directed by Harold Prince, set designed by Boris

Fig. 32 *Zorba* lighting layout plan

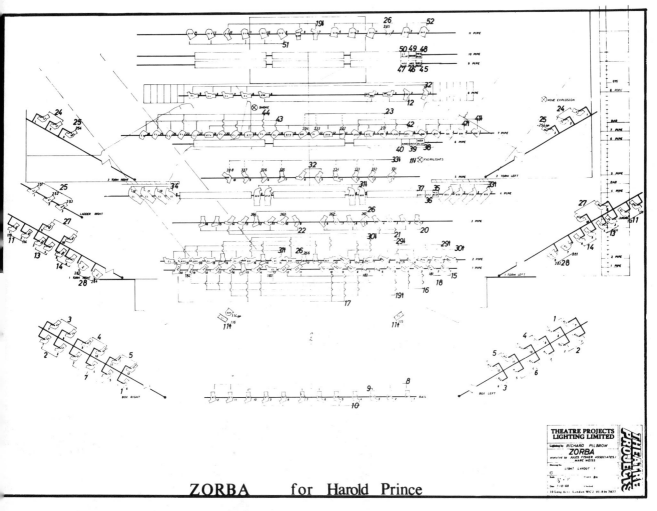

ZORBA   for Harold Prince

Aronson. Here an enormous amount of variety was required from the rear-lit cloth. It had to represent every sort of sky from a blazing Grecian day, to night and storm as well as some purely abstract projected shapes.

It has long been customary for musicals to use follow-spotlights on the principal artists. This quite arbitrary method of illumination seems to some people to convey a threatricality that contributes to the glamour of the occasion. The way in which follow-spots are handled (and the decision whether or not to use them at all) depends upon the subject and content of the show. A bright, sparkling, light-hearted entertainment can certainly benefit from an obvious and glamorous follow-spot, while in a dramatic musical the follow-spots, if used at all, should be extremely subtle. If subtlety is required, the follow-spots are best worked from a side, front of house, or proscenium position (from the old perch position rather than from the conventional rear of the auditorium). *The Man of La Mancha* and *Golden Boy* employed this technique very effectively. Indeed, the designer should remember that there are a great many effects other than the conventional hard bright circle of light to be achieved with follow-spots.

Lighting ballet and dance
In conversation with John B. Read

"One of the fascinations of lighting for dance is that here, more than in any other branch of theatre, the lighting designer's role has advanced furthest. The process of staging ballet and perhaps most particularly modern dance is almost a collaboration between partners, the choreographer and the lighting designer.

Lighting the dance gives the designer almost total freedom. His role is to manipulate light in space. That space, however, will be filled with a continually changing number of people. Dancers use their entire body as an instrument and lighting has to mould and sculpt the whole person. The dancers become a series of moving sculptures and revealing these visually to the audience in a dramatic or appropriate way is the lighting designer's task.

However, by referring to the dancer as a moving sculpture one could be in danger of ignoring the most important ingredient. That is, the individual personality of the dancer himself and the interaction between the individual personalities of all the dancers involved, the choreographer and lighting designer. The interplay between personality and the physical movement that results from it, should determine the sort of lighting and make it seem almost inevitable.

I turn up at the rehearsal studios at least twenty minutes before the run-through of the piece is due to begin. I need to sense the ambiance amongst the group, and to be accepted by them. There has to be a realization of all the almost subliminal

122

factors that show me how to light it. It is absolutely vital to sense and understand the inner interpretation that lies beneath the movement. I take down everything the choreographer says. Some, of course—Tetley, Cohan, or Ronnie Hynd—I have worked with a lot and one goes in with some sense of their intentions, but every view or thought expressed may go toward understanding. The choreographer will usually have a feeling of what he wants and the style he asks for is usually right, but occasionally I find a choreographer who asks for one thing which is belied by the work that he later produces. Sometimes it's difficult to talk about the lighting, indeed it's the last thing that he might want to discuss. Perhaps it's rather like a cat stalking a mouse and you talk about everything else except the subject under discussion. I try and find something constructive to say, then talk about something else until I can cheat my way into the subject. I cannot force them, there's sometimes insecurity to be overcome, I slowly work toward understanding.

I do not like intruding on rehearsals in the very beginning but I try and see the work when it's almost ready, to get an overall impression of the impact it will make on an audience. I plot all the movement diagramatically straight away, almost touch-typing it onto paper. Simultaneously I time with a stop-watch all the rhythms and changes and most importantly have all my senses attuned to getting the emotional feel that underlies the dance. I need all the explosions to happen in my head that first time—to get the inspiration going.

Some companies have a visual image or style which to some extent might be dictated by the circumstances in which they work. For example they might have a semi-permanent touring rig, and the need to do two or three pieces in one evening will provide some framework or limitation. But I try to start from scratch with every new piece, the style has come from the director and every item has to have the appropriate degree of individuality.

Everything is the movement. I think that the lighting should be totally unselfish, I hate tricks, all the light should be on the body and the thing I perhaps most dislike is overdesign. Trick changes out of context can destroy the concentration of the dancer.

In terms of physical layout of the equipment much will depend on the company. For example, for the London Contemporary Dance Company I use a top light in areas, a three colour choice of a high side position at the end of the overhead pipes, a side light at eye level, mid level above and a shin buster (just above floor level). In addition I use a heavy back light position but no spotbar, very little FOH and consequently no conventional acting area lighting. In addition to this I will have perhaps 20 specials. The whole thing adds up to about 200 units on eight pipes and is controlled by a touring 80 way memory board. Other companies are like this with fewer specials, perhaps with less back light. For classical ballet I use more softer acting area light, at the conventional 45 degrees and less top light and side light, largely because of the problems that are thrown up by girls in tutus. Too much top light can make them look dwarflike. Of course for the really big shows in the classical repertoire I might do a specific fairly elaborate rig.

A lot of dance involves touring and touring brings with it the need for great practicality. We need to use rugged equipment that can take the rough handling.

If I divide the stage up into conventional areas these can be nine (three rows deep of three across) or twenty (five rows deep of four across) (fig 33). In this latter case I often create one or two centre positions: one downstage 'star turn' position and one midstage. I will also divide the stage up into strips across—'in one/in two/in three/in back—and an end pipe side high light will go from centrestage to the far side in each one of these strips. Back light will cover perhaps two strips but in sections across the stage. I will probably use a minimum of four side lights: one lamp over three metres, one just below, one at eye-level and one shin buster. Another common movement that can mean special cross light, will be diagonal from downstage to upstage on the opposite side. The 'acting areas' I have mentioned for modern dance will usually only have a top light; this might be a single lamp or possibly two quite closely mounted together, but for classical 'tutu' type dance conventional spot bar coverage will be added.

The thing that I have to be careful of is the problem that classical dancers call 'experience with eye-level side lighting'. This can easily disorient them when doing spins, pirouettes and turns and they sometimes need an establishing light at a low level of brightness in some permanent position in the theatre. Also, sudden change has to be used with great care and must always be *before* any difficult sequence a dancer is about to go into. If a big lighting change, of level or direction or height, happens during a complicated movement, this can disorient the dancers completely. I always remember, in *Giselle*, the Queen of the Wilis' entrance. She looks far the best very dramatically crosslit. However her dance demands she must be able to see the floor or she's completely lost, and so a certain amount of top light at a very low level is essential. Quite often one has to make the stage look totally dark even when parts of it are lit for purely technical dance reasons.

Colour is an essential part of dance lighting. Used with care it can create the mood and atmosphere. It can help with the feeling of space around the dancer. For modern dance it can be used quite freely, but for classical work it must be used with extreme care. A heavy selection of colour, like strong top light, can distort the image of the dancer.

The biggest lantern I usually use is a five kilowatt, but I often wish for some special effect of far greater intensity. I have used

9 part acting area

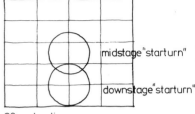

midstage "star turn"

downstage "star turn"

20 part acting area

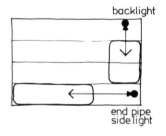

in back

in 3

in 2

in 1

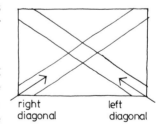

backlight

end pipe
side light

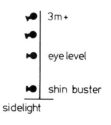

right
diagonal

left
diagonal

3m +

eye level

shin buster

sidelight

Fig. 33 Lighting ballet and dance

a whole cluster of PAR 64 lamps to build a pyramid of light upon the stage and I seek a greater *range* of brightness than is presently possible.

All too often ballet in the olden days was performed in enormous open areas with acres of canvas background and lit by rows of battens and border lights. It is infinitely more exciting to see all the light emphasis on modelling the dancer in space with the scenery taking its place discreetly in the background.

The lighting designer has the greatest scope in the field of modern dance. He can allow his imagination virtually total freedom when the dance, no longer restricted to story telling, concentrates upon the evocation of mood and emotion through sheer movement. The lighting itself can dance with the performer, weaving its pattern around him, revealing every moment and conveying every mood.

The new developments in lighting control offer the dancer a new partner able to react as fast as quicksilver or as fast as light itself."

Lighting opera
In conversation with William Bundy O.B.E.

In the previous section on lighting the dance, we saw that the battle for establishing the place of the lighting designer seems to have been almost won. In the world of lighting for opera it still rages.

One of the fascinations of operatic lighting is how little there is of it. Opera after opera seems to take place in Stygian darkness. Yet the scene has been changing; for since the mid-fifties the old European style has given way to the new American-influenced style of lighting where the lighting designer's role counts and is appreciated.

"In many ways the new style of lighting was pioneered in the UK. Under the old régime the director, the set designer and the chief electrician got together and in an all too often haphazard manner decided how they would light the scenery and when necessary the singers.

In the early fifties Tyrone Guthrie and Peter Brook both worked at the Royal Opera House Covent Garden and tried to bring the light they were used to in dramatic productions into the world of opera. Frankly, however, they were beaten by the system. The system is one largely influenced by the German Opera example. The equipment consists of very little front of house, a very heavily equipped proscenium bridge manned by electricians who would move large wattage lamps from position to position between scenes, and the rest of the stage primarily lit by rows and rows of battens. This was still prevalent until quite recently in many of the world's great opera houses and indeed it is only now in some beginning to change.

The lighting in opera is motivated by the music. On the

whole the stories are rather idiotic but the music is not. The overall trend has been away from a purely vocal and musical performance toward presenting a totally theatrical experience. With the productions of Visconti and Zeffirelli in London a demand was placed upon the singers that they should also act. Movement and performance became part of a total picture. Light was used to create atmosphere so that the whole stage was one, and directors with this power of imagination and stagecraft, put their 'stamp' on the production. Gradually the more outstanding conductors also began to realize that opera was more than just the music, and men such as Solti and Guilino began to take a keen interest in the overall staging, and lighting in particular.

Opera calls upon a total emotional commitment, the power of the music draws in the spectator and makes operatic theatre the ultimate creative visual, aural all-involving experience.

Wieland Wagner in Bayreuth demonstrated sensational possibilities for imaginative operatic lighting, because he threw away all the clutter that had come traditionally to surround Wagnerian production and made a statement that fitted perfectly with the music with simplicity and the power of light.

A director such as Zeffirelli took another route, often employing enormous realistic sets that with the lighting created an all-embracing atmospheric surround to the musical sound. With monumental realistic atmospheric staging (such as in *Tosca*—my favourite) an overwhelming impression could be made. The great designer Svoboda took yet another direction, providing not a complete environment but a powerful fragment of that environment with highly dramatic lighting.

Opera often includes large groups of people on the stage. They have to be able to sing and they have to be able to see the pit where the conductor holds the whole performance together. The audience don't need to see every face amongst the chorus, so darkness and light can be used with greater freedom than is often possible in a dramatic theatre. A picture can be created with shadow and darkness to convey atmosphere. Of course, with the new style opera, with singers being expected to act better and look better and not just be a voice, they can be lit properly and appropriately, so opera is really moving toward the dramatic style of lighting — three-dimensional lighting selectively revealing and concealing and shaping and creating atmosphere around the stage in sympathy with music.

Opera seems to have inherited immense problems. Everything is large. Sets are huge and cumbersome and time is limited. Opera singers cannot sing on consecutive nights and usually want a two day break between performances. They cannot rehearse and play the same opera in a single day, therefore there is an immense repertoire changeover problem. Even so, and despite the difficulties, operatic lighting is moving toward the three-dimensional. No longer is the front bridge sufficient, and although it took me seven years to get a back light established at the Royal Opera House Covent Garden in the famous production of *Cav and Pag*, this is the direction in which things are going. Covent Garden in 1965 went toward a dramatic multi-lantern complex of equipment. This has been widely appreciated by all the visiting foreign directors and scenographers and increasingly has an influence on the Continent of Europe.

Of course, since operatic lighting leans so heavily upon the music, subtlety of timing and complexity of timing are of great importance. The lighting designer works as one of a team with the director and designer. He must be fluid and flexible to create as the work develops. Only out of the closest collaboration can lighting make its contribution toward a totally coherent visual product that supports and uplifts and surrounds the musical and emotional experience.

So the days of the flapping backcloth revealed by rows of border lights are ever more surely numbered. Opera is traditionally the most hidebound of the theatrical arts, but the realization grows that to reveal the music fully, staging and lighting must be brought up to date. It is by lighting the singers and not leaving them in the dark, and by using the new dynamic that lighting has to offer, that opera production can enter the twentieth century.''

Problems in repertoire

One of the problems of both opera and classical ballet in England is that they are usually performed in repertoire (that is to say that a different production will be performed every night). This same problem is now being encountered in the English dramatic theatre which has recently begun to organize itself on the repertoire system. The major companies of the National Theatre and the Royal Shakespeare are being followed by the leading provincial theatres in this, for repertoire does provide a very varied theatrical diet for its audiences.

A large part of this book has been about the lighting process, the way in which the lighting is created. It may have seemed rather complex and, indeed, on a professional scale lighting can be extremely complicated. In the West End of London or on Broadway, hundreds of spotlights and man hours are involved in creating the sort of lighting that I have attempted to describe. It is not difficult to appreciate, therefore, that considerable problems arise when such complex lighting setups have to be changed between one performance and another.

Germanic practice has solved the problem to a certain extent by placing as much equipment as possible in positions that are accessible. The stages are large, the lanterns are suspended on lighting bridges, and sufficient manpower is available to focus the lanterns during the performance. This solution cannot apply in English and American dramatic theatre for three reasons. The first is that the stages are usually much smaller and the necessary flying depth for a lighting bridge is simply not available. Second, manpower today is becoming increasingly expensive and the normal theatre budget cannot cope with the large number of electricians needed.

Third, the use of light put forward in this book is based upon American and English theory and practice. This is a concept of light used in three dimensions and one that, for all its growing popularity in the English-speaking world, is still comparatively uncommon on the Continent of Europe. There the four functions of lighting are given far less consideration, and lighting is more often only for illumination and effect. The scenery may be beautifully and atmospherically lit, and the effects spectacular, but the actors themselves will be lit almost crudely (often with follow-spots). There is little attempt to bring these four component parts together and to link the actor with his setting by a three-dimensional use of light. This means that the use of multiple banks of spotlights, for backlight, sidelight and downlight, is reduced, and the problem of handling and re-handling quantities of lanterns is also automatically reduced. The growth of the repertoire system in England could be to the detriment of the relatively high lighting standards which have developed in that country over the years. The obvious solution to the repertoire situation— much simpler lighting with fewer units—can only be considered a backward step.

I believe the only way to achieve an ambitious and complex lighting plot, of the standard seen in London's West End or on Broadway, in this situation is by following the principles which I have tried to outline in this book. First, the lighting has to have method; second, it has to be carefully planned. The designer has to provide a repertoire theatre with a basic permanent layout of equipment. This layout has to provide all the acting area lighting and all the standard lighting that might be required. These should probably account for about half of the installation and should be focused and locked tight, never to be moved again for that season at least. Then, of course, there should be a liberal supply of 'specials'. From each angle a range of equipment should be available that can be shared between productions: some set permanently and some to be re-set between performances. In the old days the battens and footlights provided this basic illumination, which has now gone in these days of total spotlighting. The repertoire theatre, using good planning and the Method must provide a basic spotlight illumination which each designer can use.

For the National Theatre at the Old Vic in London, I designed a layout of equipment which can best be described as a

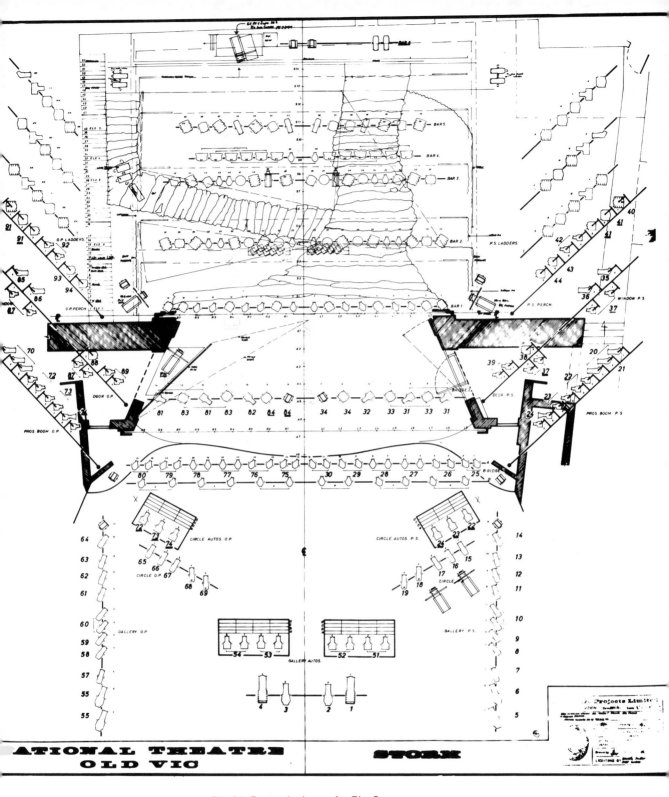

Fig. 34 Repertoire layout for *The Storm*

'saturation' rig (fig 34). It employs about sixty lamps front of house, lighting the forestage and downstage areas; fifty around the proscenium zone (which includes a large forestage); about eighty on five spot bars overhead and twenty-five each side of the stage on perch booms and ladders (these can roll up and down stage suspended from under the fly-floors). A considerable proportion of this equipment is permanently focused. Most of the front of house is fixed and this gives acting area light to the forestage and front of the main stage. Overhead, the proscenium zone is accessible and therefore able to be refocused, but the bars above the stage are, whenever possible, rationed between productions. Downlight and backlight units are left permanently and the remaining lanterns shared out between shows. If one production needs a special backlight from the fifth bar, we attempt to ensure that no other production needs to use this particular unit. Inevitably, this does not always work, and the rules have to be bent slightly, but a change can be made from one production to another in well under an hour. Some shows require special effects and special equipment and this can always be added but, as in a modern television studio, the bulk of the equipment is permanently available.

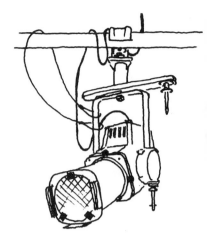

Fig. 35 Pole operated Patt 263

It is not a great problem to arrange for the changing of colours in permanently focused equipment. A bar can be dropped into the stage or raised to the grid for access when colour changing, and permanently-set front of house units can be recoloured far more quickly than it would be possible to refocus them.

The actual process of focusing the lantern (which is at present done by a man with a spanner) is rather archaic, particularly in comparison with the degree of sophistication that has been achieved at the control end. The television practice of pole-operated focusing (fig 35) has begun to move into the theatre (led by Charles Bristow at Sadler's Wells) but the maximum practical reach of a pole—about twenty feet—limits its theatrical application.

The New National Theatre, London

In 1976 the New National Theatre of Great Britain opened. The National includes three auditoria: the Olivier, the Lyttelton and the Cottesloe. The Olivier Theatre has an open stage set in the corner of a room, with the stage partially surrounded by the audience seated in a semi-circle, and with space at the rear capable of being opened out to form a 'space' stage (fig 36). The Lyttelton is a comparatively conventional proscenium theatre, only with a Germanic style semi-cruciform stage for production changes in repertoire, and an exceptionally flexible proscenium opening (fig 37). Both these theatres are elaborately equipped, in order to both allow first-class lighting to be achieved within the repertoire pattern of perhaps a twice-

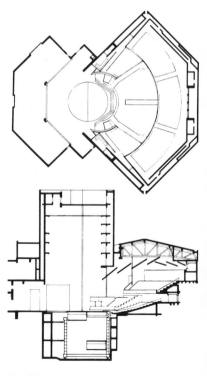

Fig. 36 Olivier Theatre

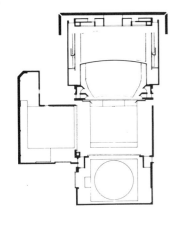

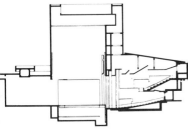

Fig. 37 Lyttelton Theatre

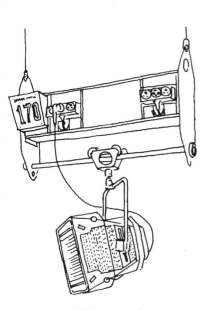

Fig. 38 Short TV-type spotbar

daily change of production and to provide superlative facilities for the lighting designer. The third theatre, the Cottesloe, is the studio theatre, a fascinating galleried flexible space that in deliberate contrast to the two main theatres is equipped comparatively simply.

Particularly in the two larger theatres, the latest advances in stage lighting are employed. What does this mean in terms of the design of the building and its equipment?

Firstly, a comprehensive range of lighting angles to the stage was made a topmost priority. Both the main auditoria have ceilings that contain five lighting bridges. Two or three vertical lighting positions are built into the side walls. In the Olivier Theatre, owing to the configuration of the ceiling (that curtails the length of the bridges), the stage, and some of the auditorium, lighting is mounted on four 'chandeliers' that are hung vertically through the ceiling. All these positions are accessible from above, and a series of walkways connect through the roof void from the front projection room (rear of the circle) right onto the fly floor and the stage.

The stages are surrounded by galleries for lighting or the handling of scenery. All rails throughout stage and auditorium are of 50 mm. ($2\frac{29}{32}$ in.) diameter pipe to allow a luminaire to be fixed in any position.

Over the stage in the Lyttelton theatre, the lighting is hung from conventional counterweight pipes (power assisted). All feed cables are dropped from the grid by windlasses that automatically take in or let out cable as the lights are raised and lowered. Over the Olivier stage, because the stage equipment is particularly designed for the use of three-dimensional scenery (scenery suspension is by 140 electronically synchronized point hoists), lighting is suspended BBC TV style (fig 38) on short, 2 to 3 m-long hoists. This allows lighting to be hung at varying heights across the stage and also allows sections of the lighting rig to be flown out to the grid in order to clear a piece of scenery positioned up and downstage at any angle.

The electrical installation follows the principle of the 'saturation' rig. At every potential lighting position a number of socket outlets appear to allow a sufficient number of lanterns for every demand made by the current repertoire. Thus the minimum number of lanterns are refocused. Some are merely recoloured and some either dedicated to a permanent focus or specifically set for one production.

A point of interest is that many of the profile spots (manufactured by CCT) have a shutter assembly that is easily removable from the lantern like a cartridge. When set, the shutter position may be locked, and thus for a small beam-shape adjustment the unit itself can be left undisturbed, and only its shutter assembly changed, which is as easy as changing a colour filter.

Every socket has its own dimmer. Thus there are 600 in the

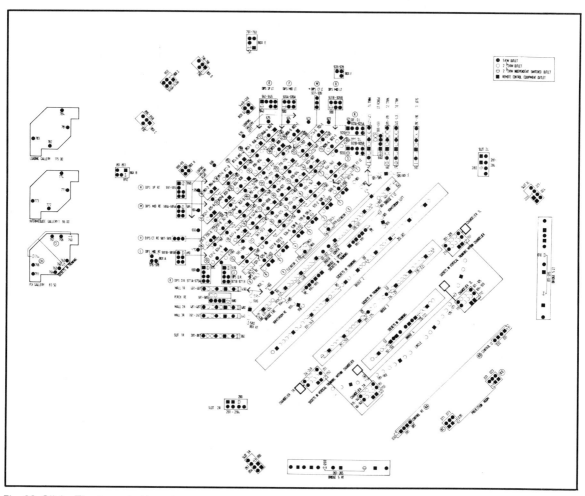

Fig. 39 Olivier Theatre socket layout

Olivier (see fig. 39) and 470 in the Lyttelton. No cumbersome—and time-consuming—patch panel is involved, for all dimmers are connected to the new computer lighting control system in each theatre, named Lightboard (see page 155). Lightboard was designed by the author and Theatre Projects Consultants and engineered by Rank Strand Electric. Two are installed at the National; since then others at the Burgtheater Vienna, the Royal Opera House Covent Garden, the Deutsches Opera Berlin and the Hamburg Opera attest to the advanced facilities Lightboard offers.

Lightboard can control up to 1000 circuits, but it is far more than a computerized patch panel—that is, a functional aid to repertoire working. More importantly it takes the principle of the memorized lighting control and makes a leap forward into the future. Many systems allow the memorization of lighting pictures and the ability to add, subtract or cross fade from one to another. Most, however, allow this process to happen at a comparatively limited number of speeds. But light is, by its nature, the most fluid ephemeral of substances—it shifts and changes subtly or blatantly, slowly or quickly, sometimes in an instant. Lightboard acknowledges this, and provides an instrument that can be played by the operator, allowing different groups of light to be under his finger-tip control simultaneously, and also allows many different sections of light to travel to any new intensity simultaneously, but at many different speeds.

For the first time, light can be manipulated with all the fluidity of natural light itself. Multi-time movements can be started together or separately, and travel at their own speeds, yet all the parts are always under the immediate individual control of the operator. Operation of one or a multiplicity of lights is through a calculator-type keyboard which a proficient operator can operate by touch while watching the stage.

No longer is it necessary to think in terms of single dimmers. Lighting can be conceived in blocks or 'pictures' of light that can be mixed, interwoven and balanced. Out of each block, the operator can still summon a single unit but he has equal ease of access to one light or to any group. Equally important, he has the ability to 'collect' all or any part of the lighting instantly under his control. At all times the state of lighting upon the stage (or in any recorded 'memory') can be displayed on video monitors which show all circuits and their levels together with their source of control.

There are many other auxiliary facilities designed both to speed the lighting process and extend the possibilities open to the designer. One section of Lightboard is portable and may be operated from the centre of the stalls or elsewhere. Another allows any circuits to be connected to a sound-to-light device for automatic flashing or fading, light movement synchronized to sound, or random light modulation.

Finally, Lightboard also allows orientation control—the remote control of luminaires (pan tilt and focus), colour change (up to eight colours) and projector control (random access slide change, and focus). This system is multiplexed around the theatre, so an appropriate unit can be connected anywhere and respond to the operator's instructions. These orientation commands can be memorized on any cue with or without an intensity change occuring before or after the physical movement.

Sadly, the mechanized lanterns themselves are still very expensive, so their number is limited—at least at the moment. But in time this technique will clearly be extended in repertory houses.

The speed of development in lighting control design around the world is amazing. Lightboard represents a unique advance and perhaps indicates the direction along which future design will travel.

9 Design problems: the open stage

Widening the viewpoint

There is every indication that the open stage, in its various shapes, is establishing itself as the predominant theatrical form of the future. There is growing recognition that the proscenium arch 'picture frame' theatre is simply a 'phase' in theatrical history and that it may be supplanted. A great deal of the impetus in this change has come from the influence of the new lighting. With lighting it has been possible to localize and contain space, not only behind a proscenium arch but within the very centre of the auditorium.

Another reason for the first wave of enthusiasm over these forms was the apparent economy they offered. No longer did a stage have to be filled with scenery, and the production costs were consequently greatly reduced. Theories were put forward that open stage theatres were by definition 'non scenic' theatres; that the very shape of the theatres and stages produced a new aesthetic that turned away from the depiction of a physical world surrounding the action. Sir Tyrone Guthrie, at his theatre in Stratford, Ontario, led the cry for stark revealing white light on the open stage.

The first flush of enthusiasm now seems to have passed and even the theorists have begun to recognize that perhaps in their enthusiasm they have thrown the baby out with the bathwater. Why, simply because the audience were seated in a different relationship with the stage, did the entire style of the theatrical occasion necessarily have to be changed? Why were the sensations the spectator received through his eyes of little importance? Why should he have nothing to look at and have to rely on the spoken word alone? If human behaviour is influenced by environment, why had it become no part of theatre to suggest an impression of environment around the actor, for him to empathize with or react against?

The true need of the theatre is for a new relationship between actor and audience, a new dynamic bringing a fresh excitement to the theatrical occasion.

Modern theatre design is producing a new type of theatre which welds the audience into a new three-dimensional relationship with the stage. This can still create a physical environment for actors and audience alike, and can be perfectly attuned to the content of the play and the intention of the director. In England the new Olivier Theatre in the National Theatre, the Barbican Theatre for the Royal Shakespeare Company and several others are moving in this direction.

The reader may be surprised that, in view of the obvious importance of these new types of theatre, I have left the

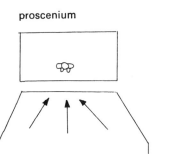

proscenium

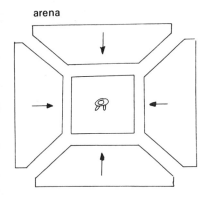

arena

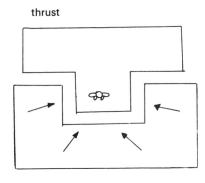

thrust

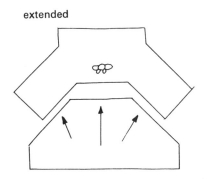

extended

Fig. 40 Types of stages

question of their lighting until so late in this book. I believe I need make no excuse for this because the fundamental truths of both the art and craft of lighting are basic to all forms of stage. The design of lighting is circumscribed by the behaviour of light, both natural and artificial in the real world, and by the limitations of available equipment. The application of light to the stage is, I feel, ultimately ruled by the demands of the playwright himself. The fact that the stage is a different shape or placed in a different relationship with the audience is not of the first importance and the differences of technique are comparatively minor and not differences of principle.

With open staging generally there is only one essential difference—the viewpoint of the audience. This viewpoint is considerably widened; for with the proscenium arch removed the audience surround the stage to a varying degree. Returning to the first principles of illumination, we remember that if the audience are to see the features of the actor's face, he must be illuminated from his front. If the audience are going to be seated right around the stage, the front is obviously 360° around the actor. Wherever he looks there will be audience. Thus the 'acting area lighting' (the basic actor illumination) will have to be extended right around the actor.

Whereas in the proscenium form we have been striving to think of our lighting three-dimensionally, we now have an absolute commitment to think in depth. In the proscenium theatre, when a scene is really successfully lit in three dimensions, the lighting will appear almost as satisfactory from the back of the stage as from the front. When we come to the open stage we simply have to ensure that every seat is getting a view of the stage perfectly lit and with perfect actor-visibility lighting. This reason alone explains the greater number of circuits in the Olivier Theatre in comparison with the Lyttelton.

The arena stage

First let us take the example of the complete arena stage: theatre in the round. Here the audience is seated right round the stage and the actors' entrances are probably through the audience, down the gangways. Arena stage theatres are usually fairly small, with an acting area of about sixteen to thirty feet wide. How can the basic lighting 'Method' be adapted to the wrap-round audience condition?

When lighting the acting area, the basic position for FOH spotlights in a proscenium theatre was seen to be approximately 45° vertically and 45° to either side of the front of the actor. This is obviously insufficient for an arena stage; and the simplest and most successful expedient is to duplicate these units at the other two points of the compass. Thus the stage will be divided into the usual areas and into each erea we will direct a spotlight from 45°, 135°, 225° and 315°. These are all shown in plan view in fig 41. The height of these units will be calculated in the same way as for the proscenium. Those lights coming in from the outer side of the stage, i.e. from over the audience, may need to be lowered to about 35° in order to light into the actors' eyes. Alternatively, we may decide to use a lower bank of fill-lights, but we will have to be careful not to go too low or we will create glare into the eyes of the audience sitting on the opposite side of the stage.

The lights over the stage, which are in effect pointing outward to the stage edge, have to be treated even more carefully. We have to light the actor from his on-stage side when he is standing on the edge of the stage, but we must avoid dazzling the people sitting in the front row. To do this we may have to lift this inner angle to as much as 55° (fig 42).

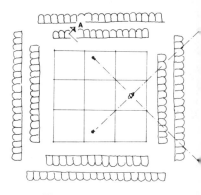

Fig. 41 Arena acting area

These four units into each area provide the basic acting area lighting but, of course, it will be noticed that they are actually doing more than their equivalent in the proscenium theatre. For example, if we sit to the front of an actor, right between the spots at, say, 45° and 135°, the two on the farther side of the stage will be back lighting him; similarly, if we sit beneath the 45° lantern, those at 135° and 225° will be directly sidelighting him, and the fourth lamp will be a direct backlight. This may seem a daunting complication, but in fact it merely adds to the excitement of lighting on the open stage. No two people have exactly the same view, either of the actors or of the lighting. To create a series of different pictures from each side of the stage, and yet to hold each as a valid expression of that moment in the play, is a fascinating exercise.

On top of this acting area lighting we may, of course, add all the other lanterns that we need. The rules of dominant and secondary light apply with equal force: motivating lights, blending and toning, special visibility, effects, etc., all have their function as before. All we have to remember is the varying effect that each will have from each different view point. What may be a dazzling shaft of back light for one section of the audience may simply be a rather flat frontal illumination for those on the other side of the stage; everything has to be tempered and judged from all parts of the auditorium.

It has been suggested that open stage lighting should revert to bold simple beams and patterns of light, or that we should return to the beautiful simplicity of a single shaft. If the play demands this very special stark treatment, it should have it, but with an audience surrounding the stage nothing could be more difficult than this approach. A single dramatic shaft of light will almost certainly only look dramatic to that section of the audience which sees the actor in profile; to the others he will either appear very flatly lit or in almost total darkness. Except for rare and brief moments of stillness on the stage, each actor has to be lit from more than one direction to ensure basic visibility. Here, of course, a basic complication arises, for it is extremely difficult to *confine* a small area on the open stage. If we are lighting from a reasonable angle of about 40°, the light

Fig. 42 Arena sections

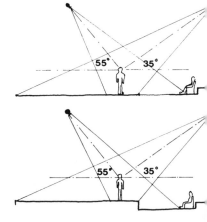

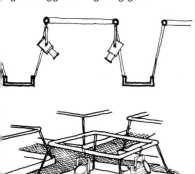

Fig. 43 Egg crate lighting grid

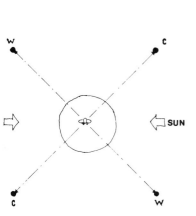

44 Open stage colour layout basis

45 Thrust stage.

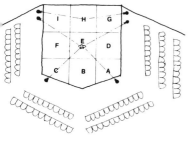

to a standing actor will throw a shadow beyond him for six or seven feet. If this has to be repeated in two directions at least, a single actor quite tightly lit can find himself surrounded by a pool of light fourteen or fifteen feet in diameter. The inability to confine light tightly is a loss, but the enterprising designer will find many other compensations in his work on the arena stage.

The theatres in which open stage work takes place are so varied that one cannot give general rules for the placing of lanterns. It will, however, be clear that most of the lighting equipment has to be placed overhead, and some form of grid over the entire area is usually the best solution. Obviously a large part of the lighting is going to come from over the audience. Although it is usually impossible to mask the lighting equipment completely, some form if catwalk ceiling to provide access, like an inverted egg crate (fig 43), can be very useful.

Colour on the arena stage has to be used with particular subtlety. Since there are usually fewer lanterns coming in from each direction they are not as mixed by the time they reach the acting areas as they are on the proscenium stage. Therefore, and particularly with the acting area units, the colours chosen should be very subtle. With four acting area spotlights I have found that a very flexible solution is to use the pairs opposite each other in contrasting tones, one warm and the other in either open white or a cool tone. In this way we can get an overall warm stage by bringing up all the acting area spots with the warm opposite colours in, using the others at a lower level as a fill-light, and vice-versa. Greater variety can be achieved by adding a further set of lanterns at, say, 90° or 180° in plan. If those at 90° are chosen to act as the dominant light, say, sunshine, they might be open white or coloured with very pale yellow. Used full with the warm acting area, the stage will be hot. Used with the cool, it will be very fresh. Conversely, the lanterns on the other side might use cool tones suggestive of moonlight. When used with the different combinations of acting area lighting, varying results will be achieved. Add to this downlight in various colour tones and considerable variety can be achieved (fig 44).

In addition to any other special lights required on the stage itself we may have to light into the aisles of the auditorium. The director will know at what point he wants his actors to be seen on their entrances and exits.

The thrust stage

With the thrust stage the audience is placed around three sides of the acting area (fig 45). On the fourth is a scenic back wall that can be either a permanent background or can be designed as a scenic element. In principle, the same lighting variations apply as for the arena stage, the exception being that it is possible (although in my experience not desirable) to reduce

137

the number of acting area spotlights to three per area, which can be placed at 120° in plan from each other instead of at 90° as previously discussed. This is a possible economy when required, but I find it limits the degree of colour flexibility obtainable with the four lantern method. The scenic back wall may need some special lighting treatment and indeed the set design may include considerable built structures which can extend over the floor of the thrust stage and even over part of the acting area. The upstage acting area angles in plan will have to be brought out more to the sides to keep approximately the correct vertical angle.

It is common for the actors to approach the stage from the front, through tunnels or vomitoria. It can be effective to position lights in these entrances, and the new thrust stage of the Crucible Theatre at Sheffield in England allows for the possibility of a trench right around the stage in which lighting units can be used. A production of *Hamlet* by the 69 Theatre Company for the Edinburgh Festival, with lighting by John B. Read, used lighting from below most effectively for Hamlet's soliloquies. Here the beams, having passed the actor, were lost in the dark ceiling above (fig 46).

Fig. 46 Thrust stage 'footlighting'

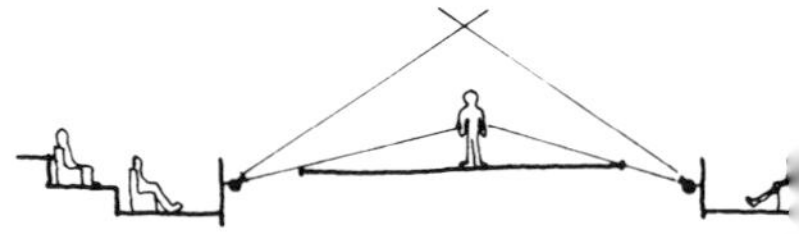

Gobos and projections can be well employed on the open stage. In the National Theatre production of *Armstrong's Last Goodnight* (directed by William Gaskill, set designed by Rene Allio at the Chichester Festival Theatre) exciting forest scenes were created with the light of gobos from profile spotlights, giving a dappled impression of the sheltered Scottish Lowland woods.

Profile spots are the principal lighting unit for the open stage, where the usual requirement is the need to contain the light to the stage as much as possible. Fresnels are best reserved for the subsidiary role of downlighting and colour-toning and even then they should be fitted with blacked risers and barn doors.

Other forms

There are many other variants of the open stage, two examples are the transverse stage which has an acting area with an audience on two opposite sides, and the quite common end-stage, of which the Mermaid Theatre in London is an example, with the audience on only one side but with no proscenium arch separating them from the acting area. These are all striving to combine all the excitement, intimacy and contact of the open stage with all the development of 2000 years of stagecraft and the potential of modern lighting.

10 Tomorrow

This book has, so far, been a statement of beliefs and practice. Many of these beliefs originated in the theories and writings of others and have filtered through my own thought and working method. I have been lucky enough to work under many varied circumstances; from being an amateur at school (with four float spots as front of house lighting) to the West End of London and Broadway, where some four or five hundred lighting units are not unknown. Before writing the first, 1970 edition of this book I studied all previous volumes on stage lighting that I could find. In that edition I wrote as follows:

> It is fascinating to see how much (or how little) has been achieved since those [books] published in the 'twenties and 'thirties. Technically, a great deal has happened, and yet when one realizes how far the creative achievement has fallen short of the dreams of Craig and Appia, one sees how much more there is yet to be done, and how this book can only be considered an interim report.
>
> Let me, briefly, have the impertinence to attempt to look into the future. As far as lighting control is concerned we are already seeing the beginning of amazing developments. The predominant difficulty in any ambitious lighting scheme has always been its switchboard operation. The instantaneous memory dimmer systems, now becoming available, certainly promise a great lessening of this problem. In 1960 I looked forward to a control system that could take, say, 300 channels, and move them to 300 different levels at 300 different speeds and so on *ad infinitum.* At the time it seemed absurd, and yet within ten years a large part of it is already possible. The leading instantaneous memory system manufacturers are already developing greater flexibility in both speed and operational control, while the recording of levels has already been achieved.

The reader will, I trust, forgive me for quoting at length what I wrote prior to 1970. Since then over eight years have passed. In some areas, notably in lighting control, much has happened. In others a more depressing picture emerges. Technically, lantern development has been perhaps least progressive. In England a new company, CCT, have made advances in the profile spot range (particularly with the introduction of zoom lens units), and in the United States Berkey have produced a new and efficient range of profiles or 'ellipsoidals'; but nowhere is revolution to be seen. The market leaders, Rank Strand (UK) and Strand Century (USA), having led the field in recent years in control, are currently striving to update and innovate upon their lantern range, and only now are new developments beginning to emerge. A less widely known company, Electro Controls of Salt Lake City, Utah, unveiled in 1977 a new type of zoom lens profile instrument, the 'Parellipsphere', that in spite of some shortcomings early on contained some interesting features that might be capable of further development. The use of the tungsten halogen lamp has certainly tended to provide a general increase of efficiency, but few radically new concepts. Efficiency of course, coupled with longer lamp life, has become increasingly important since the energy crisis and consequent inflation. The cost of lamp replacement and of electricity has become a major factor in the economics of stage lighting in a way that no one could have predicted in 1970.

The PAR lamp—particularly the wide range available in the United States—has increasingly become more commonly used. Highly efficient, long-lifed, easy-to-handle units employing PAR lamps proliferate. PAR 64s, the largest size, are often employed in circumstances where high key colour is needed (musicals, or pop and rock shows); while the small PAR 36 and 46s, having a tiny compact source of light with a wide variety of choice of beam shape, are revolutionizing display and architectural lighting, and becoming highly useful in the theatre. Low-voltage PAR lamps almost rival the German-inspired 24 volt Beamlites as the best parallel-beam shaft of light, yet even these are still far from the 'shaft of sunlight' that one longs for. However, the variety and sophistication of the sealed beam lamp perhaps indicates that future stage lighting units might increasingly rely, for their performance, upon the lamp they contain.

My feelings in 1970 about the need for a flexible multi-purpose unit continue. The American profile spot to provide a variable-shape, soft- or hard-edge beam (without radical change of size), and the German Beamlite, remain, with the PAR units discussed above, my favourite lanterns.

The subject of remote control focussing was touched upon in my earlier comments about the National Theatre. The limiting factor is still cost. Many major theatres in Germany and Eastern Europe employ a limited number of remote pan, tilt and focus lanterns. The Austrian company PANI have developed both units and memory control. Japan possesses several theatres heavily equipped with remote control lanterns—yet surprisingly the rest of Japanese stage lighting development remains comparatively primitive. Time must produce a break-through in this sphere. Present control systems employ considerable sophistication to record and repeat the intensity of stage lighting instruments. Surely in the near future systems will become available, at reasonable cost, that will control not only intensity but also the position, direction, shape and colour of every unit.

Already the necessary controls (such as Lightboard) are on the market. Manufacturers now have to produce a lantern that is accurate and capable of exact repositioning, as well as being sturdy enough to withstand the considerable heat and a life of hard knocks hanging over a busy stage—all at a cost possible for the theatre.

Without any doubt, the spectacular advances in the technology of stage lighting have been in the field of control. In 1970 I discussed the Thorn Q-File and Rank Strand IDM/DDM; but these days memory systems seem to arrive on the marketplace almost weekly.

The use of the computer, the mini computer and now the micro-processor have revolutionized stage lighting control just as they are revolutionizing many other aspects of life. The memorization of 'states', or lighting 'pictures', is almost commonplace. Micro-processor technology is already making such devices available to quite modest installations. Like pocket calculators, the many competing systems continue to decrease in cost. The potential purchaser, particularly in the United States, is faced with a bewildering choice of options. How can a decision be made?

Perhaps the first fact that has to be faced, is that micro-processors are spreading like wildfire, and that almost any qualified engineer can, should he so wish, put together a memory lighting system. For better or worse, another fact, however, prevails, and that is that the live theatre needs both value for money and reliability. Therefore the buyer should carefully consider the future of his control: chiefly whether, despite its apparent cheapness, it is supplied by a manufacturer with an ongoing commitment to the stage lighting industry. All too many installations can be purchased from companies who are only temporarily in the stage lighting business.

But given that miniaturized memory technology is advancing so rapidly, what does this mean to the art of stage lighting—or rather what can it mean?

Obviously the first benefit is that operating lighting becomes easier. No longer is the lighting designer's imagination limited by what is possible on the switchboard. Cues can follow each other with a rapidity that was previously impossible. But in addition there are other, more important benefits, which truly begin to alter the whole process of lighting. Firstly, lighting 'pictures' can be created, not with one circuit at a time, painstakingly summoned up, but with blocks or prerecorded groups of lighting. With a non-memory control, each individual circuit has to be selected and set to a level. To increase or decrease the intensity of part or all of the stage picture, every circuit involved has to be altered. With a memory system, blocks of lighting can be prerecorded and then called up while plotting as a 'block'. Thus the designer might call up: 'all cool acting area to level 8—warm downstage centre to 5—cool side light left to full, right to 5—gold backlight centre only to full—cyclorama blue less ends (circuits 119 and 129)—all units from stage left down 10%—everything up overall 10%—

and so on. These instructions (seven in all) might move several dozen or indeed hundreds of circuits, and be sufficient to light the stage successfully. As the plotting proceeds, cues already recorded may be re-used entirely or modified. For instance, 'cue 44' may consist of 'Q3 plus Q10 minus circuits 15, 27, 38—plus circuit 15 to 5 and Q18 to level 7'.

Advanced memory systems such as Lightboard facilitate this procedure in two ways. Firstly, the setting panel they employ bring into play any individual circuit or any group of circuits with 'touch-type' keyboard alacrity, giving equally easy access to any number of units. Secondly, the board offers a series of submasters that can be loaded with a lighting 'picture' instantaneously at the touch of a button. These can then be delicately balanced against each other, under the fingertips of the operator, to achieve exactly the desired relationship on stage between each part of the lighting.

Where the advanced memory system really begins to open up new possibilities for the lighting designer, is in the far more sophisticated way in which it can control the movement of light. The memory systems available in 1970 allowed at the most two speeds of movement upward and two downward. Lightboard allows on each of two separate playbacks six upspeeds and six downspeeds. Thus, a cue can be divided into twelve parts that can start simultaneously or separately, and which can move at different speeds to their destinations. These speeds may be set manually or prerecorded. Either collectively or individually, all parts of the moving lighting can be accelerated or slowed down under the direct control of the operator. Furthermore, while the two multi-speed playbacks are in operation, all the submasters (normally eight or twelve) may be used either manually or via the modulation control, which provides automatic flashing or fading, sound-to-light synchronization, random modulation, and other moving effects.

Since 1970 projection technology has advanced in various areas. New lamp sources have allowed the manufacture of high-power large scene projectors such as the HMI Pani BP4, which produces a dazzlingly vivid picture able to match almost any level of stage lighting. The increased demand for multi-screen projection (largely built around the Kodak Carousel) has led to the production of superwide-angle lenses for use with very restricted throws, and—once again employing the ubiquitous micro-processor—sophisticated control systems for a number of projectors to provide a complex sequence of easily recorded variations of slide programming.

Lightboard can control single projector random access slide change, and group change, integrated with any lighting cue. But control systems specifically for projection programmes from such companies as Audio Visual Laboratories Inc. of New Jersey, USA, also offer a remarkable range of facilities. Multi-screen set-ups with three projectors to each screen; complex interweaving timing; automatic homing; facilities for adding, skipping and reversing cues—all these readily available.

The psychedelic lightshow perhaps went into a decline with flower power, but is now reviving with the Disco boom. Extraordinary and lovely visual effects can still be achieved with gobos, colour wheels, changers, and moving effects. The laser, which is almost certainly going to effect changes in our lives in the next twenty years (akin to the computer in the 1970s), has been increasingly seen in the theatre and in rock shows, as well as starring in its own productions. The laser and the hologram will change the staging of theatre in the future. But the time has not yet quite come. Despite the public's fascination with exhibitions of these phenomena, shows built around the technology have usually been failures. A simple truth may be that all shows built around technology alone are likely to be ill-received.

This brings me to my final point, which expresses an attitude that I hope has prevailed throughout this book. Of course, the technology of lighting is important. An understanding of it is essential to the designer, and an awareness of the technology in countries beyond his own is a stimulus that is highly to be desired. The international world of stage lighting is a small one, and knowledge of the practice, techniques and tools of other countries can immeasurably increase a designer's capability. However, lighting equipment, be it computer or spotlight, is just a tool; and no tool ever produced a masterpiece. Just as the quality of the brush probably added little to Rembrandt's paintings, so lighting equipment cannot produce fine lighting. All is in the designer's imagination and talent.

Lighting design as a profession is still most firmly established in North America. There, after four generations of lighting design, and several decades of formal training in universities, the profession has a growing awareness of its position, responsibility and role. It is understood that the lighting designer's task is to reveal to the spectators *everything* upon the stage—in the style, mood and manner in which it should be revealed. He is responsible for the control of light— the means of seeing, and the most powerful influence upon the mind and emotions.

In both Britain and the States, dissatisfaction has been expressed about the formal training available. All too often this training is concerned with technology, equipment and techniques. Indeed, all too often where enthusiasts of lighting find themselves together, the conversation turns in the same direction. But these things are peripheral to lighting design. The designer has a creative role to play in interpreting the drama, dance or opera and aiding the director in his interpretation. The designer's preoccupation must be with *seeing* every facet of light, and with listening to, reading, and understanding the material upon which he is working, and grasping the purpose behind his unique art.

In Britain the profession continues to struggle, often ill-rewarded, sometimes ignored, but called upon for many productions, and for all complex ones. Perhaps most surprisingly, the German theatre has at last caught up with the argument in favour of the specialist lighting designer. The younger generation there appears to realize the limitation of lighting the traditional European way—with little pre-planning, the director simply relaying his wishes to the chief electrician—and is striving to introduce the concept of lighting design.

The technician has a vital role to play, his job is indispensable. But lighting design is a fundamentally different process, requiring intuition, sympathy, talent and, above technological knowledge, the ability to hear and to see.

The dreams of those who saw the beginning of the new stage lighting are still unrealized. The disappointment is often due to circumstances of timetabling or economics, sometimes to the mediocrity of the talent involved; but all too often it is due, even now—to a lack of awareness, among the director, set designer and production team, of the contribution lighting can make.

Next report in 1986—maybe.

Part 2
Stage Lighting Mechanics

Since 1970 many new factors have entered the designer's life. The following has been updated where possible, but cannot claim to be comprehensive. Much information has been taken from manufacturers' published data which should be referred to both for verification and for further particulars. Details about some older equipment have been retained, as the designer will still encounter it on his travels.

Introduction

Stage Lighting Mechanics provides a very brief introduction to the technical factors that affect the lighting designer's job as a craftsman. Items of lighting equipment are to the designer what paint and palette are to the painter. They are simply the tools of his trade. A knowledge of the behaviour of light and electricity, of reflection and refraction, of the design of lanterns and stage switchboards is not, in fact, essential to the lighting designer. What is absolutely imperative is that his knowledge of these areas is sufficient to enable him to function with sufficient freedom as an artist. He must know what can be done with light and, if a problem should arise in any technical area, he must have sufficient knowledge to overcome it. His know-how should enable him to choose a lantern and then ensure that it is functioning correctly; he should understand how much can be expected from the control system he is employing. His knowledge of electricity should be sufficient to allow him to plan his installation sensibly and correctly, and he must know how light behaves.

The following sections touch briefly upon many of these areas. Further details can be found in some of the more comprehensive technical books listed in the bibliography.

Light

Light is electro-magnetic radiation visible to the human eye. Light is usually measured in lumens per square foot (abbreviated to lm/ft.), alternatively known as foot candles. One foot candle is approximately the amount of light emitted by a candle on to a matt white card one foot square, one foot away. The metric unit is known as a lux. This is a card one metre square at one metre distance and a conversion can be made by multiplying foot candles by a factor of 10·76.

The amount of light reflected from the card will depend upon its colour and surface, the resulting reflection can be measured in foot lamberts (ft/L). A considerable science has been developed in the measurement and control of illumination, none of which is particularly relevant to the lighting designer working on the stage. These figures are, however, useful when judging the performance of a particular lantern relative to its fellows.

A photometer is an instrument that measures light, it is calibrated to give a reading in either lumens per square foot or foot candles. This instrument can be useful for checking lantern performance or for simply investigating relative brightnesses about the stage but, apart from this 'interest' factor, it is of little use to the stage lighting designer.

If the original white card is moved from a distance of one foot to two feet from the candle, the light on the card will decrease not to a half, but to a *quarter* of the original. This is known as the **Inverse square Law** and it should remind one of the golden rule that light spreads in three dimensions.

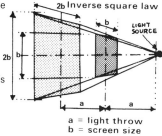

2b Inverse square law

LIGHT SOURCE

a = light throw
b = screen size

Reflection

Objects are only seen by the light they reflect. If an object has a matt uneven surface, the light striking it will be reflected in many directions. This is known as *diffuse reflection*. If it has a flat shiny surface the light will be directly reflected. This is known as *specular reflection*. The principle of reflection is, of course, used inside a lantern both to control and to collect the maximum possible amount of light emitted by the lamp. For this the reflector has to be curved and it is the shape of this curve and the degree to

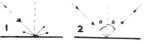

1 Diffuse reflector
2 Specular reflection (a = a)

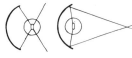

Spherical reflectors

which it surrounds the light source that determines the amount of light collected and, in consequence, the efficiency of the lantern itself. A diffuse reflector is used for soft edged lanterns such as floods; specular reflectors are used in various types of spotlight. Spherical, elliptical and parabolic reflectors are common but other more complex shapes can also be used highly reflective surface on the reflector itself can pre problems by reflecting the filament image. To avoid this reflector may be entirely made up of small flattened facets all tangent to its basic shape.

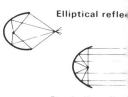

Elliptical refle

Parabolic reflec

Refraction

When a light ray passes through any transparent material, bent or reflected. This happens at the join between two mate for example between air and glass, glass and another shee glass, and so on.

A lens is simply a piece of glass that uses this principle bends the light passing through it in the direction required. Ra light from a point source can be placed at the focus of a lens w will then refract them into parallel rays; the distance between lens and this focal point is known as the focal length of the ler description of a lens gives its diameter first and then its f length. The shorter the focal length, the larger will be the im projected and this is termed a wide angle lens. The wide angle will have to be moved much closer to the lamp to bring the b into sharp focus. Normal stage spot lights use one or two le but when one enters the field of projection complex combinations are employed.

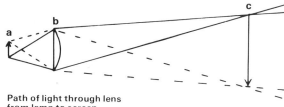

Path of light through lens
from lamp to screen
a   lamp
b   lens
c   inverted image in focus
d   out of focus screen

Electricity

Electricity is dangerous, particularly since it can't be seen, a should be treated with respect. The lighting designer must ei have skilled help or he must acquire sufficient knowledg electricity to enable him to handle it himself. He should alv check that all wiring connections are neatly and firmly made he must know how much load he can apply to any partic circuit.

Ohms Law, which is to be found in every electrical textbo tells us that amps = volts divided by ohms. So also, v multiplied by amps = watts; and, conversely, amps = w divided by volts. The voltage is probably standard (in the UK volts, in the USA 120 volts). The amp is a unit of the rate of flo electricity, used to describe the capacity of the socket outle cable; watts describe the amount of energy consumed by a la The designer should be able to work out quite simply what loa can apply in what circumstances and what size cables he require to feed it.

1000 watts is known as 1 kilowatt (1 kw) and 1 kilowatt per is 1 unit on the electricity meter.

Cable sizes in the UK are:
23/0076 = 6 amps, 40/0076 = 13 amps, 70/0076 = 18 amps

ɘ range of visible light is measured from 4000 to 7000 Angstrom.
our is perceived when we receive only part of this visible range.
ɘ spectrum, first studied by Isaac Newton (1666), breaks up a ım of white light into component parts.

ıe distribution of colours in spectrum

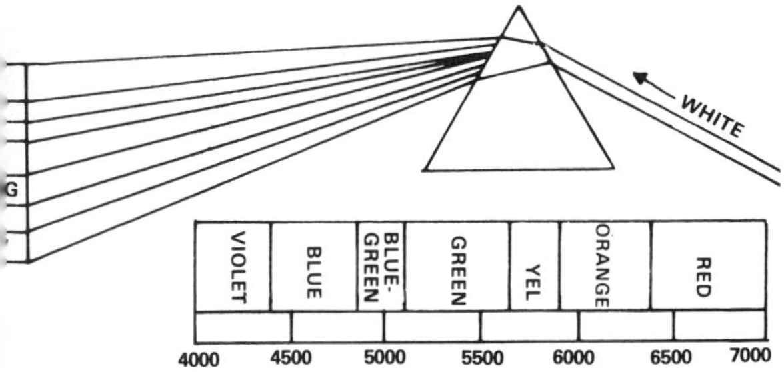
WHITE
G
VIOLET
BLUE
BLUE-GREEN
GREEN
YEL
ORANGE
RED
4000
4500
5000
5500
6000
6500
7000

B. In reality there are hundreds of pure (saturated) colours ıich blend imperceptibly, so the divisions above are arbitrary.

yond the red end is invisible infra-red.
low the violet end is invisible ultra-violet.

ddditive mixing

imary colours of light are red (6)*
blue (20)
green (39)

ɔeams of red, blue and green light are mixed together the result ll appear white

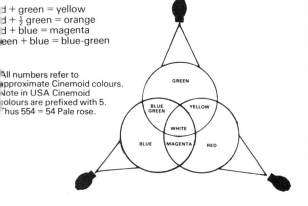

d + green = yellow
d + $\frac{1}{2}$ green = orange
d + blue = magenta
een + blue = blue-green

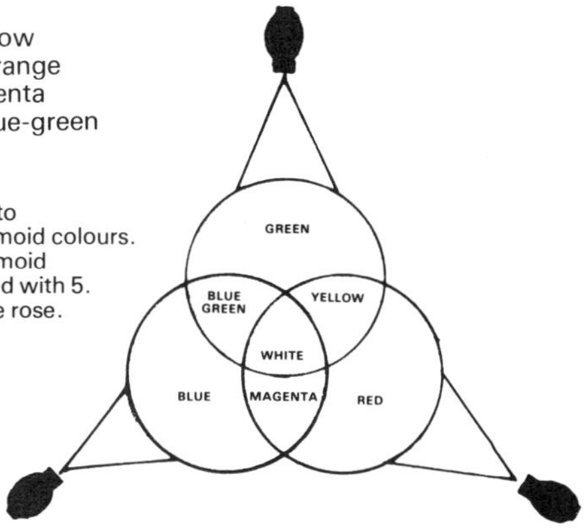
GREEN
BLUE GREEN
YELLOW
WHITE
BLUE
MAGENTA
RED

ll numbers refer to ıpproximate Cinemoid colours. Vote in USA Cinemoid :olours are prefixed with 5. Thus 554 = 54 Pale rose.

ɘcondary colours of light are yellow (1)
blue-green (16)
magenta (13)

ıch primary colour is complementary to its opposite secondary, us
d + blue green = white

dditive colour mixing chart (showing approx. Cinemoid ɉuivalent)

ED (6) +	GREEN (39) +	BLUE (20) = WHITE (Double watts)	
ull	$\frac{1}{3}$	Out	= orange (5)
	$\frac{2}{3}$	O	= amber (4)
	F	O	= yellow (1)
	F	O	= pea green (21)
	F	O	= light green (22)

RED (6) +	GREEN (39) +	BLUE (20) =	WHITE
O	F	O	= GREEN (39)
O	F	$\frac{1}{3}$	= deep green (24)
O	F	$\frac{2}{3}$	= peacock —
O	F	F	= blue-green (16)
O	$\frac{2}{3}$	F	= light blue (18)
O	$\frac{1}{3}$	F	= mid blue (32)
O	O	F	= BLUE (20)
$\frac{1}{3}$	O	F	= violet —
$\frac{2}{3}$	O	F	= mauve (26)
F	O	F	= magenta (13)
F	O	$\frac{2}{3}$	= claret —
F	O	$\frac{1}{3}$	= scarlet —
F	O	O	= RED (6)

To achieve **tints**

F	$\frac{1}{2}$	$\frac{1}{2}$	= deep salmon
F	$\frac{3}{4}$	$\frac{1}{2}$	= light salmon
F	F	$\frac{1}{2}$	= warm grey
$\frac{3}{4}$	F	$\frac{1}{2}$	= green tint
$\frac{1}{2}$	F	$\frac{1}{2}$	= pale green
$\frac{1}{2}$	F	$\frac{3}{4}$	= steel grey
$\frac{1}{2}$	F	F	= steel blue
$\frac{1}{2}$	$\frac{3}{4}$	F	= cold white
$\frac{1}{2}$	$\frac{1}{2}$	F	= lavender
$\frac{3}{4}$	$\frac{1}{2}$	F	= pale rose
F	$\frac{1}{2}$	F	= deep rose
F	$\frac{1}{2}$	$\frac{3}{4}$	= pink

Note Colour mixing with primaries is in practice extremely inefficient and wasteful of light *unless* one of the primaries themselves is required.

Subtractive mixing

The secondary colours of light are the primary colours of pigment.
Yellow pigment reflects yellow, red and *green* light.
Blue pigment reflects blue, blue-green and *green* light.
Mix blue and yellow *pigments,* only *common* colour is reflected. i.e. green.

If a blue object is lit with a white or blue light it will appear blue. *A red light which does not include any blue will make the object appear black*

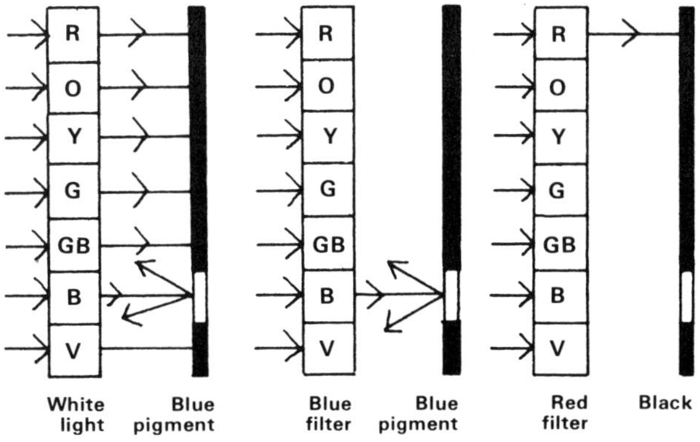
R
O
Y
G
GB
B
V
White light
Blue pigment
Blue filter
Blue pigment
Red filter
Black

Similarly, if yellow and blue filters are placed together in one lantern the resultant colour will be mixed subtractively.
A yellow filter transmits yellow, red and *green* light.
A blue filter transmits blue, blue-green and *green*.
Yellow and blue filters placed together transmit only common colour, i.e. *green*. Colours are identified in a lighting plot by their numbers. Two (or more) colours mixed subtractively are described with a minus sign. e.g. 17 - 38.

Colour media

The most common method of colouring light on stage is to place a coloured transparent material immediately in front of the light.

1. Plastic In recent years various plastic colour media have come on the market giving an ever-increasing choice of colour, quality and cost.

The oldest and best-known is the cellulose acetate, *Cinemoid*, which is long-lasting, moisture-resistant and tough. A similar medium is *Roscolene*. Neither, however, holds up well to the high-wattage t-h sources. It is possible to prolong colour life by perforating the medium with tiny holes, which will not show in the beam, but will allow some heat to escape.

For high-intensity sources there are *Roscolux* (US) and *Roscolux* and *Supergel* (UK). These are either polyester- or polycarbonate-based media supplied by Rosco. Berkey make a Mylar-based high heat material, *Gelatran*. Rank Strand supply *Chromoid*, and Lee Filters make a polyester-based range of colour and colour-correction filters. The latter, often used in film and TV lighting, are useful for correcting unwanted carbon-arc and discharge lamp colours. Similarly, Rosco supply a range of plastic-based diffusers and reflectors.

2. Gelatine Still used in the USA, but not in the UK. Unfortunately, it tears easily, and becomes very dry and brittle. Since the colours do not usually last long, gelatine has to be replaced frequently. However, its great range of colours and low price appeal to many users, particularly when the colour need not be used for an extended period.

3. Glass Glass has been superseded in many cases by the high-intensity plastics. It is rarely used in the UK but still in the US (particularly in high wattage PAR lamp battens) and in Europe. Glass has to be cut as required for each special use. It can be obtained in narrow strips for very hot-beam lanterns. It is comparatively difficult in Europe to obtain a satisfactory range of glass colours, and even when they are available it is difficult to obtain accurate colour matching on consecutive orders. In the US, Light Services Inc. of New York supply a very wide range of excellent colours.

There follows an infinitely debatable colour comparison chart. The colours were viewed by several designers using a 1000 watt quartz source — in a busy design office, not in a laboratory.

As colour dyes and bases develop and change so quickly, samples and batches can vary despite strong efforts by manufacturers towards quality control. Sample books of colours can be obtained from the suppliers listed at the back of the book.

N.B. Numbers in parentheses after a colour refer to the order of colour identification numbers on the same horizontal.

Cinemoid	Roscolene	Roscolux UK	Roscolux US	Supergel	Chromoid	Gelatran	Lee	Colour
								GOLDS
	803	602	02					Bastard Amber (1,2)
52							52	Pale Gold
							152	Pale Gold (1,2)
						16		Pale Gold
	802							Bastard Amber
			03	03				Bastard Amber
47								Dk Bastard Amber (1,2)
		610	17					Apricot
								Light Flame (1,2)
								PINK HUES
54								Pale Rose
51								Gold Tint
						06		French Rose
75			01	01			175	Lt Bast'd Amb. (1,2),
								P. Golden Rose [P.G.R.(3)]
			30	30				Lt Salmon Pink (1,2)
								PINK
						03		Light Pink
	825							No Colour Pink
						05		Chorus Pink
			35	35				Light Pink (1,2)
53								Pale Salmon
							153	Pale Salmon
9							109	Light Salmon
								Light Salmon
					107		107	Rose Pink, Light Rose
						15		Nymph Pink
			31	31				Salmon Pink (1,2)
7								Light Rose
	834							Salmon Pink
		626	34					Flesh Pink (1,2)
	826							Flesh Pink
	835							Medium Salmon Pink
	830							Medium Pink
56								Pale Chocolate
						17		Rosy Amber
			40	40				Light Salmon (1,2)
						19		Peach
78								Salmon Pink
					178			Salmon
							157	Pink
			32	32	157			Med. Sal. Pink (1,2),
66							166	Pale Red (1,2) [Pink (3)]
		632	41					Salmon (1,2)
			24	24				Scarlet (1,2)
	836							Plush Pink
27								Smoky Pink
								ROSE
		625	37					Pale Rose Pink (1,2)
			38	38				Light Rose (1,2)
10								Middle Rose
			36	36				Medium Rose (1,2)
						04		Flesh Pink
11							111	Dark Pink (1,2)
	827	631	44					Br. Pink (1), Mid. R.(2,3)
	829							Bright Rose
						83		Deep Pink
	828							Follies Pink
						13		Brite Pink Hue
	837							Medium Magenta
12								Deep Rose
						14		Cherry
48								Bright Rose
								RED
	832							Rose Pink
						09		Magenta

Cinemoid	Roscolene	Roscolux UK	Roscolux US	Supergel	Chromoid	Gelatran	Lee	Colour
13							148	Bright Rose
								Magenta
							113	Magenta
			45	45	111			Rose (1,2,3)
							113	Magenta
			46	46				Magenta (1,2)
		620	42					Deep Salmon (1,2)
			26	26	106			Light Red (1,2), Red (3)
6							106	Primary Red (1,2)
		621						Light Red
						08		Light Red
14	821							Ruby, Light Red
	823							Medium Red
								AMBERS/ORANGE
		613	16					Light Amber (1, 2)
		614	18					Flame (1, 2)
			20	20				Medium Amber (1,2)
	811							Flame
							134	Golden Amber
34								Golden Amber
33					97			Light Golden Amber
	813							Deep Amber
						20		Light Amber
			21	21				Dark Amber
		615						Golden Amber (1,2)
	815							Deep Straw
							105	Golden Amber
5								Orange
58								Orange
								Deep Orange
	817							Dark Amber
		618	23	23				Orange (1,2,3)
			22	22	135			Autumn Glory
						22		Deep Amber (1,2) Dee
						10		Fire [Golden Amb.
35								Deep Golden Amber
			25	25				Orange Red (1,2)
							164	Flame Red
	818							Orange, Medium Red
64								Medium Red
	819							Orange Amber
								YELLOW/AMBERS
			06	06				No Color Straw (1,2)
		607	07	07	150			Pale Yellow (1,2,3,4)
		604						Pale Yellow
50								No Color Straw
73								No Color Yellow
	804							Straw Tint
		605	08					Pale Gold (1,2)
	805							Light Straw
							103	Straw
3								Straw
	808		09	09	98			Med.S.(I), P.Amb. Go
2							102	Lt Amb. [(2,3),P.G
			14	14				Lt Amb. [Amb
	810							Medium Straw (1,2)
4								N.C. Amber
						34		Medium Amber
						36		Old Gold
			15	15				Deep Straw (1,2)
46							104	Deep Amber
	809							Chrome Yellow
			11	11	149			Straw
49								Lt S. (1,2), Canary (3)
						40		Canary
								Medium Lemon

olour media

Left chart

Roscolene	Roscolux UK	Roscolux US	Supergel	Chromoid	Gelatran	Lee	
		10	10	101			Med. Yellow (1,2),
	609	12			41		Mellow Yellow [Y. (3)
							Straw (1,2)
						101	Yellow (1,2)
806							Medium Lemon
807							Dark Lemon
							GREEN
	669	87				213	Pale Yellow Gn (1,2)
							White Flame Green
							Green Tint
869					46		Pale Yellow Green
							Pale Green
							Pale Green
	671	88				138	Light Green (1,2)
							Pale Green
							Pea Green
						121	Lee Green
							Yellow Green
878					47		Yellow Green
							Moss Green
						122	Fern Green
	672		89				Moss Green
				122			Moss Green
							Moss Green
871							Light Green
							Light Green
						124	Dark Green
							Dark Green
					52		Moss Green
						139	Primary Green
874							Medium Green
				139			Green
							Primary Green
		90	90			53	Dark Yellow (Gn 1,2)
							Dark Green
	674	91					Primary Green (1,2)
		94	94				Kelly Green (1,2)
							BLUE (toward green)
						218	1/3 C.T. Blue
						203	1/2 C.T. Blue
							Ariel Blue
							Steel Tint
					73		Steel Blue
							Steel Blue
							Water Blue
848						117	Mist Blue (1,2)
		61	61				Steel Blue
849							Pale Blue
		63	63	117			P. B. (1,2), Steel B. (3)
					77		Daylight, Elec. B.
					74		Shark Blue
854							Steel Blue
		70	70				Nile Blue (1,2)
853							Pale Blue
					68		Middle Blue
					75		Azure Blue
		72	72	140			Christel Blue
							Azure B. (1,2), Sea B. (3)
		71	71				Giselle Blue
							Pale Navy Blue
860							Sea Blue (1,2)
							Light Blue
							Bright Blue
						118	Light Blue
					76		Timothy Blue
					71		Moon Blue
							Turquoise
		76	76	162			Lt Gn B. (1,2), Turq. (3)
857							Medium Blue
							Peacock Blue
						115	Peacock Blue
		73	73	115			Peacock Blue (1,2,3)
					51		Blue-Green
					67		Aqua Blue
							Blue-Green
		95	95	116			Medium Blue Gn (1,2),
877							Med. B.-Gn [B.-Gn (3)
	673	92					Turquoise (1,2)
					49		Kelly Green
	676	93					Blue-Green (1,2)
							BLUE (toward red)
866		85	85	93			Deep Blue (1,2), B. (3)
	661	83					Deep B., Dk Urban B.
							Medium Blue (1,2)
							Dark Blue
					61		Deep Blue
					60		Zenith Blue
						119	Dark Blue
							Sky Blue
863							Medium Blue [O.K. Blue (4)
862		79	79	119			True B. (1), Br. B. (2,3),

Right chart

Cinemoid	Roscolene	Roscolux UK	Roscolux US	Supergel	Chromoid	Gelatran	Lee	
	857							Medium Blue
	861							Surprise Blue
						64		Medium Blue
		657	80					Primary Blue (1,2)
							132	Medium Blue
32								Medium Blue
	856							Light Blue
					91			Middle Blue
		81	81		92			Urban B. (1,2), Caspian
		82	82					Surprise B. (1,2) [B. (3)
		659	77					Green-Blue (1,2)
	851							Daylight
			68	68				Sky Blue (1,2)
								Bright Blue
			67	67				Light Sky Blue (1,2)
			65	65				Daylight Blue (1,2)
	850							No Color Blue
	855	654						Azure Blue
								Daylight Blue
						65		True Blue
	852							Smokey Blue
61								Slate Blue
						69		Area Blue
						70		Daylite Blue
		651	64					Light Steel Blue (1,2)
						72		Light Sky Blue
							201	Full C.T. Blue
							202	1/2 C.T. Blue
		649	62					Booster Blue (1,2)
		648	60					No Color Blue (1,2)
								VIOLET
			53	53				Pale Lavender (1,2)
			54	54				Special Lav. (1,2)
			55	55	171			Lilac (1,2,3)
71								Lavender
	842							Special Lavender
						86		Violet
	841							Special Pink
								Pale Violet
							142	Pale Violet
42								Violet
	844							Lavender (1,2)
			57	57		87		Misty Lilac
		642	51					Surprise Pink (1,2)
	840							Special Lavender
			52	52	136		136	Lt Lav. (1,2,3), P.Lav. (4)
						80		Surprise Pink
36								Pale Lavender
		638	47					Lt Rose Purple (1,2)
						82		Dark Lavender
								PURPLE
			48	48				Rose Purple (1,2)
						84		Belladonna Red
	838							Dark Magenta
			49	49	96			Medium Purple (1,2,3)
						81		Persian Blue
	839							Rose Purple
26								Mauve
							126	Mauve
25								Purple
								LAVENDER
			58	58		79		Lavender
						88		Deep Lavender (1,2)
	846							Nightshade
	843							Medium Purple
						62		Medium Lavender
						66		Congo Blue
						63		Alice Blue
								Dark Blue
							208	BROWN/CHOCOLATE C.T.Org + .6 Neut Density
56							156	Chocolate
5								Pale Chocolate
						93		Cocoa
		682	99					Chocolate (1,2)
							211	.9 Neut. Density
							210	.6 Neut. Density
60								Pale Grey
55								Chocolate Tint
	880							Light Grey
							209	.3 Neut. Density
		680						Light Grey (1,2) 97
							221	FROST Blue Frost
							220	White Frost
							216	White Diffusion
31		102	102					Lt F. (1), Lt Tough F. (2,3)
		103	103			99		Tough F. (1,2), F. (3)
29	801	101	101		99		129	Heavy Frost (1,2)
								F. (1), Lt F. (2,3), [Tough F. (4)

Control

The heart of every stage lighting installation is the control system. By means of dimmer control stage lighting is balanced to achieve the desired pictorial effect. All control boards provide this facility with a varying degree of sophistication.

Rank Strand Junior 8 (UK)
This is the cheapest and simplest form of dimming control. It uses four resistance dimmers, each of which can have one or two loads of up to 1000 watts connected to them. Thus eight channels can be switched full on, off, or on-dimmer; in the latter position they are used in pairs.

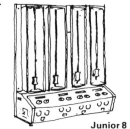

Junior 8

Rank Strand Mini-2 + (UK)
Complete packaged range of two-pre-set desks, portable six-dimmer packs or permanent twelve-dimmer racks. Provide a wide range of local or remote control up to 36, 2000W channels in multiples of six or twelve.

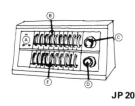

Mini-2 +

Rank Strand Type JP 20 (UK)
The earliest junior version of the English remote control board. It provides twenty dimmers of two or five thousand watts capacity. There are two pre-sets with a master dimmer for each. The later versions also have a master blackout switch for each pre-set.

JP 20

Key. A Neon pilot lamp and control cartridge fuse. **B** Pre-set one dimmer levels. **C** Pre-set one master. **D** Pre-set two master. **E** Pre-set two dimmer levers.

The JP Type control system is commonly used with up to thirty or forty channels and with either two or three pre-sets.

Rank Strand Type SP 20/80 (UK)
Next comes the SP range. These again have two or three pre-sets and are commonly found with up to eighty dimmer channels. The principal difference from the JP is that each channel is provided with a switch which allows circuits to be grouped on to either an A or B master or on both. Thus each pre-set will have an A and B master, a circuit, if switched to group A on one master, will be on that same master on the other pre-sets. On later models separate switching is provided for each pre-set to allow individual groups to be made up as required within each.

Key. A Pre-set one dimmer levers.
B Pre-set two dimmer levers.
C Grouping Switch (black and white latching push buttons).
D Pre-set two master faders.
E Pre-set one black and white master faders.
F Neon pilot and dead black-out switch.

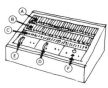

SP 20

Rank Strand Micro 8 II (UK)
Portable, self contained control for eight channels of up to 1000W. Each of the eight circuits can be switched full-on, on-dimmer, or off and share four 2 x 1000W variable load triac dimmers controlled by four faders and master fader.

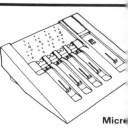

Micr

Strand Century Edkotron (US)
This low cost packaged control system, no longer manufactu is still quite commonly used. Each dimmer unit has six dimmer 1800 or 3000 watt capacity. The control unit will operate these will also have a master lever to control all proportionately. master unit can control up to six control units (i.e. acting a grand master) or it can be used between pairs of control units cross-fader from one to the other.

Strand Century Theatron (US)
This provides a two scene pre-set with or without group sub masters. Interlocking levers for master dimming of each pre-set or single handle cross fading are provided.

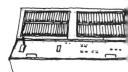

Theat

Rank Strand AMC (UK)
Multi-pre-set, multi-group control based upon ten channel modules with three pre-sets, each with three groups. Up to twelve of these modules link by plug-in ribbon cable to a master module with a dipless cross-fader controlling the master faders for the nine groups. An alternative time master module has 1-60 seconds/minutes auto timing for both sides of a split cross-fade

Each channel has additional flexible selection to an inhibit fa or to a direct master independent of the grand master fader.

Key. A Ten way three pre-set three group channel module w switch for inhibitor group and independent. **B** Master modu Nine group faders, two group master faders, cross-fader, D switch, grand master fader and inhibitor fader.

Electrosonic Rockboard (UK)
A two pre-set portable control developed from custom-made boards for major rock bands. Each pre-set has three groups and grand master fader with black-out switch. Additionally each channel has a touch flash on-to-full button, pin matrix to allow ten independent master faders, or programmable pattern 'chaser' or 'ripple' effect with variable speed.

Electrosonic Rockboa

Additional options are a touch switch independent sub-mast selection and a group clear push facility.

Key. A Two pre-set channel levers and group switches. **B** Fla buttons. **C** Pre-set masters. **D** Pin matrix controllers. **E** Chase/ripple control.

en working with more than sixty or eighty channels, a more histicated method of pre-setting and grouping becomes very irable.

nk Strand type LP Luminous Pre-Set Console
s is a three pre-set console with separate grouping facilities to h pre-set; it is commonly available in sizes ranging from 40 to channels. A unique feature is the internally illuminated nnel lever which combines group switching selection and ication within the scale of each dimmer lever. On each of the e pre-sets any dimmer may be grouped to a red master, a ite master, to both simultaneously or off. Selection is made by ssing the appropriate master push together with the scale of control lever. Indication of grouping is given by a red and/or ite light inside the scale itself. Master pushes to switch all to ite or all to black are provided, as well as matching pushes ich allow the grouping on one pre-set to be instantly copied on any other. The six master faders (a) can be grouped to either of two grand master faders (b) or can work independently. other fader can be provided to override a permanently selected up of circuits on all pre-sets. This could, for example, be a ster controlling all front of house channels.

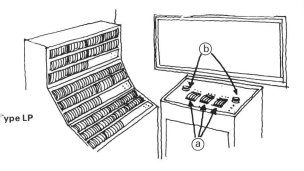

ype LP

te. The LP control was clearly a substantial improvement upon se previously mentioned, since grouping was readily dependent on each pre-set. For many years controls in the UK d provided a grouping facility common to all pre-sets and, hough this approach had its supporters, it only resulted in ntinual complications during production (when trying to sort t where the switching should be when using each particular pre-t).

Rank Strand introduced in 1969 a development of the Type SP ntrol called the 'Threeset'. This provides three pre-sets with ree separate groups within each pre-set, the group selection ing made by a three-position switch above each channel lever. development of this, known as 'Light Set', combines these cilities with the advantages of the LP system above, and thus at st recognizes the needs of lighting design practice for dependent grouping within pre-sets.

A forerunner of these developments was one of the first yristor controls for the National Theatre at the Old Vic which as devised with independent group switching to each pre-set d, over several years, clearly proved itself one of the most utstandingly simple from the point of view of both the operator d the lighting designer.

ype MGP Multi-Group Pre-set (not shown)
his control, which is an elaboration of the LP type, allows the perator to memorize up to 40 *groups* of circuits. This avoids the ecessity for selecting groups by touching each channel lever idividually. The memory action brings groups of circuits on to the d master only. These can then be faded in and the channels arked' on the white master, provided that it is at the same level s the red. This system allows a very large number of circuits to be asily controlled by one operator, since he has only to concern imself with those channels whose scales are illuminated. Up to 40 channels can be comparatively easily handled.

Strand Century C-I Control. 5 or 10 scene pre-set (US)
This control consists of a master console and a five or ten scene pre-set panel. This provides an individual control for each channel on each complete scene pre-set. These are all internally illuminated. A one hundred channel control might have 1000 levers to set up. Once pre-sets are set, the master fade control can proportionally cross-fade all the lighting from one pre-set scene to the next, and so on.

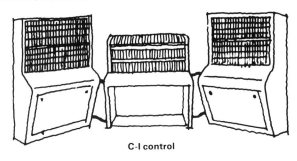

C-I control

Siemens Regulator (GERMANY)
This control, which is extremely common in Western Germany, has one main desk with a lever to operate each channel (a). Each lever is motor-driven and when the separate pre-set panel (c) is activated by the master control (b) every dimmer lever is driven to its set position. Thus not only is the lighting on stage altered, but so also is the actual lever display on the dimmer board. The pre-set levers are mounted in groups of four, side by side. Picking out a pre-set is made easier by bringing the appropriate levers forward mechanically from behind a shield where they can otherwise be seen but not worked. Additional pre-sets are now available in the form of punched card equipment (d).

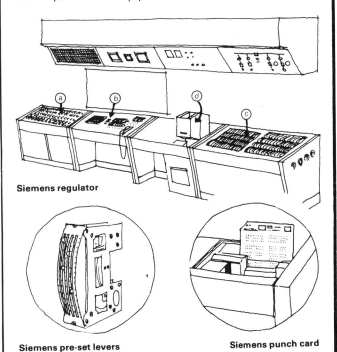

Siemens regulator

Siemens pre-set levers　　　　**Siemens punch card**

It was obvious for many years that, as lighting became more sophisticated, more sophisticated methods of control would have to be devised. The timely arrival of the memory systems has immeasurably improved the capability of lighting control.

A major breakthrough in lighting control systems has come with the development of instantaneous memory facilities. Using the techniques of the computer world, this development means that a switchboard is capable not only of providing a means of operating the dimmers, but of 'remembering' the dimmer levels of each cue set up by the designer. At a lighting rehearsal every state of light can be simply recorded, not on pencil and paper but at the touch of a button within the switchboard itself. Two principal versions led the market in England but a great deal of activity along these lines is going on all over the world.

Thorn Theatre Q File (UK)
This revolutionary system was first designed for the substantial television lighting control market in the United Kingdom and has subsequently been modified and improved for the theatre. In a space under two square feet up to 1000 circuits can be controlled and their every level memorized. This extremely compact desk is made possible by a radically new method of controlling the individual channels. Instead of the usual one lever per circuit, only one is provided for the whole installation, and the circuits are connected to it by a numerical push button selector. When a circuit number is selected the dimmer lever moves automatically and instantly to the position at which that dimmer happens to be; it can then immediately be modified manually as desired. The lack of the usual large complement of levers is at first somewhat daunting, but the operator very quickly becomes used to the new method; the operation of the numerical selector becomes extremely easy and almost as fast as touch typing. Once a lighting picture has been built up with the individual channel controller, the whole can be instantly recorded. The memory controller part of the system divides into three parts. Each memory is given a number (usually up to 100, but 200 are available) and any memory can be instantly recalled by selecting its number from the memory selector. To switch that memory straight on to the stage, the *stage store* is used. This store has various controls, all of which immediately affect the live lighting upon the stage. Memories can be switched on (deleting anything recorded previously) and added to or subtracted from the current lighting, but it must be stressed that all of these are switch cues. To fade in or out, the memory chosen is transferred to the *pre-set store:* there are two of these. Once in either pre-set store, the lighting can be cross-faded, add-faded or subtracted at any speed selected (from one second to seventy minutes). Within each pre-set, lights fading up can travel at a different speed from those fading down: thus four groups of lights can travel simultaneously at different speeds, overlapping, accellerating or slowing down as the operator requires. All fade operations are instigated at the push of a button, once the speeds have been set, but the start and finish of a cue and its speed can be instantly overriden by the operator. Furthermore, operation of the individual channel controller will instantly override whatever is happening in either stage or pre-set stores.

Rank Strand System DDM (UK) (not shown)
The Rank Strand System DDM has many of the features which described above. However, an individual channel controll provided for each circuit. This takes the form of an intern illuminated rocker switch. When the upper part of the rocke pressed, the light concerned will increase in brightness; press on the lower part will make the light grow dimmer. When a light picture has been achieved it can be recorded, at the press o simple button; and up to 250 memories can be record in this way. These memories may be recalled in any order selecting their number and fading them in. Two playbacks provided which allow two up speeds and two down spee simultaneously.

These two systems alone represented memory control in 19 The following indicate the speed of development at every leve complexity.

Rank Strand Compact (120, 80 or 48 ways) (UK)
A self-contained, mobile intensity memory control with a choice ferrite core memory or lower capacity MOS memory. Eith provides fast random-access of stored cues; for repertoire libra storage a matching separate desk with cassette recorder available.

Channel control is by keyboard selection to the fader whe which does not have to be matched to the existing intensity befo providing fingertip control. After recording live, blind, or the to output in mid-fade, any memory can be recalled to replace t previous lighting, all the memories can be added together subtracted one from another. The cross-fade can be dipless contoured, and on completion the next cue can be called automatically. Auxiliary controls for direct fader lever control a placed in a foldaway panel that conceals the pin matrix auxiliary channel selection. The Compact 120 channel selector h an '@' (at) button to allow fast direct entry of intensity levels, example channel 18 @ level 7.

Also provided are an '&' (and) key that allows combinations channels to be called up, and an '&M' (and memory) key th allows previously recorded memories to be recalled as a group control by the fader wheel.

The Compact 80GT has the above facilities but also the cap bility on playback to insert a new cue or series of cues in automatic sequence wherever it might be required.

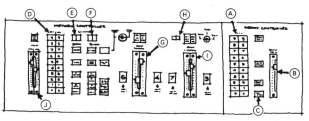

Thorn Q File

Key. Circuit controller: A Numerical selector. **B** Dimmer lever. **C** On/Off Switch. **Memory Controller: D** Memory Numerical Selector. **E** Stage store indicator and action buttons. **F** Pre-set store A and B indicator and action buttons. **G** Pre-set A and B speed controllers. **H** Pre-set store C and D indicator and action buttons. **I** Pre-set store C and D speed controllers. **J** Master dimmer levers.

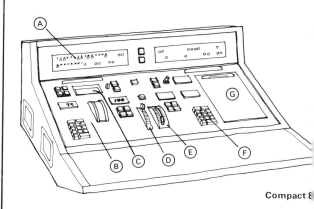

Compact 8

Key. A Channel mimic. **B** Channel selector and wheel. **C** Chann intensity indicator. **D** Grand master. **E** Twin-lever cross-fader. Cue select. **G** Pin matrix and foldaway auxiliary chann controllers.

...orn Q-Master (UK)

...-160 channels (Q-Master 1000); Ferrite core, 50/100 memories. ...-240 channels (Q-Master 2000); Interchangeable magnetic discs, ...0-600 memories.

...Q-Master control employs one manual fader per channel. ...anually set up states may be transferred to any of three masters, ...us giving three pre-sets, without using the memories. Memories ...n record the state of lighting on the stage at any time or a blind ...te set up on the manual controls. Three independent playbacks ...ow use of three memories separately yet simultaneously. ...emories may be added or subtracted on a single master. ...tomatic fades and cross-fades may be employed with timings ...ntinuously adjustable from 1 second to 1 hour. Variable ...ightness mimic lamps above each channel show channel level. ...l memorized channels may be overriden manually at any time.

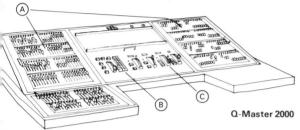

Q-Master 2000

...ey. A Channel levers. B Memory select. C Three independent ...aybacks.

...rand Century Multi-Q (US)

...programmable software lighting control system for 32 or more ...annels. The desk features two dipless cross-fade units each with ...tomatic sequence (A-B, C-D) and manual speed override. An E- ...split fader allows a third profiled fade to take simultaneous ...ect. A single keyboard provides pre-set (memory) numbers, ...annels, their level and optional speed of movement. Cues may ...inserted or deleted. A complete set of manual faders may be ...ed for setting up lighting or as back-up. An additional back-up ...odule allows for independent cross-fading between up to 16 pre- ...ts selected by thumbwheel. A VDU provides mimic information.

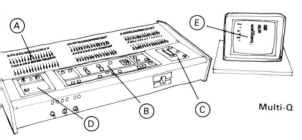

Multi-Q

...ey. A Channel levers. B Control module. C Splitfade module. D ...ack-up module. E Video display.

...rand Century Micro-Q (US) (not shown)

... modular control giving a manual two-scene pre-set with or ...thout a complete memory system for the smaller installation ...om 8 to 96 channels).

...Channel control modules (two pre-set of eight channels each) ...ay be added together and mastered by the manual control ...odule which provides a split dipless cross-fader, an independent ...d manual master. Houselight modules and non-dim ...dependent modules are available.

...The memory control module provides a keyboard for channel, ...vel, pre-set and time entry. A split dipless cross-fader, scene ...aster fader and grand master fader provide flexibility of timing. ...ew cues may be inserted in sequence. Channels may be selected ...r use onto a ten-way submaster module.

Kliegl Bros. Performance (US)

This control uses a numerical keyboard for channel selection with the useful addition of a 'Thru' (through) button for calling up several circuits (all circuits between 21 and 30 being 21 'Thru' 30). An 'AT' button allows levels to be set via the keyboard; alternatively a linear belt controller may be used without the need for matching to set levels.

Up to 24 group masters may be added to the system to give the operator proportional manual control over any group of circuits. Proportional patching (up to 1000 outlets to 200 dimmers) is available electronically.

There is a grand master fader and black out button. The memory select unit allows new cues to be inserted by the use of a decimal point and thus · 1 to · 9 may be added between any whole number. Two manual cross-fader units are provided, A and B being split dipless cross-faders and C and D being manual masters for proportional control of assigned memory or for 'pile on' operation. Further, one or two automatic time-fader units give a timed fade to memories assigned to the unit, with cross-fade, plus-fade, minus-fade, fade-out all at prerecorded speeds, which, however, may be accelerated or retarded by an associated linear belt controller. A complete set of manual levers for alternative channel control is hinged within the top of the desk. A video mimic may be added to display the state of lighting on the stage, the pre-set store, any manual master, the manual cross-fader or any time fade unit the system contains. Floppy disc recording may be used for library storage. A portable remote desk is available.

Key. A Channel select. B Grand master. C Time fade control. D Split fader. E Manual pile-on masters. F Memory select keyboard. G Manual levers under. H Floppy disc.

Performance

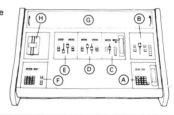

Skirpan Lighting Control Corporation Autocue (US)

The first mini-computer lighting control in the United States, Autocue remains unique in its basic operating principle.

The system employs a dynamic video display that shows a great amount of information about the lighting, such as each dimmer channel and its intensity, cue numbers, fader designations and a series of instructions (black-out, clear display, store, next cue or back a cue, etc.). With a light pen, the operator can touch the appropriate portion of the screen and thus activate the change of light. For example, a level of light between 0 and 10 can be touched with the pen. Thereafter, every circuit number touched will immediately go to the chosen level, and once at that level it can be edged up or downward by further use of the light pen. Similarly a cue number can be selected and the whole state of lighting recorded by further use of the pen.

In addition to the video display unit and light pen, a performance control panel is placed in an adjacent position, which provides the normal operating controls for running the show. Push-button dimmer and cue selection can be done on this panel, and some of the light pen functions on the VDU are duplicated by push button switches, allowing the operator a choice of operating modes. Two time faders, two manual cross-faders, two pile-on faders, and two encapture (or inhibitor) faders permit the control of pre-recorded cues, channels or groups of channels.

The VDU can be operated in a rehearsal or show display mode and it can also display a list of the shows on the auxiliary long-term storage cassette. Other functions, such as load patching display, a display of dimmers in use, the control of remote control units, and even the movement of audio switching functions and stage machinery, are available extras. Remote control consoles that can be operated around the stage or studio are available.

Control

Rank Strand Duet (UK)

The first micro-processor-based system from this company in the U.K. is a stylish, low-cost system for from 48 to 120 channels with 199 memories. The Duet's self-contained console, which is the heart of the system, has a number of optional peripheral units. This include two forms of mimic, a simple LED display showing those circuits above zero and a complete read-out on a VDU of all circuits and their levels. For long-term bulk storage of memories there is a separate floppy disc unit and, for those who prefer the now more old-fashioned method of channel access by an individual controller per channel, there is an auxiliary wing providing a simple two pre-set desk, the contents of which can be recorded by the main console. A ten-group pin patch panel providing flexible pile-on or inhibit grouping by a pin matrix to ten fader levers, a portable rigger's control for remote control of any channel and a ten submaster group desk, complete the optional units presently available.

Key. A Keyboard. This keyboard (as in Lightboard) is used to call up any single channel, memory or pre-recorded group of channels without their assigned levels. It is also used to select cues in a playback mode. Levels may be set within the keyboard

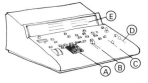

Rank Strand Duet

directly by use of the '@' button or by the adjacent wheel. The '+' and '−' buttons together with a 'Thru' button allow several unrecorded channels to be called up together. **B** Manual Playback. **A** and **B** masters provide a dipless or contoured cross-fade from memory to memory. **C** A timed playback allows a pre-recorded or manually set timed cross-fade to occur separately or simultaneously. **D** Grand master fader and black out switch. **E** LED mimic display.

Rank Strand MMS (UK)

An internationally sold modular memory system that can be extended by extra channels, memories and facilities. May be used for 80 to 360 channels.

Channel selection may be by numerical keyboard (which will also call up pre-recorded memories and set levels); or push button selection, to the Rank Strand patented fader wheel. Mimic display, which may be by video, shows lighting on stage or in any playback or pre-set. Playbacks may be by manual dipless split cross-fader or by rate (timed) cross-fade (1 sec. to 60 min.), which also has up-fade, down-fade and group-fade (pre-recorded circuits without recorded level for proportional modification), or any combination. Ten independent submasters may be used in conjunction with a pin matrix. New memory numbers may be inserted into a sequence individually or to repeat a series. Tape cassettes are used for library storage, print-out is available, and a portable control for use in lighting rehearsals provides all facilities in a briefcase.

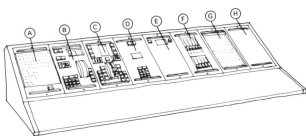

Rank Strand MMS

Key. A Mimic display. **B** Channel control. **C** Rate playback (manual or further rate playbacks are optional). **D** Memory selector. **E** Ferrite core memory. **F** Back-up masters **G** Pin matrix for **F** above. **H** Blank to allow for future expansion.

Rank Strand Octet (UK) (not shown)

The Octet has eight addressable playback stores, two being recorded time or manual split cross-fader, the other six be submasters that can proportionately reduce to zero or boost fifty per cent the intermediate levels of channels within that sto There is keyboard selection, with or without fader wheel, channel, memory, group and level, and video monitors disp channel levels in any or all stores. Grand master fader and t independent ancillary faders for circuits selected by pin mat complete this recent control.

Hub Electric Co. Inc. Encore 100 (US)

A 100 cue memory for 32, 64, or 96 channels. A single keyboard controls channel and memory selection and a single cross-fader may be operated manually or to a pre-set time.

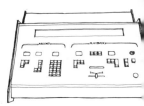

Encore

Berkey Colortran Channel Track (US) (not shown)

This system, the latest from Berkey, offers the now familiar cho of channel control via individual lever or key pad. The key pad select channels individually or in sequential or random grou Designated channels may be sub-mastered as required. Chan Track allows the operator to see the level of the chosen chan throughout all recorded memories in a single display. The syst has a pair of timed faders allowing proportional dipless cro fades, split time faders with different start/stop times, plus a minus fades, pile-on fades and timed fades within fades. A furt pair of manual faders permit cues to be operated manually throu a proportional dipless split cross-fader. Master controls provided for both the memory and manual sections of the contr

ADB Memolight 120/240/360 (BELGIUM)

Each channel may be operated either by its own manual fader by pushbutton selection (which is also the mimic) to a sin channel fader. There is a master fader for all the manual levers a a grand master fader. Four playback groups providing two lin cross-faders are controlled manually or automatically, and allo fade within a fade. For correction the manual control may be us to reduce any circuit to a lower level or out, and the push but with the single channel control will increase any selected circ with no sudden change of light on stage.

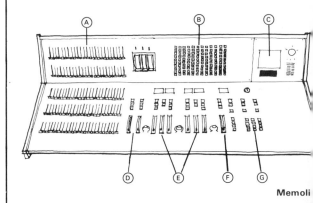

Memoli

Key. A Manual levers. **B** Manual master and grand master. **C** F playback groups and time setters. **D** Single channel fader. **E** Sin channel selector and mimic. **F** Memory selection buttons. Floppy disk (ferrite core optional extra).

AB Elektronik AB AVAB 2000 (SWEDEN) (not shown)

is control from Scandinavia employs a programmable mini-
computer with floppy disk as external memory. Control of over
00 circuits with up to 1000 memories is available. A video screen
ows the state of lighting on stage or in any memory. It also
plays any internal faults or denotes lamp failure, lamp usage
ch as burning time), as well as any plain language information.
rd copy print-out is available as well as a pocket-sized radio-
ntrol portable unit which can even be used at the top of a
der! A number of submaster and cross-fade routes are available
d channel selection is by numerical keyboard and 'joystick'
ntrol.

AB Elektronik AB AVAB 2001 (SWEDEN) (not shown)

portable 'brief-case' micro-processor control. Lighting is set up
a keyboard and three joystick controls that act as level setters
to accelerate or slow down a movement of light. Automatic
eing allows a chain of cues to 'loop' as required concurrently to
e main lighting programme. A manual pin patch back-up
ovides colour-coded diode pins to give up to nine pre-set levels.

emens Sitralux B30 (GERMANY)

is Siemens control employs a standard computer, a data
minal for display of channel or other information, a floppy disc
long-term storage and a teletypewriter. The control employs
sh buttons for mimic and channel selection (laid out
ographically if required) and a master section. The controllers
the master section use a plug-in digital fader wheel combined
th an analog display indicator showing the level of each
ntroller. Each controller has a push on/off switch.

The master section has a controller for all stage circuits and all
nt of house circuits, a cross-fade master, eight submasters (A
H), and a channel controller and a numerical keyboard.

Channels may be called up by their mimic pushes or by the
yboard. Levels can be set again by the keyboard or by a
mmon channel controller. Each part of the lighting — or all of it
may be assigned to any submaster A to H. The contents of the
bmasters may be combined onto any one, broken up into
osen component sections or transferred from one to another.
e submaster controllers may be used either to bring in their
signed lighting manually or to pre-set a fade-in and fade-out
e. Buttons in/out, one above each submaster, implement
ves under pre-set time mode. A cross-fader control provides a
less cross-fade between any two submasters or groups of
bmasters.

the VDU.

This, the latest control from Siemens, recognizes more clearly
e flexibility of circuit grouping needed by the lighting designer;
s has little or no connection with the geographic location of the
cket outlets within the theatre.

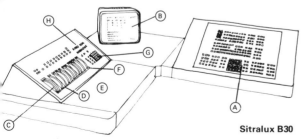

Sitralux B30

ey. **A** Channel mimic and selector pushes. **B** VDU **C** FOH and
age masters. **D** Cross-fade master. **E** Submasters. **F** Channel
ntroller. **G** Numerical selector of channel intensity and memory
umber. **H** Submaster selector.

B. An auxiliary special effects controller, the 'Siepromat', is also
ailable. This selects circuits via a pin matrix to fade, switch or
cker automatically, or for pulsing or cycling effects.

Rank Strand Lightboard (UK) (see Plate 73)

This control derived its simple name 'Lightboard' from its
fundamental simplicity, yet also from the possibility it offers the
lighting artist to play or paint with light — in time.

The intention was to produce a control which would satisfy
various criteria: 1. It would be fundamentally simple in its basic
operation; 2. It would be capable of being 'played' by a skilled
operator with 'heads up' attention on the stage; 3. It would
recognize the gifts that memory control brings: a *group* of lights is
just as important as a single channel, and the operator requires
finger-tip control of various live *blocks* of light for comparative
balancing; 4. Light has to be capable of moving with great subtlety
or complexity, but also, at any time, of being, in part or in whole,
combined (or separated) for override control; 5. The control
should provide detailed information about every part of the
lighting; 6. In a multi-lantern repertoire rig, the patch panel had to
be eliminated, yet the operator is interested only in those channels
actually employed in the current production and does not wish to
be distracted by the others not in use; 7. The orientation and
control of position and colour of lanterns must be integral to the
control, as must projection slide change, effects and so on.

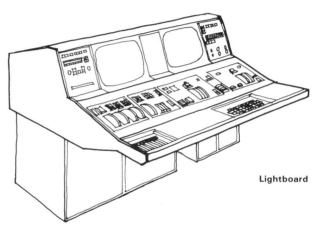

Lightboard

Palettes

The left-hand palette is the basic instrument with which lighting
cues are prepared in the control room. An optional right-hand
palette may be removed and used elsewhere for lighting
rehearsals.

A palette consists of two sections: the setting panel and the
sub-masters.

The setting panel contains a keyboard on which any lighting
channel or channels, or pre-recorded memory (a combination of
circuits with or without their levels for proportional movement),
may be called up and adjusted. This adjustment of level may be
with the controller wheel or within the keyboard itself. The setting
panel can be used live or blind. Any action may be reversed.

Once any pattern of lighting has been created on the setting
panel it may be transferred to one of the sub-masters. New
lighting can then be prepared and balanced between any submasters which might be in use.

The sub-masters may also be used during performance as
manual controllers in a conventional manner for fading or
switching circuits selected, or they may be programmed via an
auxiliary modulation panel to give a random or programmed cycle
of light, possibly linked to a sound source input, for instance for
flashing or shimmering effects.

The sub-masters may be operated independently or subject to
the overriding control of the playbacks. They may also be 'loaded'
automatically from a single memory number. One submaster may
be invoked to 'master' the other in use if required.

Playbacks

These are identified as 'green' and 'red'. They provide the
principal method of operating the lighting during performance.
Part or all of the lighting may be cross-faded (all other lighting

fading out), moved up or down in level, raised to full or faded to out. Any action may be temporarily or permanently stopped at any time and/or reversed so that all circuits return to their starting levels. Playback cross-fades or fades to out may apply to circuits assigned to that playback or all circuits.

The playbacks may be operated in a manual or automatic mode. In manual, the controller wheels are used to move the lighting manually like normal dimmer levers. In automatic, the controllers become time-setters that may be used to pre-set the speed for a change and then, if necessary, be operated while the cue is in motion to accelerate or decelerate the movement of light. Times may be pre-recorded and up to six different up and down speeds of light may be separately or collectively invoked on either playback at one time. On the latest Lightboards any or all of these movements may be separately or collectively accelerated or decelerated.

In order to simplify the operational concept of the systems, channels operate on the principle of 'latest takes precedence'. In other words, if a channel on one controller is subsequently used elsewhere in the system it is instantly under that new control. On the newest Lightboards, however, a 'collect' button is added to each controller so that if he wishes the operator can recollect under his control the original contents of a submaster despite their subsequent modification.

An 'automod' facility may be used in an emergency (if, for example, a spotlight is knocked out of position during performance — or a lamp fails) to provide a replacement in any cue at the same or a similar level.

Cue select

The central panel contains a keyboard on which cues may be selected for either playback. This panel also selects the recorded time facility and the sequential call-up of cues for playback or recording. Decimal points may be used to insert up to nine new cues between any two recorded cues.

Video displays (black-and-white or colour)

The two principal video screens illustrate the state of lighting, indicating the circuits in use and their level. The bottom section of the screen provides information about the contents of each controller on the palettes and playbacks. Associated with the optional right-hand palette is a third display which is also removable. It should be noted that the video display *can* show only circuits in use in any particular production. Thus, if only thirty circuits are used, thirty are displayed; if 280 circuits, 280 are shown.

Tape recording

Lighting cues may, at the same time as recording onto the core store, be recorded on tape automatically, or at the discretion of the operator. This tape can be used as a library store or later to edit the order of cues between any primary cue. Alternate programme tapes allow the operator to check the correct functioning of every part of the system.

Auxiliary facilities

(a) Cue Title. A typewriter keyboard is contained under the front part of the desk and may be used to type onto the video displays a 'cue title' list or other information that may be of use to the operator.
(b) Auxiliary Masters. Totally independent of the main system, a series of manual faders with a pin matrix provides control over any combination of lighting circuits.
(c) Written Record. Facilities are available to provide a permanent record of the lighting plot.

Orientation control

The optional panel at the right-hand end of the control system employs a keyboard to call up a remote control luminaire or a projector with slide change. By use of the keyboard and the controller, the pan, tilt and focus of luminaires or the slide change and focus of projectors may be operated and recorded on any cue number. The subsequent operation of this panel can be mastered from the 'green' playback. Separate facilities for colour change control are provided on the main setting panel.

The system may be expanded to include:
Up to four palettes, with up to six submasters on each.
Up to eight video displays, either monochrome or colour.
A removeable stalls control, with one complete palette and playback.
A multi-channel modulation unit allowing control of up to si groups of lighting from an audio cassette, flasher unit, o external audio input.
Any number of hand-held designer/technician radio-contro keyboards affording control of the lighting whilst maintainin complete freedom of movement.

Strand Century Light Palette (US) (see Plate 52)
Latest in the advanced control system field is Strand Century Palette. This is the first system to take some of the operation advances of Lightboard and provide them through a micro processor-based 'computer'.

Light Palette allows channels or cues to be selected from single keyboard, and employs three sets of keyboards to carry o all operations, even perhaps customer reprogramming of the micr processor. It has two wheels, one of which affects the level selected circuits or cues, and the other the speed of operation any movement of light. There are two cross-faders, X and Y, an four master levers, thus allowing six operations to take plac simultaneously. There is also a series of submasters that can b assigned to selected circuits, but these have some limitations a they are effectively only *inhibitors* of circuits, taking out certa groups of circuits from cues in operation in the main part of th system.

Once cues have been set up and masters assigned to any actio the speed of change of light can be recorded as well as a delay c any chosen period between one change and another. Going eve further, the actual profile of the fade can be pre-selected to allow for example, lamps with a long warm-up time to be brought in i different manner from their fellows. The whole show, whe recorded, uses the video screens, not only as an indicator c channels in use and their levels, as in Lightboard, but also as th cue-sheet itself. Thus, one screen lists the cues in use and thos about to be employed with their timing, delays, profiles, etc., an their submasters. The touch of a single 'Go' button will start a cu with all its component parts, into action. The speed of all or part c the action may be overridden manually or taken over complete for manual control. Operated in an 'auto-record mode' Ligh Palette will remember any change of timing by the operator an subsequently put the new fade timing into effect.

Light Palette provides many of the facilities of Lightboard although perhaps lacks some of the latter's ergonomic simplicit Its use of the micro-processor to memorize whole cues and displa them in such an advanced manner is a step forward. It should als be noted that the control allows the pre-set of patching from large number of dimmers to a chosen number of operable contr channels, making it a good control for an important repertoi theatre.

Light Palette

Memories . . . an interim conclusion

Memory systems, like calculators, get smaller — and usually cheaper.

Briefcase memory systems like the Berkey Memory 2 provide 00 memories for 32, 64 or 96 channels with single manual or timed cross-fade. ADB's Memo 48 gives 100 memories for 48 channels with two pre-sets and single cross-fade and even has a thermal teleprinter — in the lid.

From here to the major systems of Rank Strand and Siemens seems a long step. But the most sophisticated facilities are continually coming down-market as the micro-processor advances, and as prices drop.

The computer in all its manifestations is still a beginner. Soon in the theatre — very soon — it will work scenery, box offices, sound, and many other things. It will also be more and more accessible to every lighting designer. Let him have the imagination, awareness and talent to use this miraculous device for what it is intended: to display and complement performances with sympathy and understanding.

The Broadway Theatre

It is an extraordinary contradiction that the Broadway Theatre, which houses perhaps the highest standards of lighting design in the world, operated until recently with the most antiquated control equipment. 85 per cent of the London West End theatres are equipped with remote control switchboards, but in New York these are still an innovation; there each theatre is simply a shell into which the producer has to take every bit of lighting equipment he requires for each production. A further complication is that many Broadway houses are only equipped with a DC supply, thus making it difficult to use Thyristor dimming equipment. This problem, together with the need to make everything portable, has held the Broadway equipment scene back, with its heavy and cumbersome resistance dimmer boards using mile after mile of temporary cabling to the lanterns.

But at last, with *A Chorus Line* (Plate 65), the memory control has come to Broadway. Let us hope that economics will not too long delay the demise of that dinosaur, the piano board.

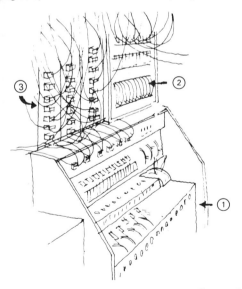

American piano board/pre-set/plugging box

Piano boards (1)

The main form of dimmer control was the piano board, so called because the dimmers were built into metal-lined boxes which resemble upright pianos. There are two principal sizes of piano board. One has twelve dimmer plates, each with a capacity of 5000 to 6000 watts. The other, more commonly used, has fourteen

dimmers with a capacity of 1500 to 3000 watts each. Each circuit has a switch and fuse and there is a master switch to kill the entire board. The dimmers can all be locked to a common shaft so that all can be faded in or out with a master handle. It is common practice to operate the boards by standing them in two rows, facing each other. Then the operating electrician stands between two facing boards, working them both.

Pre-set boards (2)

Placed on top of the piano boards are auxiliary or pre-set boards. These have either eight 750 watt dimmers or twelve 500 watt and are used to control single spotlights or any small wattage load, which can then in turn be fed by any of the larger dimmers of the piano board beneath it. In this way four lamps can be set at different pre-set levels, then brought to these levels simultaneously and proportionally by bringing in the master dimmer.

If lanterns are required to work together and yet do not have to go to different levels, they can be grouped up through a 'plugging box'. These boxes are also mounted above the piano board and have a series of porcelain sockets to receive cables from the stage. From the box one feed goes to a dimmer in the board below. Standard plugging boxes have two, four or six sockets, each individually fused. (3)

It should be noted that all these dimmers are usually of the resistance type and accordingly have to be loaded up to approximately their correct wattage if a satisfactory dimmer curve is to be obtained. Efforts have been made to introduce auto-transformers and this is a step towards a much-needed development.

The Patch Panel

This is a device whereby a few dimmer channels can be readily connected to a large quantity of socket outlets from a central location. It is, in fact, simply a large plugging board. In the United States it is common practice in a large installation to have every single outlet brought back to a Patch Panel and then every control board channel can be 'patched' to its chosen outlet for a specific show. In Europe it is usual for the control board itself to have a greater quantity of dimmer channels, and there is consequently less reliance on patching. The Patch Panel can be an extremely valuable adjunct to an installation. In any type of theatre there are sure to be a number of circuits that are only infrequently used. These can certainly be satisfactorily patched and it is in this way that a Patch Panel should be considered, as a valuable extension of an installation rather than as an unnecessary link in every single circuit.

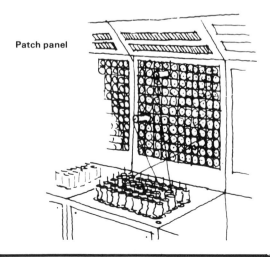

Patch panel

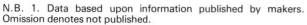

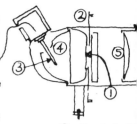

N.B. 1. Data based upon information published by makers. Omission denotes not published.

2. Lamp stated is that in common use.

3. Beam angle = 50% max. intensity.

4. Field angle = 10% max. intensity.

5. Multiplying factor. Multiply throw by this figure to obtain diameter of beam at any throw.

E.g. Patt 23 with 30° F/A @ 5m throw:

5m × ·54 = 2·7m diameter, 15ft × ·54 = 8· 1ft diameter.

6. Peak candela figure is principally of interest for comparative purposes. To establish output of luminaire at any throw use the inverse square law: Divide the Peak candela figure by the square of the throw.

E.g. Patt 23 with 17,000 Candelas @ 5m throw:

$$\frac{17,000}{25 \text{ (throw squared)}} = 680 \text{ lux}$$

7. W = width of lantern

L = length of lantern

H = height of lantern

HY = height of lantern, including the lantern yoke

Wt = weight

Dimensions are given first in millimetres, then inches.

Weight is given first in kilograms, then pounds.

Profile spots provide a beam of any profile which is determined by the shape of the gate aperture (1), and by the use of either built-in shutters (2), or an iris diaphragm, or a gobo or template (a special cut-out metal mask). The maximum amount of light possible is collected from the lamp (3) by a reflector (4) and passed through the gate. The light from the gate is then brought into hard or soft focus by a lens (5). The narrower

Section Lekolit

the beam angle provided by the lens, the greater will be th intensity.

The ideal profile spot will provide an even overall beam that can shaped easily as described and which can then be brought fro hard to very soft focus without undue alteration of the beam size

250/500 watts General backstage and small theatres

750/1000 watts General backstage and FOH medium large theatres

2000 watts Long range

Key to Notes: 1 Shutters. 1a Bifocal shutters. 2 Template slot. Iris included. 3a Iris available. 4 Step Lens. 5 Colour whe available (or changer). 6 Diecast body. 7 Rotating front.

Unit		F/A	B/A	Multi-plying Factor	Lamp	Peak Candela	W	L	H	HY	Wt kg/lb	Notes
Rank Strand (UK) 240 volt	Patt 23	30°	17°	·54	T1 500W T17 500W	17,000	285 11·2"	355 13·9"	235 9·25"	310 12·2"	3·2 6·8	1,2,3a,5,6
	Patt 23W	36°	36°	·65	T1 500W T17 500W	6,500	285 11·2"	355 13·9"	235 9·25"	310 12·2"	3·2 6·8	1,2,3a,5,6
	Patt 23N	11°	11°	·19	T17 500W T13 650W	58,000 84,000	285 11·2"	500 19·6"	235 9·25"	310 12·2"	5·6 12·3	1,2,3a
	Patt 823	22°	18°	·38	T13 650W	52,500	285 11·2"	445 17·5"	235 9·25"	310 12·2"	5·6 12·3	1,2,3,4,5,6
	Patt 813	20° 35°	16° 23°	·35 ·65	T13 650W	80,000 40,000	285 11·2"	490 19·2"	235 9·25"	310 12·2"	7·0 15·5	1,2,3,5,6,Zoom
	Patt 263	28°	18°	·35	T4 1000W	32,600	242 9·5"	565 22·2"	280 11"	395 15·5"	7·5 16·5	1,2,3a,5
	Patt 264	17°	17°	·30	T4 1000W	80,000	242 9·5"	565 22·2"	280 11"	395 15·5"	7·5 16·5	1,1a,2,3a,5
	Patt 764W	28°	20°	·51	T9 1000W	52,500	315 12·4"	610 24"	220 8·6"	415 16·3"	8·1 17·8	1,1a,2,3a,5
	Patt 764	20°	14°	·35	T11 1000W	82,000	315 12·4"	610 24"	220 8·6"	415 16·3"	8·1 17·8	1,1a,2,3a,5
	T Spot 64	22°	18°	·38	T11 1000W	60,000	310 12·2"	560 22"	190 7·4"	462 18·1"	9·0 19·8	1,1a,2,3a
	T Spot 54	30°	24°	·54	T11 1000W	34,000	310 12·2"	560 22"	190 7·4"	462 18·1"	9·0 19·8	1,1a,2,3a
	Patt 774	12°	10°	·21	T11 1000W	134,000	305 12"	800 31·4"	250 9·8"	350 13·7"	12·6 27·7	1,1a,2,3
	Patt 253	24°	24°	·42	CP41 2000W		430 16·9"	770 30·3"	465 18·3"	570 22·4"	24·5 54	1,2,3,6
	Patt 808	14° 24°	12° 18°	·24 ·42	CP43 2000W	300,000 155,000	380 14·9"	1000 39·3"	285 11·2"	515 20·2"	21·5 47·3	1,2,3,Zoom
	Patt 293	13°	8°	·22	A1/218 2000W	235,000	430 16·9"	1005 39·5"	465 18·3"		27·2 59·9	1,2,3,6
	Patt 793	13°	8°	·22	CP56 2000W	400,000	430 16·9"	1005 39·5"	465 18·3"		27·2 59·9	1,2,3(1a available)
C.C.T.(UK) 240 volt	Minuette				M40 T18		160 63"	330 13"	140 5·5"	180 7"	2·2 6·4"	1,2
	Silhouette 30	22° 40°	20°/13° 31°/17°	·39 ·72	T9 T11 1000W	42,600/67,500 30,000/60,500	270 10·6"	510 20"	250 9·8"	420 16·5"	8·8 19·4	1,2,3,5,6,Zoom
	Silhouette 15	16° 23°	9°/6° 19°/9°	·28 ·40	T9 T11 1000W	180,000/251,000 70,000/190,000	270 10·6"	703 27·6"	250 9·8"	420 16·5"	11·8 26	1,2,3,5,6,Zoom
	Silhouette 10	9° 20°	9°/6° 16°/9°	·16 ·35	T9 T11 1000W	251,000/330,800 119,400/239,500	305 12"	860 33·8"	305 12"	420 16·5"	17 37·4	1,2,3,5,6,Zoom
	Silhouette 40	32° 46°	27°/19° 38°/22°	·57 ·84	T9 T11 1000W	32,000/48,000 20,000/40,000	270 10·6"	510 20"	250 9·8"	420 16·5"	8·8 19·4	variant 530: 6

23.
500W. First
best-selling
profile.

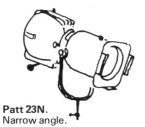

Patt 23N.
Narrow angle.

Patt 264.
1000W. Bi-
focal shutters
for mixed
hard and soft
beam edges.

T Spot.
1000W.

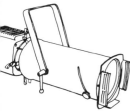

774. 1000W.
ow angle.

Patt 253. 2000W.

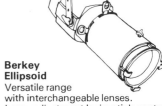

C.C.T. Silhouette.
range. Highly
versatile zoom lens
with interchangeable
lens fronts.

**Berkey
Ellipsoid**
Versatile range
with interchangeable lenses.
Lamp adjustment by joystick control.

Unit		F/A	B/A	Multi-plying Factor	Lamp	Peak Candela	W	L	H	HY	Wt kg/lb	Notes
T.(UK) olt	Silhouette 2000 40	32° 46°	28° 41°	·57 ·84	CP43 2000W	43,800 25,600	270 10·6″	580 22·8″	340 13·3″	490 19·2″	13·4 29·5	1,2,3,5,6,Zoom
	Silhouette 2000 30	23° 40°	18° 36°	·40 ·72	CP43 2000W	86,000/97,000 32,000/38,000	270 10·6″	580 22·8″	340 13·3″	490 19·2″	13·4 29·5	1,2,3,5,6,Zoom
	Silhouette 2000 15	12° 23°	9° 17°	·20 ·40	CP43 2000W	248,000 167,000	270 10·6″	770 30·3″	340 13·3″	490 19·2″	16·2 35·7	1,2,3,5,6,Zoom
	Silhouette 2000 10	10° 19°	8° 13°	·17 ·33	CP43 2000W	390,000 216,000	310 12·2″	920 36·2″	340 13·3″	490 19·2″	21·7 47·8	1,2,3,5,6,Zoom
ey Ellipsoid (US) olt	40°	40°	15°	·73	FEL 1000W (or 240 volts)	112,000 (78,000)	381 15″	698 27·5″	381 15″	622 24·5″	9·1 20·1	1,2,3a,6
	30°	30°	11·0° (11.5°)	·54	FEL 1000W (or 240 volts)	154,000 (112,000)	381 15″	698 27·5″	381 15″	622 24·5″	9·1 20·1	1,2,3a,6
	20°	20°	8·3° (14°)	·35	FEL 1000W (or 240 volts)	224,000 (136,000)	381 15″	698 27·5″	381 15″	622 24·5″	8·8 19·5	1,2,3a,6
	12°	12°	5·5° (6·6°)	·21	FEL 1000W (or 240 volts)	324,000 (198,000)	381 15″	698 27·5″	381 15″	622 24·5″	8·6 19·1	1,2,3a,6
	10°	10°	4·3° (6·6°)	·17	FEL 1000W (or 240 volts)	585,000 (377,240)	381 15″	775 30·5″	381 15″	622 24·5″	9·6 21·1	1,2,3a
	5°	5°	2·6° (5°)	·09	FEL 1000W (or 240 volts)	1,000,000 (576,000)	381 15″	1054 41·5″	381 15″	952 37·5″	13·7 30·3	1,2,3a
ey Mini-ellipse (US) olt	50°	50°	22°	·93	500Q/CL 120V	19,476	330 13″	430 17″	125 5″		3·9 8·7	1,2,3a
	40°	40°	22°	·73	500Q/CL 120V	31,600	330 13″	430 17″	125 5″		3·9 8·7	1,2,3a
	30°	30°	11°	·54	500Q/CL 120V	58,000	330 13″	430 17″	125 5″		3·9 8·7	1,2,3a
nd Century Lekolites (US) olt	3½″ × 6″ 2115	32°	25°	·58	FDA 400W	9,900	229 9″	295 11·6″	229 9″	273 10·7″	3·6 8	1,2
	3½″ × 8″ 2125	24°	18°	·42	FDA 400W	15,300	229 9″	318 12·5″	229 9″	273 10·7″	3·6 8	1,2
	4½″ × 6½″ 2211	50°	38°	·93	EGC 500W	17,500	289 11·4″	406 16″		613 24·1″	5·9 13	1,2,6
	6″ × 9″ 2321	40°	24°	·73	EGF 750W	48,000	289 11·4″	406 16″		613 24·1″	6·8 15	1,2,3a,6
	6″ × 12″ 2331	28°	16°	·5	EGF 750W	88,000	289 11·4″	406 16″		613 24·1″	6·8 15	1,2,3a,6
	6″ × 16″ 2333	20·5°	16°	·35	EGF 750W	154,800	289 11·4″	433 17″		613 24·1″	5·9 13	1,2,3a,6
	6″ × 6″ 2341	28°	18°	·5	EGF 750W	74,700	289 11·4″	406 16″		613 24·1″	5·9 13	1,2,3a,4,6
	6″ × 6″ 2335	22·5°	14·5°	·4	EGJ 1000W	150,000	305 12″	876 34·5″		699 27·5″	19 42	1,2,3a,4

Unit		F/A	B/A	Multi-plying Factor	Lamp	Peak Candela	W	L	H	HY	Wt kg/lb	Notes
Strand Century Lekolites (US) 120 volt	6″ × 9″ 2327	32°	16°	·57	EGJ 1000W	87,200	305 12″	876 34·5″		699 27·5″	19 42	1,2,3a
	6″ × 12″ 2337	22·5°	12·5°	·4	EGJ 1000W	176,000	305 12″	876 34·5″		699 27·5″	19 42	1,2,3a
	8″ × 9″ 2457	15°	7·5°	·26	EGJ 1000W	307,200	305 12″	965 38″		699 27·5″	20·4 45	1,2,3a,4
	10″ × 12″ 2567	10·5°	7·5°	·19	EGJ 1000W	420,000	305 12″	965 38″		699 27·5″	21·8 48	1,2,3a,4
	12″ × 12″ 2669	10·5°	7·5°	·19	BWA 2000W	640,000	356 14″	1016 40″		724 28·5″	23·6 52	1,2,3a,4
Kliegl Bros. Kieglight (US) 120 volt	6″ × 3¾″ 1355W	27°	27°	·5	EHG 750W	52,000	345 13·5″	560 22″	230 9″	495 19·5″	6·4 14	1,2,3a,4
	6″ × 8″ 1355	18°	18°	·32	EHG 750W	125,600	345 13·5″	560 22″	230 9″	495 19·5″	6·4 14	1,2,3a,4
	8″ × 12″ 1355/8	12°	12°	·21	EHG 750W	246,400	345 13·5″	675 26·5″	230 9″	495 19·5″	7·3 16	1,2,3a,4
	6″ × 8″ 1360	18°	18°	·32	EHG 750W	125,600	345 13·5″	560 22″	230 9″	495 19·5″	6·8 15	1,2,3a,4,7
	6″ × 3¾″ 1360W	27°	27°	·5	EHG 750W	52,000	345 13·5″	560 22″	230 9″	495 19·5″	6·8 15	1,2,3a,4,7
	8″ × 12″ 1360/8	12°	12°	·21	EHG 750W	246,400	345 13·5″	675 26·5″	230 9″	495 19·5″	8·2 19	1,2,3a,4,7
	6″ × 6″ 1357	27°	27°	·5	DWT 1000W	59,200	410 16″	660 26″	250 10″	700 27·2″	10·8 24	1,2,3a,4
	6″ × 8″ 1357/6	18°	18°	·32	DWT 1000W	120,000	410 16″	660 26″	250 10″	700 27·2″	9·4 21	1,2,3,4
	8″ × 12″ 1355/8	13°	13°	·22	DWT 1000W	251,200	410 16″	800 31·5″	250 10″	700 27·2″	10·8 24	1,2,3,4
	10″ × 15″ 1357/10	9°	9°	·16	DWT 1000W	415,000	410 16″	900 35·5″	250 10″	700 27·2″	12·6 28	1,2,3,4
	12″ × 16″ 1357/12	8°	8°	·14	DWT 1000W	420,000	410 16″	940 37″	300 12″	700 27·2″	12·6 28	1,2,3,4
Electro Controls Parellipsphere 170 (US) 120 volt		35° 22°	21° 13°	·65 ·38°	EGJ 1000W	99,413 161,967	325 12·7″	629 24·7″	261 10·2″	442 17·2″		1,2,3a,6 Zoom
Reiche & Vogel Ellipsenspiegel (Germany)	EL650	18°	18°	·33	GX9 650W	64,800	300 11·8″	500 19·7		430 17″	12 26·5	1,2,3,5,7
	EL 2000	17°	17°	·30	GY16 2000W	200,000	520 20·4″	840 33·1″		650 25·6″	28 62	1,2,3,5

3½″ Lekolite.

6″ Lekolite.

8″ Lekolite. 1000W.

12″ Lekolite. 2000W.

Parellipsphere 170. Zoom lens profile With several new features.

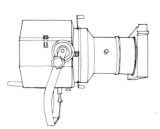

Reiche & Vogel 650W.

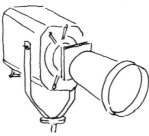

Reiche & Vogel 2000W.

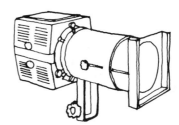

Niethammer HPS 111.

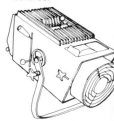

Pani HV 650.

Profile Spots

Unit		F/A	B/A	Multiplying Factor	Lamp	Peak Candela	W	L	H	HY	Wt kg/lb	Notes
Emil Niethammer (Germany) 220 volt	HPS 111	11°	11°	·19	1000W	264,000						1,2,3
	HPS 217	17°	17°	·30	2000W	242,000						1,2,3
Pani (Austria)	HV 650	22° 11°	22° 11°	·38 ·19	G6. 650W		345 13·5"	568 798 22′ 31·4"		360 14·1"	13 28·6	1,2,3,5,6,7
	HV 1000	15° 10°	15° 10°	·26 ·17	G6. 1000W	225,000 375,000	345 13·5"	568 798 22′ 31·4"		360 14·1"		1,2,3,5,6,7
	HV 2000	22° 11°	22° 11°	·38 ·19°	GY16. 2000W		385 15·1"	775 1040 30·4′ 41"		450 17·7	25 55	1,2,3,5,6,7

Follow spots

Unit		F/A	B/A	Multiplying Factor	Lamp	Peak Candela	W	L	H Max.	Wt (with stand) Kg/lb
Rank Strand (UK)	Patt 793	13°	8°	·22	CP56 2000W	400,000	430 16·9"	1005 39·3"	1975 77·7"	40·7 90
	Patt 265* Halospot	18·5°	10·5°	·32	400W Merc. 600W Merc	304,000 410,000	290 11·5"	735 29"	360 14"	13 28·5
	Patt 765	14°	11°	·24	1000W CSI	770,000	430 16·9"	1050 41·3"	1975 77·7"	68·2 150
C.C.T. (US)	CSI Sil 10*	** 9° 20°	9°/6° 16°/9°	·16 ·35	1000W CSI	1,050,000	305 12"	1035 40·7"	403 15·8"	24·0 53
	CSI Sil 15*	** 16° 23°	9°/6° 19°/9°	·28 ·40	1000W CSI	730,000	250 9·8"	878 34·5"	403 15·8"	18·5 41
Berkey (US)	Colorspot I	9°		·16	FEL 1000W	800,000	810 32"	890 35"	1800 71"	51·7 114
	Colorspot II	9°		·16	1200W HMI	2,400,000	810 32"	890 35"	1800 71"	87·8 193
Strong (US)	Trouperette	** 7° 22°		·12 ·38	1000W 120V	396,500 82,500	660 26"	840 33"	1960 77"	34 74
	Trouper	** 4·5° 26°		·08 ·50	Carbons	1,792,000 32,000	710 28"	1600 63"	1650 65"	102 225
	Supertrouper	** 2·9° 14°		·05 ·25	Carbons	12,000,000 460,000	737 29"	2050 80·5"	2000 79"	179 395
	Xenon Supertrouper	** 4° 8°		·06 ·14	1600W Xenon	10,544,800 2,422,800	812 32"	1968 77·5"	2082 82"	225 496
Reiche & Vogel (Germany)	Lichtkanone				4000W HMI					
Pani (Austria)	CV 1000*	** 10° 17°		·17 ·30	1000W CSI		345 13·5"	798 31·4"	360 14"	

*Without stand dimensions

**Zoom

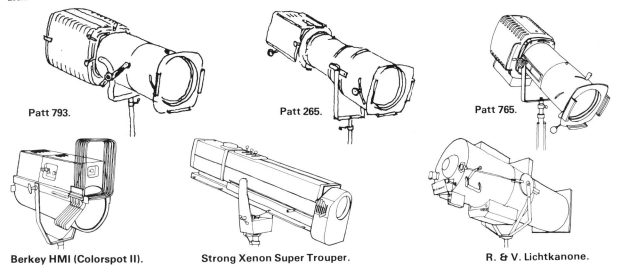

Patt 793. **Patt 265.** **Patt 765.**

Berkey HMI (Colorspot II). **Strong Xenon Super Trouper.** **R. & V. Lichtkanone.**

Fresnel spots
Soft edged beam. Adjustable in spread by relative movement of lamp and lens. Barn doors can be fitted to give some control of beam shape and stray light. Stepped lenses can be obtained with blackened risers, described as COLOUVERED, to reduce stray and scatter light. These are usually preferred for general purposes.

250/500 watts General backstage small theatres
750/1000 watts General backstage/FOH
2000 watts Special purpose medium & large
5000-10,000 watts Special effect

1 Short focus fresnel lens
2 Lamp
3 Spherical reflector
4 Movable tray carrying lamp and reflector

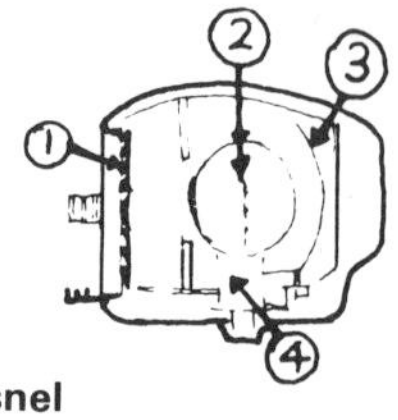

Section Fresnel

Unit		SPOT FOCUS F/A	B/A	Multi-plying Factor	Peak Candela	FLOOD FOCUS F/A	B/A	Multi-plying Factor	Peak Candela	Lamp	W	L	HY	Wt Kg/lb
Rank Strand (UK) 240 volt	Patt 45	14°	8°	·24	21,560	45°	36°	·83	3,780	T1 500W	230 9″	290 11·4″	320 12·5″	3·7 8·4
	Patt 123	26°	16°	·46	16,960	51°	42°	·95	5,400	T1 500W	265 10·4″	265 10·4″	320 12·5″	2·6 5·7
	Patt 223	18°	10°	·32	92,030	70°	60°	1·4	9,900	T6 1000W	345 13·5″	320 12·5″	395 15·5″	6·8 14·9
	Patt 743	15°	8°	·26	124,460	70°	60°	1·4	10,980	T9 1000W	345 13·5″	320 12·5″	395 15·5″	6·8 14·9
	Patt 243 BP	16°	10°	·28	280,280	50°	40°	·94	41,565	CP41 2000W	405 15·9″	430 16·9″	500 19·6″	14 30·8
	Patt 803	13°	8°	·22	65,000	65°	50°	1·27	4,500	T13 650W	270 10·6″	300 11·8″	330 12·9″	5·5 12
C.C.T. (UK) 240 volt	Minuette	20°	9°	·35	20,500	74°	64°	1·5	3,100	M40 500W	160 6·3″	212 8·3″	243 9·5″	2·0″ 4·4″
	650	15°		·26		55°		1·04		T12 650W	290 11·4″	290 11·4″	350 13·7″	4·8 19·1
	1000	15°		·26	113,400	55°		1·04	17,000	T11 1000W	290 11·4″	290 11·4″	350 13·7″	4·8 19·1
	2000	15°		·26	243,000	51°		·95	37,200	CP43 2000W	355 13·9″	356 14″	460 18·1″	8·7 19·1
	5000	12°		·21	500,000	54°		1·0	90,000	CP29 5000W	355 13·9″	356 14″	460 18·1″	8·7 19·1
Strand Century (US) 120 volt	3″ 3142	16°	8·5°	·28	5,800	58°	38°	1·11	2,227	250Q CL/DC	174 6⅞″	149 5⅞″	225 8⅞″	1·8 4
	6″ 3342	17°	8°	·3	80,100	45·5°	32°	·84	16,000	BTL 500W	241 9½″	225 8⅞″	318 12½″	3·2 7
	8″ 3413	16°	9°	·29	392,000	33°	21°	·59	68,800	BVW 2000W	324 12¾″	359 14⅛″	482 19″	7·8 17
Kliegl (US)	4½″ 3604	18°		·32	40,400	54°		1·0	9,500	BWM 750W	184 7¼″	196 7¾″	285 11¼″	4·1 9
	6″ 3606	18°		·32	70,425	62°		1·2	29,600	EHG 750W	254 10″	342 13½″	393 15½″	5·9 13
	8″ 3608	14°		·24	186,400	54°		1·0	23,600	CYV 1000W	304 12″	339 13⅜″	444 17½″	9·1 20
Berkey (US)	6″ 100-412	19°	10·5°	·33	13,600	54°	44°	1·0	20,400	BWN 1000W	279 11″	292 11½″	330 13″	
	8″ 100-362	13°	6·5°	·22	336,000	44°	36°	·81	38,000	CXZ 1500W	317 12½″	279 11″	482 19″	
Reiche & Vogel (Germany)	H650		9°		90,000		55°		9,000	650W	400 15·7″	330 12·9″	570 22·4″	
	H200N		15°		250,000		53°		19,200	2000W	430 16·9″	400 15·7″	610 24″	
	55N		19°		432,000		43°		104,000	5000W	675 26·5″	570 22·4″	895 35·2″	
Pani (Austria)	ST5000		6°		750,000	60°	16°	1·15		5000W	500 19·6″	530 20·8″	710 27·9″	28 61

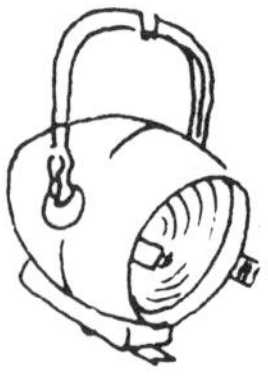

Patt 123.

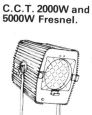

C.C.T. 2000W and 5000W Fresnel.

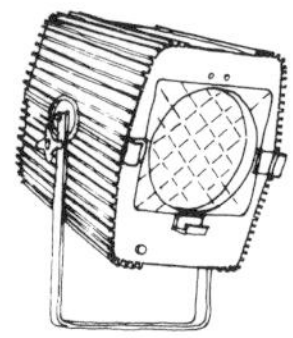

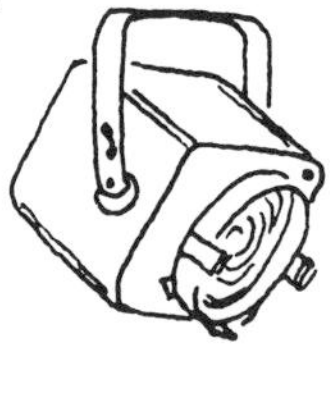

Patt 743.

8″ Fresnelite spot.

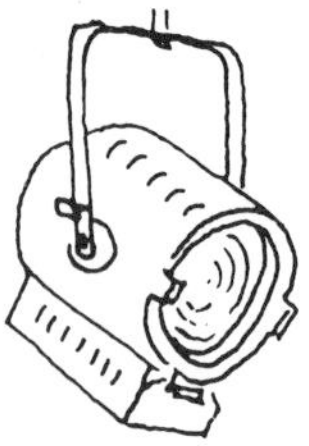

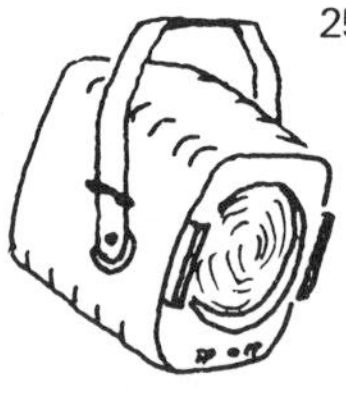

Patt 243.

Century Beam Projector 250W – 1000W.

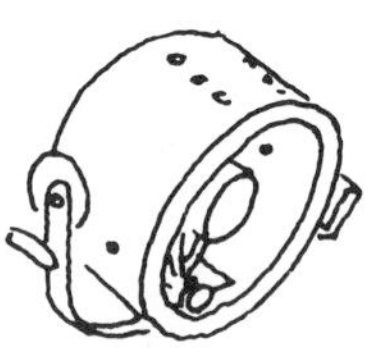

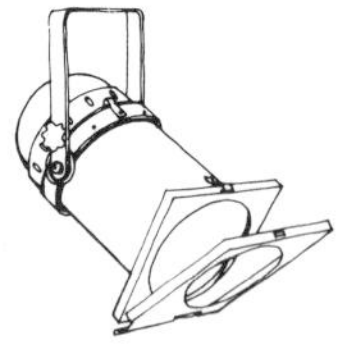

C.C.T. Parhead ('Rockette').

Lanterns

The beam light or beam projector provides a very narrow and intense beam of light, using a parabolic reflector and no lens. The Fresnel spotlight focused right down to a small spot is not a true substitute, since it does not give the sharp, clear beam of the beam light.

Basically this lantern is a small searchlight for theatrical use, and it should be employed for strong shafts of high-intensity light. It can be used through windows to suggest sunlight; or, on a large stage, banks of beam lights can be employed for backlight, side-light, etc. The lantern has a reflector (1) which sends all the rays that strike it forward in a near-parallel beam. To stop direct diverging light coming from the lamp (2), a spherical reflector (3) can be placed in front to re-direct rays back to the parabolic reflector. In some types of beam light, the spherical reflector may be incorporated within the lamp itself, i.e. crown-silvered lamps. Circular baffles fulfil the same purpose, intercepting and absorbing unwanted stray light.

A good beam light provides a greater light intensity at lower cost and weight than a profile or Fresnel spot with comparable wattage. Using a low-voltage lamp (and transformer) gives even better results.

Unit		F/A	B/A	Multi-plying Factor	Lamp	Peak Candela	W	L	H	Wt kg/lb
Rank Strand (UK)	Patt 750	9°	6°	·16	T11 1000W	329,760	380	325	385	4·2
		18°	18°	·31			15″	12·7″	15·1″	9·2
Strand Century (US)	10″	15°	8°	·26	BTR 1000W	292,000	365	264	305	6·1
		125°	12°	·44		121,500	14·3″	10·3″	12″	13·5″
	15″	16°	9°	·28	BVW 2000W	592,000	460	368	584	
		30°	22°	·53		120,800	18·1″	14·5	23″	
Reiche & Vogel (Germany)	250W	12°		·2	250W 24V	450,000	285	305	425	12
							11·2″	12″	16·7″	26·4
	500W	8°		·13	500W 24V	800,000	335	345	495	15·15
							13 2″	13·5″	19·4″	34
	1000W				1000W 24V					18
										39·6
Pani (Austria)	P500				500W 24V		275	375	400	5·9
							10·8″	14·7″	15·7″	13
	P1000				1000W 24V		320	430	480	8·0
							12·5″	16·9″	18·8″	17·6

PAR lamps and reflector lamps are not simply another form of floodlight. The PAR lamp, which is available in a vast range of types up to 1000 watts at various voltages in the United States, is newer in England but is a most important stage lighting tool. These lamps used in a batten (border-light) can be very effective as backlight or downlight. This is particularly useful for the musical stage since a batten can skimlight a cloth and downlight the area in front of it at the same time. If adjacent surfaces are not intended to be lit, the batten should be used with some form of cut-off mask similar to a barn door on a Fresnel.

Used individually in 'Parheads' the PAR lamp provides a compact, powerful fixed beam spotlight, which in the larger PAR 64 size is marvellous as a provider of high-key colour.

The following schedule shows the common range of lamps and their beam angles. It should be noted that most lamps have a rectangular beam; by turning the lamp through 90° in the fitting some variety of effect can be achieved. Also partially listed, where they are of interest to the theatre, are a wide range of low voltage PAR lamps made for such purposes as aircraft landing lights. (See manufacturers' catalogues for more information.)

Lamp		B/A	Candela
PAR 36	5·5V 25W	*4·5° × 5·5°	30,000
	12V 25W VWFL	33° × 40°	250
	12V 25W WFL	26° × 37°	500
	12V 25W NSP	8° × 10°	4,500
	12V 50W VWFL	37° × 40°	600
	12V 50W WFL	28° × 36°	1,300
	12V 50W NSP	9° × 11°	9,200
PAR 38	240V 150W FL	40°	3,000
	240V 150W SP	15°	7,500
	120V 150W WFL	61°	1,400
	120V 150W FL	31°	4,000
	120V 150W SP	14°	11,500

Lamp		B/A	Candela
PAR 46	5·5V 25W	*4·5° × 5·5°	55,000
PAR 56	120V 300W WFL	18° × 37°	11,000
	120V 300W MFL	11° × 23°	24,000
	120V 300W NSP	8° × 10°	68,000
	120V Q500W WFL	20° × 44°	19,00
	120V Q500W MFL	10° × 26°	43,000
	120V Q500W NSP	7° × 13°	96,000
PAR 64	120V Q1000W WFL	24° × 48°	40,000
	120V Q1000W MFL	12° × 28°	125,000
	120V Q1000W NSP	7° × 14°	290.000
	120V Q1000W VNSP	6° × 12°	400,000

* Field angle quoted.

Patt 60.

Patt 49.

AC 1001.

Strand Century 14″.

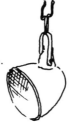

Kliegl 18″ Scoop.

Unit		Lamp	Max. Beam	W	L	HY	Wt kg/lb
Rank (UK) 240v	Patt 137	100/200W	105°	324 12·75″	241 9·5″	292 11·5″	3·6 8
	Patt 60	300/500W	80°	367 14·5″	367 14·5″	400 15·75″	5·5 12
	Patt 49	1000W	120°	383 19″	292 11·5″	540 21·25″	9 20
	Patt 749	1000W T11	105°				10 22
C.C.T. (UK) 240v	AC 1001	625/750/1000 1250W		360 14·2″	120 4·7″	340 13·3″	2·8 6·16
	AC 1004C	4 × above		700 27·5″	120 4·7″	750 29·5″	11 24·2
	AC 1004L	4 × above		1260 49·6″	120 4·7″	340 13·3″	11 24·2
Strand Century (US) 120v	10″	100/400W	113°	273 10·75		508 20″	
	4271 14″	500/1000W	130°	406 16″	349 13·75″	508 20″	4·1 9
	4273 18″	750/2000W	110°	470 18·5″	392 15·5″	616 24·5″	4·1 9
Kliegl (US) 120v	3450 12″	300/500W	102°	368 14·5″	317 12·5″	546 21·5″	3·6 8
	3451 16″	500/1000W	102°	470 18·5″	394 15·5″	597 23·5″	3·6 8
	1155 18″	1000/2000W	106°	520 20·5″	381 15″	749 29·5″	3·6 8

Strand Century (US)

Roundel Batten 200/300W
16·5 cm (6½″) reflectors to any length, 3 circuits
Heat resistant glass roundels
W = 222 mm (8¾″)
H = 295 mm (11⅞″)

Roundel batten.

Rank Strand (UK)

'S' type battens 150W
1·8m (6′) length, 8 compartments, 3 or 4 circuits
W = 587mm (11⅛″)
H = 587mm (11⅛″)

S type batten.

Ianiro (Italy)

Strand Century (US distributor)
Rank Strand (UK distributor)

'Iris' Cyclorama Quartz Lighting System
Modular — 1,2,3 or 4 unit
   combinations
625W(240V)/1000W(120, 240V)/
   1250W(240V)/1500W(120V)
W = 922mm (36 5/16″)
H = 868mm (34 3/16″)
L = 248mm (9¾″)

The tubular tungsten-halogen lamp permits a very slim unit. Intense heat, however, requires the use of one of the new heat-resistant colour media.

Iris Cyclorama 4 unit/4 circuit system.

Berkey (US)

Q — Batten/G-Row 4 = 500/625/800W
W = 914mm (36″)
H = 324mm (12¾″)
L = 206mm (8⅛″)

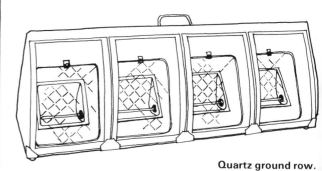

Quartz ground row.

Rank Strand (UK)

PATT 252 1000/2000W projector
6″ condenser lens
For 3¼″ × 3¼″ or 3¼″ × 4″
slides or moving effects
(see Mechanics pp 170-2).
W = 415mm (16⅜″)
L = 400mm (15⅞″)
H = 385mm (15⅛″)
HY = 505mm (19⅞″)
Wt = 16·5 Kg (36lb)

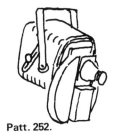

Patt. 252.

PATT 752 4000W 110V projector
For 13 cm × 13 cm or 18 cm × 18
cm slides.
High power scene projection with
wider beam spread resulting from
large slide. Slide can be rotated in
holder through 20°.
W = 600mm (w/base) (27″)
L = 795mm (31¼″)
H=804mm (31⅝″)
Wt = 56·5 Kg (125lb)

Patt. 752.

Reiche & Vogel (Germany)

2000W Projector
For 13 cm × 13 cm slides or
moving effects. 3 elements
interchangeable lens assembly
8·25 cm with small fan.
W = 383mm (19″)
L = 762mm (30″)
HY = 600mm (23⅝″)

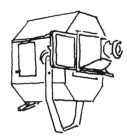

Reiche & Vogel 2000W.

*5000W Projector 240V or 110V high power wide angle scene
projector*
For 13cm × 13cm or 18cm × 18cm slides. Vernier adjustment on
pan and tilt. Slide rotatable in holder through 20°. Vignette blades
to facilitate joining projections.
W=600mm (w/base) (23⅝″)   L = 1110mm (43¾″)
HY = 864mm (34″)   WT = 132·7kg (292lb) inc. transformer.

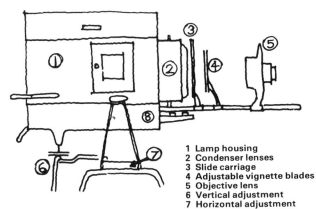

1 Lamp housing
2 Condenser lenses
3 Slide carriage
4 Adjustable vignette blades
5 Objective lens
6 Vertical adjustment
7 Horizontal adjustment
8 Fans

5000W projector.

Pani HMI BP4 (Austria)

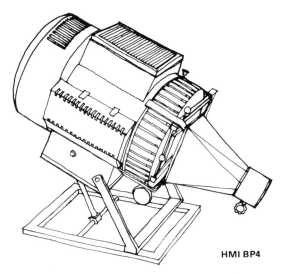

HMI BP4

4000W HMI lamp 380/220V 50HZ
23cm dia. 3 element condenser lens with
carrier for 18cm × 18cm slides.
A breakthrough in high power projectors, offering far greater light
output than ever before available in a projector.
Objective lenses 14·2, 18, 22, 27, 33, 40 or 50cm focal length.
L × 1000mm (3′3″) Wt = 86kg (189lb) excl. objective lens
and external regulation unit.

RDS Effects Projection System (Japan)

David Hersey Assoc. (UK distributor)

Flexible system employing
either a 1000W Quartz
Halogen or a CSI lamp house.
This can be mounted in the
conventional horizontal
arrangement or in a vertical
projection unit. Primary
effects units include: slide
carriage, disc machine, spiral
and film loop machines.
Secondary effects include:
flicker, prism, kaleidoscopic
and rotating mirror devices. A
wide range of variable slide or
gobo, still or moving effects
can be achieved.

**Carousel.
Effect Projection System**

Kodak (US)

*Carousel S Projector 150W
tungsten halogen*

For 80 2″ × 2″ slides.
Interchangeable lenses 60mm,
85mm, 100mm, 150mm,
180mm, 250mm, & 70mm —
120mm zoom

Carousel S-AV Projector 250W 24V tungsten halogen
80 2″ × 2″ slides and same lenses as Carousel S

Lantern symbols

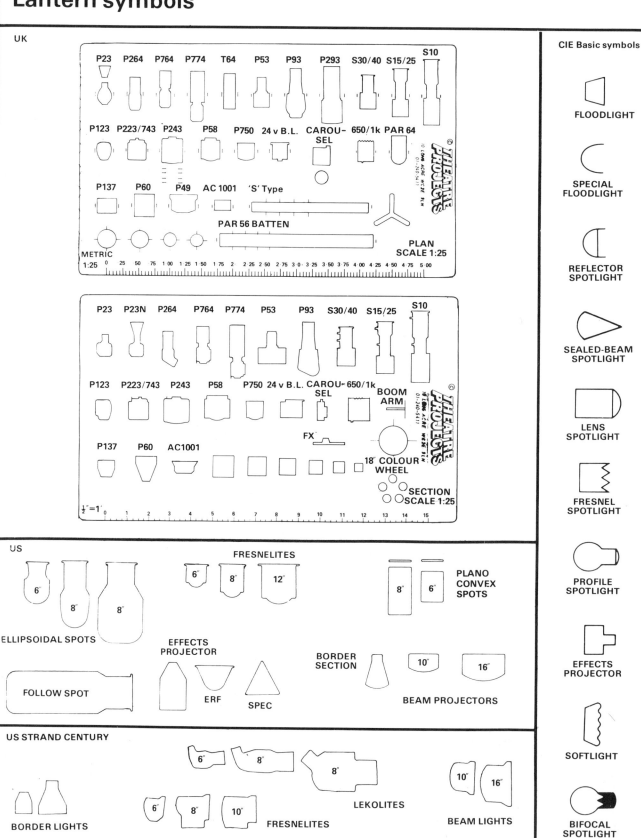

UK

P23 P264 P764 P774 T64 P53 P93 P293 S30/40 S15/25 S10

P123 P223/743 P243 P58 P750 24 v B.L. CAROU-SEL 650/1k PAR 64

P137 P60 P49 AC 1001 'S' Type

PAR 56 BATTEN

METRIC 1:25

PLAN SCALE 1:25

P23 P23N P264 P764 P774 P53 P93 S30/40 S15/25 S10

P123 P223/743 P243 P58 P750 24 v B.L. CAROU-SEL 650/1k BOOM ARM

P137 P60 AC1001 FX

18″ COLOUR WHEEL

SECTION SCALE 1:25

½″=1′

US

FRESNELITES

6″ 8″ 12″

PLANO CONVEX SPOTS

8″ 6″

6″ 8″ 8″

ELLIPSOIDAL SPOTS

EFFECTS PROJECTOR

BORDER SECTION

10″ 16″

FOLLOW SPOT

ERF SPEC

BEAM PROJECTORS

US STRAND CENTURY

6″ 8″ 8″

10″ 16″

BORDER LIGHTS

6″ 8″ 10″

LEKOLITES

BEAM LIGHTS

FRESNELITES

CIE Basic symbols

FLOODLIGHT

SPECIAL FLOODLIGHT

REFLECTOR SPOTLIGHT

SEALED-BEAM SPOTLIGHT

LENS SPOTLIGHT

FRESNEL SPOTLIGHT

PROFILE SPOTLIGHT

EFFECTS PROJECTOR

SOFTLIGHT

BIFOCAL SPOTLIGHT

Calculation of lighting angles

Calculation of lighting angles

The acting area is first divided into modules of a chosen size, in this instance I have chosen 8′: the most useful size is usually between 6′ and 12′.

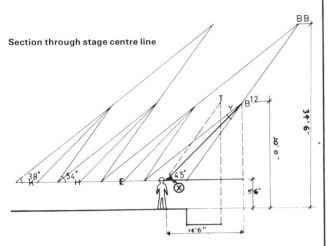

Section through stage centre line

The actor is placed in the centre of the acting area in position B. Assuming his eye level to be 5′ 6″ above the floor, all angular calculations will be taken from this height. First we will draw in the vertical angle at which the lamp is required: I have called this angle 'X', and in this case we want it 45° from the horizontal. We then draw a line upward till we reach the ceiling, in this case at 20′. This is the supposed level at which the lanterns can be rigged. We then draw lines to the up- and downstage sides of area B; this gives an angle of 54° at the front and about 38° at the back. This exercise can be repeated for the other areas of the stage E, H and K. The drawing, being a section through the stage centre line, shows the spotlight beams as they would be if the lanterns were going to be mounted directly to the actor's front. We would need a lantern of 16° width (angle Y) and the lantern would be mounted (in plan) 14′ 6″ away from the centre point of the module. But we have already decided that we want to place the lantern not in front of the actor but 45° to his side.

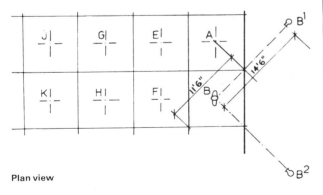

Plan view

If we move to the plan, we can first draw the acting area modules and mark the actor at point B. We know that to achieve the angle X vertically, we have to place the lantern 14′ 6″ away if the ceiling height is at 20′. We can draw this in plan, as shown, and this will give the true position of lanterns B1 and B2. Transferring this back to the section, we can mark this true position as position T. The last piece of information we can extract is the real beam angle that is required. We see from the plan that the actual area that the lantern has to cover is not 8′ wide but 11′ 6″ wide, being the

diagonal across the square module. Accordingly, if we draw a section through the actual beam of the lantern, we find that the true beam angle required is 25°.

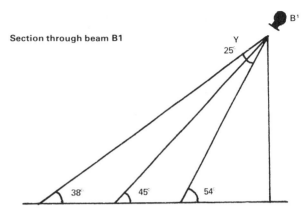

Section through beam B1

We can also see from the original section the effect of an increased ceiling height. If we go to the level at 34′ 6″, we will see that the whole area of the stage can be covered from two positions instead of four to give the same angles. But we must remember that it may be very undesirable to have such large areas. Furthermore, equipment needed for a long throw such as this would have to be more powerful and would consequently be expensive.

We have noted earlier that the angle of 45°, used on its own, can be rather severe when lighting some actors' faces. We should also, therefore, employ some lower lighting angle of about 20°-25° as a 'fill-light', but if this is not available the front of house lighting angle should almost certainly be lowered to around 35°.

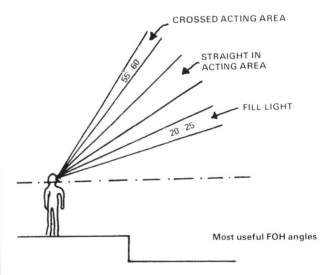

Most useful FOH angles

We can see that a position which is lighting one part of the stage at one angle is very likely to serve, in another way, for another part of the acting area. Thus the 55°-60° position provides crossed acting area lighting to the front edge of the stage but straight-in light at the 45° angle farther back.

In conclusion it must be stressed that the angles which we have been discussing are the basic ones for *illumination*. Any and indeed almost every other angle may be required for effect lighting.

Rigging

Front of house lighting positions

An electrician should have easy access to every position where lighting equipment is rigged. Front of house overhead lighting should, wherever possible, be positioned on bridges, along which the electrician can work, running above the auditorium.

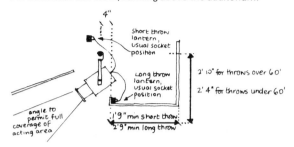

There should be separate access from outside the auditorium and the electrician should be able to get up to the bridge during a performance without disturbing the audience. The exact design of these positions has to be considered most carefully; the lantern must not only light the front of the stage but should be able to cover the whole stage area. The adjacent areas of ceiling must not interfere with the beam and it should be remembered that the electrician setting the lantern must be able to see the part of the stage at which he is aiming. The ceiling around a lighting bridge must be finished in a dark non-reflective colour. The same rules apply to slots in the side wall of the auditorium; the lantern fixing should be adjustable in height and a vertical ladder or staircase should give access to a series of levels about 7′ apart all the way up the slot.

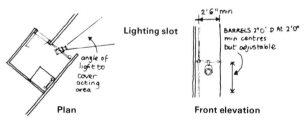

Plan   **Front elevation**

Lanterns for a low angle light to the stage will probably be fixed around the front edge of any circle in the auditorium. This position will be less commonly used and the lanterns can simply be hung on a pipe cantilevered out from the gallery front. If possible the lantern should be concealed in some form of housing designed as part of the circle front; this is particularly important if the lantern is used with any colour change equipment (which is quite large and rather cumbersome in appearance). If the lanterns are enclosed the electrician, when setting them, must be able to get at the locking nuts, masking shutters and focus. Similarly, a trapdoor to reach a lantern is useless if its open flap prevents the electrician seeing the stage.

Proscenium — downstage areas

The area immediately behind the proscenium, both overhead and to the sides, is a vitally important position. Although this statement may seem at first to conflict with what has already been said about the 45° angle, it does not, in fact, do so. The 45° angle is essential for lighting the face but it is light from more acute

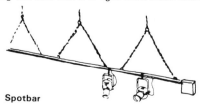

Spotbar

angles that produces the more dramatic and interesting lighting composition. Light coming from the proscenium zone itself is usually the most important in a proscenium production.

This is the place for the traditional spotbar, a pipe of gas barrel or aluminium (external diameter 50mm or $1\frac{29}{32}$″) from which lanterns are hung with a barrel clamp. The pipe may be wired internally as shown or the feed cables may be strapped along it externally.

On a complex production it is quite common to find two spotbars right at the front of the stage stacked one above the other. The first bar is used principally for lighting upstage and the second for downlighting and crosslighting. In this position I usually prefer to use profile spots. Their size depends upon the type of production and the height at which the spotbar is to be hung (which in turn depends upon the proscenium height).

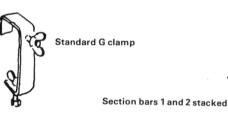

Standard G clamp

Section bars 1 and 2 stacked

There are inevitably times when the set designer is simply unable to provide space for lighting behind the proscenium. One such production was Lionel Bart's *Blitz* set, designed by Sean Kenny. In this moving scenery, which included a massive bridge spanning the whole stage, came right down to the fire curtain. There was no question of hanging either spotbar or booms within the stage area. Since the production was a very large one we were able to rig a substitute spotbar and booms on either side, outside the proscenium arch. These formed, in effect, an entire proscenium of lighting units. (See Pl. 14)

The position just outside the proscenium is an extremely useful one, and new proscenium theatres being planned should certainly consider a front of house lighting position in the form of a bridge in the auditorium ceiling, and slots in either wall, immediately adjacent to the proscenium and in front of it.

Upstage areas

The design of the top of the set, including any ceiling borders or top masking, will dictate how far upstage we can light from the number one spotbar (1st pipe) position. On a deep stage we will find that the upstage areas have to be lit from a second or third spotbar hung farther back. If the angles to the upstage areas are very steep, we may need further fill-light from the front. Any acting areas above the stage on rostra will need particular attention and a section drawn through the set will help when working out lighting positions for these. If any action takes place beneath an upper level, the overhang may cut off the ordinary lighting and it will be necessary to conceal some small units (e.g. 100 w Fresnels) within the rostrum to light this 'inner-stage'.

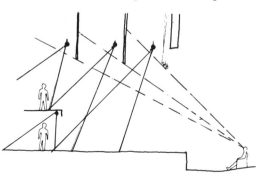

Section showing upper level platform

168

Rigging

Backlight

Backlighting can present other problems since we are even more dependent upon the top masking. No masking at all makes things much easier for the designer, since it imposes no limitation on the angles to which he can set his lamps. If borders or ceilings have to be contended with, we once again must sit down at the drawing

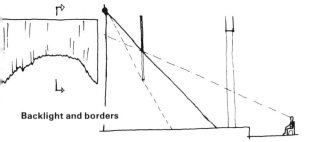

Backlight and borders

board and work out the problem in section. Particular attention must be paid to the bottoms of the borders if they are shaped in any way. The audience's sight-line must be drawn not to the lowest point but to the highest, as this is the highest point they will be able to see. This forces the backlight bar upwards, and yet at another point along the bar we may have to light under the lowest point. If this is really restricting, the lanterns can be rigged at different heights along the bar.

Sidelight

The simplest way to sidelight is to put the lantern on a telescopic stand. This is easily accessible for colour-changing and moving out, unless we are imitating an off-stage low-level light source, there is rarely any need for this angle of light. Natural sunlight at an almost horizontal angle is very rare, only occurring at the last moments of dawn or sunset, and even then it is very often obscured by neighbouring houses, trees and hills. Horizontal light brings other problems: actors cast shadows on one another; they get in one another's light and as they exit towards the 'sunset' they become strangely and suddenly brighter.

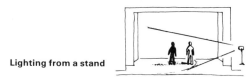

Lighting from a stand

Sidelighting, except in exceptional cases, should be mounted above head height and the most practical method is to rig the lanterns on a vertical boom. This allows everything to be firmly fixed: the top of the boom can be suspended from fly floor or grid, under tension, and the bottom can be screwed or coach-bolted to the stage.

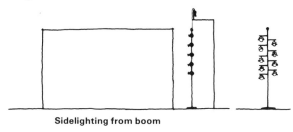

Sidelighting from boom

In England a boom is normally used with an 11"-long boom arm. I prefer the American rigging method, where a standard C-clamp is used around the boom with an extension pipe which allows easy adjustment of the distance of the lantern from the boom. The English adjustable clamp is a rather clumsy piece of equipment which is difficult to adjust and to lock securely.

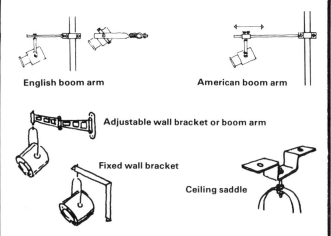

English boom arm　　　**American boom arm**

Adjustable wall bracket or boom arm

Fixed wall bracket

Ceiling saddle

If the vertical pipe to the ground is an obstruction the lanterns will have to be suspended on a 'ladder'. This is a ladder-like frame which is suspended from two points above. A ladder cannot be made rigid very easily, although stiffeners can be used and fixed to any available firm surface. The advantage of a boom is that by careful arrangement of the boom-arms more lanterns can be fixed in a tighter space than on a ladder.

If many lanterns are needed and yet the boom cannot come down to the floor, a compromise can be achieved and the boom flown off the floor with suitable hanging irons and fixings to hold it rigid.

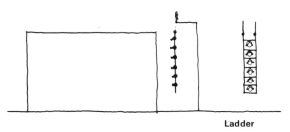

Ladder

The ladder can be very useful in a repertoire theatre because, instead of hanging it conventionally, it can be suspended from a track which allows it to be moved up and down stage under the fly floors. It is an added help if, on an adjacent track, an access ladder for the electrician is provided.

The fly gallery is, of course, a useful lighting position and it, like all other galleries in the theatre, should be equipped with a 2" diameter lighting rail in addition to the fly rail. The only problem with the fly gallery itself, is of course, that it is the place where the flymen work and it does not help them if it is cluttered up with electrical equipment. Ideally a theatre should be equipped with a separate lighting gallery on either side of the stage just underneath the fly gallery. In this way conflict between flymen and electrician should be avoided. In any event the bulk of the electrical services should be kept on the non-working fly gallery side of the stage.

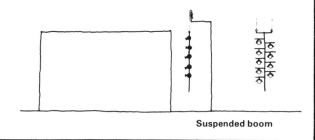

Suspended boom

Projection

Working out a projection scheme is relatively simple if the projector is placed square on to the screen: it is more complex if angular projection is called for, or if the screen is shaped in any way. However, all variables can be calculated in advance and, with care and accuracy, slides can be made pre-distorted to cope with all complications. It is sometimes possible to try out the projector in the theatre before the actual production and to reach a solution by a process of trial and error. If this is not possible, it may be best to take the problem to a company specializing in slide making.

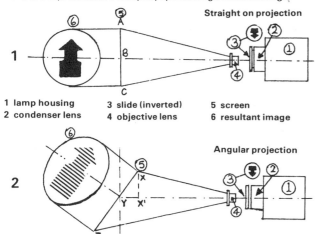

Straight on projection

1 lamp housing
2 condenser lens
3 slide (inverted)
4 objective lens
5 screen
6 resultant image

Angular projection

With straight on projection (1), we need to know the equipment to be used, the slide size and the desired distance between projector and screen. We will probably know the projector involved and the slide size. Thus we will know the beam angle that can be obtained with the widest angle lens. This will then show how close to the screen we can go to get the maximum brightness of picture.

We must be very careful to establish exactly how much of the slide is adequately illuminated. Some projectors, particularly those using larger slides, have a considerable fall-off of light toward the corners of the slide, and it is most unwise to try to use the whole slide right up to its edges. The performance of the projector to be used should be carefully checked before the work of calculation begins.

Simple formulae can be used to calculate such things as length of throw, desired size of slide or image size.

Projection calculations

$$\frac{d}{ES} = \frac{T}{SI} \qquad \frac{1}{d} + \frac{1}{T} = \frac{1}{f}$$

$$\frac{ES}{f} = \frac{SI}{T} \qquad \tan \tfrac{1}{2}\,BA = \frac{\tfrac{1}{2}ES}{T}$$

Key
T = throw from projector to screen
ES = effective slide size
SI = image size
d = distance slide to optical centre of objective
f = focal length of objective lens
BA = beam angle

Once we have established the beam angle of any particular objective lens and slide combination, we can begin to establish an angular projection set up (2). We will see that when the screen is moved at an angle in any one plane the image becomes elongated. The greater the angle of screen to projector, the greater will be this distortion. While this can be corrected at the slide, we must beware of another and sometimes greater problem: the depth of focus of the objective lens. We will see that not only is the image distorted but it also goes out of focus at its edges. There is virtually

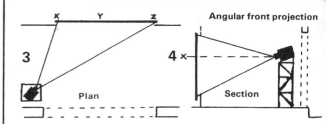

Angular front projection

nothing that can be done about this loss of focus when projecting at an acute angle and indeed it is the limit set by the depth of focus that probably dictates the maximum angle at which we can attempt to project.

If we draw our beam angle of light in plan with the screen angled as shown (3), we get the picture as shown (5). However, we must always remember that the beam of light with which we are working is three-dimensional. While we are covering the screen from X to Z in width, we must remember that only at Y will the picture be the same height as it was in our other example (1) at position B. At Z the picture will be larger than at Y and at X the picture will be smaller. This might mean that the projector has to be taken farther away from the screen in order to get sufficient picture height at position X. If we are attempting to get a square image, the height of the picture will be dictated by the height that is possible at the point of the shortest throw, X1, (4). Once this principle has been established, it is possible to draw a series of sections through varying points of the beam to establish exactly how the picture shape changes as the relationship between the screen and projector changes due to angular distortion.

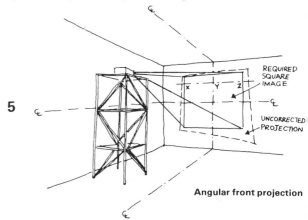

REQUIRED SQUARE IMAGE

UNCORRECTED PROJECTION

Angular front projection

The effect of an irregularly shaped screen can be calculated in exactly the same way. If, for example, we are projecting on to a curved cyclorama, we first draw the beam in plan (from projector to cyclorama) at the height of the projector. We can mark in the centre line of the beam and draw sections through it to establish the exact size of the image. If we are projecting over or around the scenery that might interfere with the projected image, this should be drawn in on the beam sections to establish the shape of possible resultant shadow.

Since it is likely that the projector will have to be placed as close as possible to the screen to secure maximum brightness, a wide angle lens will have to be used. However, the curvature of a wide angle lens may distort straight lines on the slide: thus if the straight lines are of great importance, a very wide angle lens should be avoided. A quick experiment will soon show how satisfactory the lens intended is actually going to be.

Common slide sizes:
35 mm, 2″, 3¼″, 5·2″ = 13 cm, 7·2″ = 18 cm.
N.B. Effective slide size is smaller than actual by at least the width of slide binding.

Optical effects

Gobos

A very useful form of projection, which does not require a true projector, uses any profile spot in conjunction with a gobo. This is a piece of very heat resistant material, metal or mica, that is cut into a design or shape and placed in the gate of a profile spotlight. This can then be focused by the lens and projected on to any surface. While a certain number of stock gobos can be bought from stage lighting manufacturers, a considerable variety of patterns can be obtained by using pieces of expanded metal. Alternatively, a special design can be cut in sheet metal. This effect is obviously most suitable for providing any shadow type effect, for example, a silhouette of light from a window off stage. It can be useful for rough cloud effects and perhaps most particularly for the broken effect of light through the leaves of trees. An extensive use of gobo light can be extremely fascinating and complex patterns of gobos built up from many spot-lights can produce extraordinary effects. Thus the designer can get away completely from the ever-present conical beam of the spotlight.

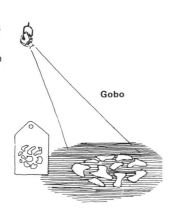

Gobo

The introduction of photo-etched stainless steel gobos has made possible the use of far more sensitive design and subtler effects.

Linnebach Lanterns

The Linnebach lantern is used to project large patterns at close range by direct light from a concentrated source. The lantern can be custom built, but Rank Strand make an adaptation of the Patt 223 lantern. The beam spread will be very wide, possibly about 60° to 90°, and only a simple pattern should be used. The details of the slide must be larger than the filament of the light source. The edges of the picture will be blurred and the intensity irregular. The slide, which is a large one, has to be placed some distance from the light source and the greater the distance, the more clearly defined will be the picture. Distortion can be corrected by either placing the slide parallel to the screen or painting a distorted slide.

Linnebach lantern

Effects should always be used with great discretion. While there are moments that require extravagant effect these are rare and the designer should beware of using any moving effect unless it is absolutely essential to the play.

Clouds

Projected clouds should almost always remain stationary. It is far better to use a slide, gobo or Linnebach projection of clouds to break up a sky surface without movement, rather than use the all-too-familiar moving-effect disc. These discs come in two standard types: 'stormy' and 'fleecy'. They should nearly always be used out of focus at a very slow speed. Only in the midst of a great storm or high wind do we normally notice clouds in movement. It is always better to use several cloud projectors, one overlaid on another. In this way one can achieve a break-up in the projected effect and show the difference in speed of various levels of cloud.

Lightning

Sheet and fork lighting are the most commonly required on the stage. For the latter we actually project the fork of lighting itself and for the former we simulate the flash upon the stage.

Fork lighting can be done in two ways. An attachment, which has a metal side on which the fork of lighting is cut, can be fitted to the front of the normal effects projector. By operating the shutter very rapidly one achieves a realistic flash. (It should be noted that a steel blue tint is often valuable here.) The second method is to use a small hand-held device known as a 'blitz-light' or 'Blitz-gerat'.

This device, made by Reiche & Vogel of Berlin, is a small projector which uses an electronic flash gun for its light source. At the press of a button it emits a very bright, very brief flash of light through the objective lens system. A series of fork lightning slides can be slipped into the slide magazine and then projected.

Blitz-light

The effect of sheet lightning or a lightning flash can be achieved most simply by rapidly switching a cold or light blue circuit of batten or floodlight. More effectively, one or several floods can be used with photographer's photo flood lamps, which can be operated from a push button. Rapid manipulation of these can produce blinding sheets of light. In the old days lightning was produced with a stick of carbon and a steel file, a dangerous but undoubtedly spectacular method.

Rain

Projected rain, in my opinion, is the worst effect in the catalogue. It is produced with a disc on which lines have been scratched and the resulting image is not only very dim, it is also extremely unrealistic. Once again, a multiplicity of projected effects tends to make the thing a little more acceptable, but the only way to produce rain really successfully on the stage is with real water. This is often not as difficult as one might imagine. The water is fed into a pipe, which has tiny holes drilled along its length, above the stage. From this it should fall into some form of trough, the size of which will be determined by the length of pipe and the height at which it is hung. Great care must be exercised to avoid any danger of the water coming into contact with electrical equipment, and the effect should be operated well away from dip traps. Cross lighting the water will produce the most marvellous effect.

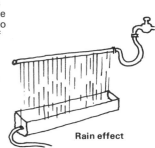

Rain effect

Snow

Effective projected snow is almost as unsatisfactory as rain. The same rules apply, and truly realistic snow can only be created by something actually falling from above. This can be confetti-like paper, fragmented Jablight or even soap flakes. Trial and error will determine the best material to use. The snow is placed in a snow bag, which is traditionally made from a length of canvas, in which a number of small holes have been cut, hung between two battens. The bag is hung on two separate sets of lines from the grid and when these are moved gently the loose material finds its way through the holes and flutters down to the stage.

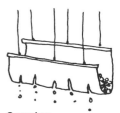

Snow bag

Optical effects

Suns and moons
Because of its brightness the depiction of the sun itself, unless seen through fog and mist, is virtually impossible. We can, however, represent the moon. A moon box, a metal box with some lamps inside it and with a cut-out shape of the moon on its front, can be hung behind a translucent cloth. Unless the cloth is a proper rear projection screen, it may be necessary to have a

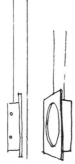

Moon box

diffuser over the face of the box to obscure the actual filament of the lamps. By hanging the box either very close to or away from the cloth, varying degrees of soft or hard edge images can be produced. This 'light box' can of course be made in any shape desired and it is a very simple method of getting any lit shape in a painted cloth (e.g. distant lit windows). Alternatively one can direct a profile spot with a round mask on to a translucent cloth. (See chapter 6, the *Brand* set-up). A moon shape can also, of course, be projected with a profile spot from the front. To get a more exactly defined image, a projector with a moon slide can be used; indeed one of the most satisfactory of all optical effects is a 'moon with passing cloud'. This has a moon slide and a cloud disc in one machine and, when used with other cloud effects, gives the most extraordinarily realistic effect.

Stars
Most usually this is done with miniature 'Christmas tree' lights that are poked through a cloth from the rear so that just their tips show through. A very tiny dab of blue or black paint will reduce the light and give a most realistic impression. A gauze hung downstage of the effect will enhance it by creating a shimmering sensation. Stars can also be projected, but here great care must be taken since even the smallest star painted on a slide can appear as large as a football on the screen. Another very simple method is to make tiny balls of silver paper and hang them on black thread downstage of the night sky cloth. Then cross-light very carefully with a narrowly slotted profile spot.

The use of fibre-optics to produce economically a vast quantity of minute light sources from a single programmable central source is a fascinating way of making stars. Alan Ayckbourn's *Joking Apart* (Globe Theatre, London, 1979) used this new device for distant firework effects.

Flames and smoke
Successful flame projection depends upon the number of projectors used and upon a sufficiently short throw to get a very bright image. A rotating disc, mounted on the front of a Patt 123 500 watt Fresnel, can produce an acceptable substitute for the more expensive flame effect projector. By muddling up the projected image with smoke and other means of producing flame effect, such as blown strips of silk, neon flicker lamps and so on, a marvellous conflagration can be produced.

Smoke box

There are several ways of producing smoke. A smoke box is simply a container, with a heating element, into which one places smoke powder (obtainable from a stage lighting supplier). When the box is heated the powder will give off a good volume of white smoke that is not too acrid for actors or audience to stand. The only problem is in cueing the effect, since it takes some time to warm up and will not switch off instantly because the heating element

Smoke gun

takes time to cool down. More effective is the smoke gun. This device consists of a container which is filled with a special oil-based liquid which can be heated. The liquid vaporizes into smoke which can then be shot out over the stage. Care has to be taken with both the oil used and the design of the gun itself to avoid actual droplets of non vaporized oil being left on the floor, scenery or costumes. The smoke tends to rise, but it can be made heavier

and of greater volume by fixing a tray containing dry ice to the front of the gun. As the heated oil vapour passes over the dry ice, a thick white smoke is produced. This method was used in the production of *Blitz* shown in various photographs in this book.

Dry ice can be used on its own to produce a very heavy white low-lying fog. A fog machine is a metal tank with a heating element which will bring the tank water to boiling point. When solid carbon dioxide is lowered in to the boiling water, a large volume of thick fog is produced: this can be directed around the stage by means of a hose.

One of the problems of using 'live' smoke or fog is controlling them and getting rid of them. It is absolutely essential to try the effect out when the theatre is at least partially full with a dress rehearsal audience. The theatre's heating and ventilating system and the general condition of air currents can only be truly assessed when the audience is in the auditorium. The first dress rehearsal with audience of the 'notorious' production of *Blitz* was conducted in the presence of Her Royal Highness Princess Margaret. During the air raid sequence the smoke billowed in ever-increasing clouds from the stage and the entire royal party (and auditorium) disappeared, only to emerge some scenes later.

A projected smoke effect is very similar to that of cloud, but is used travelling vertically rather than horizontally. It is little substitute for the real thing.

Sea waves and ripples

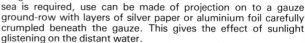

Wave effect

The optical projected effect of sea waves is one of the most effective on the market. Instead of a circular rotating disc, this uses a fixed slide with vertically moving ripply break-up glasses. The result is the most extraordinarily accurate representation of a gently rolling seascape. This can be used not simply on a screen or backcloth, but upon the floor of the stage to give an evocative undulating motion. The ripple of water in a stream or, more importantly, the effect of light reflected from rippling water, can be done with a similar type of optical effect, or by using a tubular lamp around which a perforated drum revolves. This has the advantage of being a much wider angle effect and can consequently be used for a very short throw. Another way of producing the effect of reflected light from water is to put a tray containing water on the floor outside, for example, a window, and to aim a spotlight in to it. Gentle undulation of the tray will literally re-create the effect of light on water. If a distant view of the sea is required, use can be made of projection on to a gauze ground-row with layers of silver paper or aluminium foil carefully crumpled beneath the gauze. This gives the effect of sunlight glistening on the distant water.

Water ripple

Candles, torches, oil lamp and gas
The only really effective way of producing candle or torch light on the stage is to have the real thing. Happily, fire authorities are now at last beginning to realize that times have changed since the demise of gas lighting and that one or two naked candle flames are not a signal for the whole theatre to be burnt down. This is not to say that the danger should be ignored, however, and if real flame is used the greatest possible precautions should be taken at all times. If one has to produce an imitation candle, a torch lamp can be used concealed within a twist of tissue paper while the battery is concealed in the imitation candle itself. Ideally, of course, the lamp should disappear when the flame is blown out and some ingenuity with a retractable lamp holder is called for. In recent years, a fine imitation candle flame has become available. This is a very thin lamp, mounted on a delicate spring, which gives a reasonable impression of the flicker of a candle flame.

Torches are virtually impossible to imitate electrically. Various attempts have been made with battery operated lamps, silk streamers, hidden blowers, etc. None have been really successful. If the fire authorities will not relent in their disapproval of the flambeaux torch, it should be avoided.

Theatrical lighting terms

English	French	Italian	German
Theatre			
theatre	théâtre	teatro	Theater
play	pièce de théâtre	lavoro teatrale	Theaterstück
opera	opéra	opera	Oper
act	acte	atto	Akt (Aufzug)
scene	scène	scena	Bild (Szene)
interval	entr'acte	intervallo	Pause
performance	représentation	rappresentazione	Vorstellung
lighting rehearsal	répétition de lumières	prova delle luci	Beleuchtungsprobe
Staff			
stage director/ producer	metteur-en-scène	regista	Regisseur
director	directeur	direttore	Direktor
actor	acteur	attore	Schauspieler
opera singer	chanteur	cantante	Sänger
assistant stage manager	inspecteur	ispettore	Inspizient
ballet dancer	danseur, danseuse	ballerino, ballerina	Tänzer, Tänzerin
conductor	chef d'orchestre	direttore dell'orchestra	Kapellmeister (Dirigent)
technical director	directeur technique	direttore tecnico	Technischer Leiter
stage carpenter	chef-machiniste	capomacchinista	Theatermeister
stage hand	machiniste	operao addetto alla scena	Bühnenarbeiter
chief electrician	chef électricien	capo-elettricista	Beleuchtungsmeister
property man	accessoiriste	addetto agli accessori	Requisiteur
stage decorator	décorateur	decoratore	Dekorateur
Stage			
auditorium	salle	sala	Zuschauerraum
orchestra pit	foss d'orchestre	orchestra	Orchesterraum
stage	scène	palcoscenico	Bühne
back stage	arrière-scène	retroscena	Hinterbühne
side-stage	scène latérale	quinta	Seitenbühne
stage floor	plateau, plancher	tavolato	Bühnenboden
fly gallery	galerie d'équipes	galleria laterale	Arbeitsgalerie
grid, gridiron	cintre	soffitto del palcoscenico	Schnürboden
revolving stage	scène tournante	scene girevole	Drehbüne
under machinery	machinerie du dessous	macchinario del sottopalco	Untermaschinerie
trap	trappe	botola	Versenkung
rake	pente	pendenza	Bühnenfall
rostrum	praticable	praticabile	Stellage, Gerust
step	marche	gracino	Stufe
stairs	escalier	scala	Treppe
counterweight line	équipe à contrepoids	carrucola a contrappeso	Gegengewichtszug
counterweight	contrepoids	contrappeso	Gegengewicht
rope, cord	fil	corda	Seil
wire rope, wire cable	cable	fune	Drahtseil
pipe	porteuse	trave centrale	Laststange
batten	perche supérieure	pertica superiore	Oberlatte
flying equipment	vol	apparecchio aereo	Flugvorrichtung
winch	treuil	argano	Winde
lift	ascenseur	ascensore	Aufzug
proscenium opening	ouverture	apertura	Bühnenoffnung
curtain	rideau	sipario	Vorhang
proscenium	avant-scène	proscenio	Proszenium
scenery	tableau, décors	scenario	Szenerie
Lighting			
stage lighting	éclairage de scène	illuminazione della scena	Bühnenbeleuchtung
switch	interrupteur	interruttore	Schalter
fuse	fusible	fusibile	Sicherung
control station	jeu d'orgue	cabina di manovra	Steilwerk
dimmer board	commande du jeu d'orgue	quadro elettrico	Bühnenregler
dimmers	resistances	resistenze	Widerstände
resistances			
transformer	transformateur	trasformatore	Transformator
plug	fiche	spina	Stecker
sockets	prises	scatole	Anschlussdosen
circuit	circuit	circuito	Stromkreis
direct current	courant direct	corrente continua	Gleichstrom
alternating current	courant alternatif	corrente alternata	Wechselstrom
voltage	voltage	voltaggio	Spannung
floats, footlights	rampe	luce della ribalta	Rampenlichte
borderlight	herse	luce delle bilance	Oberlicht
stage flood	appareils transportables	sostegni trasportabili	Versatzständer
acting area floodlight	lanternes de scène	luce a fascio sul palcoscenico	Spielflachenleuchten
with lens	avec lentille	con lente	mit Linse
flood lanterns	casserole	riflettore a fascio	Flutlichtleuchten
focus lanterns	projecteur	riflettore	Scheinwerfer
spotlight			
spot	projecteur d'avant-scène	proiettore d'avanscena	Vorbuhnen Scheinwerfer
perch spot	perche	proiettore di proscenio	Proszenium Scheinwerfer
arc spotlight	projecteur à arc	proiettore ad arco	Bogenlicht Scheinwerfer
cyclorama lantern	lanterne d'horizon	lampada per l'orizzonte	Horizontlaterne
cyclorama lighting	éclairage d'horizon	illuminzione dell'orizzonte	Horizontbel- euchtung
stand, tripod, telescopic stand	pied	sostegno	Ständer, Stativ
lamp	lampe	lampada	Glühlampe
direct lighting	éclairage direct	luce diretta	Direktes Licht
diffused lighting	éclairage diffus	luce diffuse	Diffuses Licht
ultra violet light	lumière ultra-violette	luce ultra violetto	Ultraviolettes Licht
glass medium	écran de verre	schermo di vetro	Glasscheibe
colour medium	écran de gélatine	schermo di mica	Gelatinescheibe
colour-frame magazine (box)	magazin à écrans de couleurs	scatola degli schermi	Farbscheiben magazin
colour-wheel	disque à écrans	disco degli schermi	Farbscheibenrad
diffusing screen	diffuseur	diffusore	Streuscheibe
shutter	obtirateur	otturatore	Abdeckschieber
mask, diaphragm	cliché	diframma	Blende
iris-shutter	diaphragme iris	diaframma dell' iride	Irisblende
mirror	glace, miroir	specchio	Spiegel
reflector	réflecteur	riflettore	Reflektor
lens	lentille	lente	Linse
objective lens	objective	obiettivo	Objektiv, Öbjektivlinse
condensing lens	condensateur	condensatore	Kondensator
focus	foyer	fuoco	Brennpunkt
Colour			
light	clair	chiaro	hell
dark	obscur	scuro	dunkel
colour	couleur	colore	Farbe
white	blanc	bianco	weiss
yellow	jaune	giallo	gelb
lemon	citron	giallo limone	zitronengelb
orange	orange	giallo arancio	orange
red	rouge	rosso	rot
pink	rose	rosa	rosa
magenta, violet	mauve, violet	violetto	violett
blue	bleu	blu	blau
light blue	bleu clair	blu chiaro	hellblau
azure blue	bleu ciel	azzurro	azur
dark blue	bleu marine	blu scuro	dunkelblau
moonlight blue	bleu de lune	blu lunare	mondblau
green-blue	bleu vert	blu verdastro	blaugrün
water-blue	bleu d'eau	blu marino	wasserblau
green	vert	verde	grun
sunlight	lumière du soleil	luce solare	Sonnenlicht
moonlight	clair de lune	chiaro di luna	Mondlicht
morning	matin	mattino	Morgen
noon, midday	midi	mezzogiorno	Mittag
evening	soir	sera	Abend
night	nuit	notte	Nacht
General			
long	long	lungo	lang
short	court	corto, breve	kurz
wide	large	largo	weit
narrow	étroit	stretto	schmal
broad	large	largo	breit
on	sur	su	auf
up	en haut	in su, in alto	hinauf, oben
under	sous	sotto	unter
right	à droite	a destra	rechts
left	à gauche	a sinistra	links
downwards	en bas	in giu	abwarts
slow	lent	lento	langsam
fast, quickly	vite, rapide	rapido	schnell
low	bas	basso	niedrig
lower	plus bas	piú basso	niedriger
high	haut	alto	hoch
higher	plus haut, supérieur	piú alto, superiore	höher
too much	trop	troppo	zu viel
too little	trop peu	troppo poco	zu wenig
more	plus	piú	mehr
less	moins	meno	wenig
a quarter	un quart	un quarto	ein Viertel
good	bon	buono	gut
bad	mauvais	cattivo	schlecht
right	juste	giusto	richtig
wrong	faux	falso	falsch
repeat!	répétez!	ripetere!	wiederholen!
once	une fois	una volta	einmal
the last time	la dernière fois	l'ultima volta	das lezte Mal
alright, OK	en ordre, ça va	in ordine, va bene	in Ordnung
cue	signal, réplique	segno, segnale, suggerimento	Zeichen, Signal, Stichwort
attention!	attention!	attenzione!	Achtung!
begin, go	en marche, on commence	si inizia	los, anfangen
stop!	halte!	alto!	halt!
to hang, to clamp	suspendre	appendere	aufhängen
to mount	équiper	provvedere	ausstatten
to set up	poser	collocare	aufstellen
to earth	mettre à la terre	mettere a fersa	erden

Suppliers

United Kingdom

Berkey Colortran
P.O. Box 5
Burrell Way
Thetford
Norfolk IP24 3RB
Tel: Thetford (0842) 2484
Lanterns and control

CCT Theatre Lighting Ltd
Windsor House
26 Willow Lane
Mitcham, Surrey CR4 4NA
Tel: 01-640 3366
Lanterns and control

Concord Lighting
International Ltd
Rotaflex House
241 City Road
London EC1P 1ET
Tel: 01-253 1200
Display lighting

Electrosonic Ltd
815 Woolwich Road
London SE7 8LT
Tel: 01-855 1101
Control

W. J. Furse and Co. Ltd
Theatre Division
Traffic Street
Nottingham
Lanterns and control

David Hersey Associates Ltd
15 Between Streets
Cobham
Surrey KT11 1AA
Tel: Cobham (266) 7117
Projectors and gobos

Lee Filters Limited
Central Way
Walworth Industrial Estate
Andover
Hants, SP10 5AN
Tel: Andover (0264) 66245
Colour filters

Philips Electrical Ltd
Lighting Division
Century House
Shaftesbury Avenue
London WC2
Lamps

Rank Strand Electric
P.O. Box 70
Great West Road
Brentford
Middlesex TW8 9HR
Tel: 01-568 9222
Lanterns and control

Theatre Projects Services Ltd
10 Long Acre
London WC2
Tel: 01-240 5411
*Design and equipment hire
sales*

Thorn Lighting Ltd
Angel Road Works
Edmonton
London N18 3AJ
Tel: 01-807 9011
Control

United States

American Stage Lighting
Co. Inc.
1331c North Avenue
New Rochelle, N.Y. 10804
*Lanterns, accessories and
control*

Audio Visual Laboratories Inc.
500 Hillside Ave.
Atlantic Highlands
New Jersey 07716
Computerized slide programming

A.V.E. Corporation
250 West 54th Street
New York, N.Y. 10019
Projection equipment

Berkey Colortran
1015 Chestnut Street
Burbank
California 91502
Tel: 213-843 1200
Lanterns and control

Electro Controls Inc.
2975 South 300 West
Salt Lake City
Utah 84115
Tel: 801-487 9861
Lanterns and control

Electronics Diversified Inc.
1675 N.W. 216th
Hillsboro
Oregon 97123
Tel: 503-645 5533
Control

Four Star Stage Lighting
Inc.
585 Gerard Ave.
Bronx
New York, N.Y. 10451
Tel: 212-993 0471
Lighting hire

Grand Stage Lighting Company
630 West Lake Street
Chicago
Illinois 60606
Tel: 312-332 5611
Lanterns and control

Hub Electric Company Inc.
940 Industrial Drive
Elmhurst
Illinois 60126
Tel: 312-832 5790
Control

Kliegl Bros
32-32 48th Avenue
Long Island City
New York, N.Y. 11101
Tel: 212-786 7474
Lanterns and control

Kodak
Eastman-Kodak
Rochester, New York
Projection equipment

Lighting Services Inc.
150 East 58th Street
New York, N.Y. 10022
Tel: 212-838 8633
Display lighting

Rosco
39 Bush Avenue
Port Chester, N.Y. 10573
Tel: 914-937 1300
Colour filters

Showco
9011 Governors Row
Dallas,
Texas 75247
Tel: 214-630 1188
*Lighting and sound hire
and rigging*

Skirpan Lighting Control
Corporation
61-03 32nd Avenue
Woodside, New York
N.Y. 11377
Tel: 212-274 7222
Control

Strand Century Inc.
5432 West 102nd St
Los Angeles
California 90045
Tel: 213-776 4600
Lanterns and control

Strong Electric
521 City Park Avenue
Toledo, Ohio 43697
Follow spots

Vanco Stage Lighting, Inc.
3240 Bronx Avenue
Bronx
New York, N.Y. 10467
Tel: 212-655 0666
Rentals, supplies, systems

Europe

Austria
Ludwig Pani
Kandlgasse 23
A1070 Vienna
Lanterns and remote control

Belgium
ADB
Leuvensesteenweg 275
B – 1930 Zaventem
Tel: 02-720 50 80
Lanterns and control

Denmark
J. C. Priebe
Kløverset 79
Haderslen
Lanterns

France
Compagnie Clemançon
23 rue Lamartine

Paris IXe
Lanterns and control

Cremer
183 rue Lecourbe
Parix XVe
Lanterns and control

Italy
Ianiro
Via Coulonia 10-A
Rome
Lanterns

Sweden
Avab Elektronik AB
V. Hamngatan 1
41117 Göteborg
Control

W. Germany
Rank Strand Electric
3340 Wolfenbüttel — Salzdahlu
Salzbergstrasse 2
Tel: 05331-7951
Lanterns and control

Reiche & Vogel — B. Deltschaf
1000 Berlin 20 (Spandau)
Blumenstrasse 10
Tel: 030-335 70 61
Lanterns and remote control

Emil Niethammer
Industriestrasse 29
Stuttgart-Vaihingen
Lanterns

Siemens AG
D-8520 Erlangen
Control

Asia
Rank Strand Asia Ltd
1618 Star House
3 Salisbury Road
Tsim Sha Tsui
Kowloon, Hong Kong
Tel: 3-685161
Lanterns and control

Australia
Rank Industries Australia Pty
Ltd
Strand Electric Division
19 Trent Street, Burwood
Victoria 3125
Tel: 29-3724

Canada
Strand Century Ltd
6334 Viscount Rd
Mississauga, Ontario
Tel: 416-677 7130

Bibliography

Books

Bellman, Willard F.
Lighting the Stage: Art and Practice
Chandler Publishing Co.,
New York and London,
2nd edn 1974

Bellman, Willard F.
Scenography and Stage Technology
Thomas Y. Crowell Co., Inc.,
New York, 1977

Bentham, Frederick
The Art of Stage Lighting
Pitman Publishing Ltd,
2nd edn 1976

Bergman, Gosta M.
Lighting in the Theatre
Almqvist & Wiksell Förlag,
Stockholm, 1977

Bowman, Wayne
Modern Theatre Lighting
Harper & Bros,
New York

Fuchs, Theodore
Stage Lighting
Little, Brown & Co.,
Boston, 1929

Kook, Edward
Images in Light for the Living

Theatre
Century Lighting Inc.,
New York

McCandless, Stanley
A Method of Lighting the Stage
Theatre Arts Books,
New York, 1958

McCandless, Stanley
A Syllabus of Stage Lighting
Drama Book Specialists
(Publishers),
New York, 1968

Ost, Geoffrey
Stage Lighting
Herbert Jenkins Ltd,
London, 1957

Parker, W. Oren & Smith,
Harvey K.
Scene Design and Stage Lighting
Holt, Rinehart & Winston,
New York

Pecktal, Lynn
Designing and Painting for the Theatre
Holt, Rinehart & Winston,
New York, 1975

Reid, Francis
The Stage Lighting Handbook
Pitman & Sons Ltd,
London, 1976

Rosenthal, Jean and Lael
Wertenbaker
The Magic of Light
Little, Brown & Co.,
Boston, 1972

Rubin, Joel E. and Watson,
Leland H.
Theatrical Lighting Practice
Theatre Arts Books,
New York, 1954

Selden, Samuel and Sellman,
Hunton D.
Stage Scenery and Lighting
Appleton-Century-Crofts Inc.,
New York, 1959

Warfel, William B.
Handbook of Stage Lighting Graphics
Drama Book Specialists
(Publishers),
New York, 1974

Williams, Rollo G.
The Technique of Stage Lighting
Pitman & Sons Ltd,
London, 1952

Periodicals

Bühnentechnische Runschau
Andreas-Herz-Str. 7
D 8011 Baldham
B. Munchen

Lighting Dimensions
3900 South Wadsworth Blvd
Denver, Colorado 80235
Tel: 303-988 4670

Sightline
Association of British Theatre
Technicians Journal
9 Fitzroy Square
London W1
England

Tabs
Rank Strand Electric
P.O. Box 70
Great West Road
Brentford, Middlesex
England

Theatre Crafts
Suite 812
250 West 57th Street
New York, N.Y. 10019

Theatre Design and Technology
Journal of the U.S.S. Institute
for Theatre Technology
1501 Broadway
Rm. 1408
New York, N.Y. 10036

Index   *Figures in italics refer to illustration plates*

Index